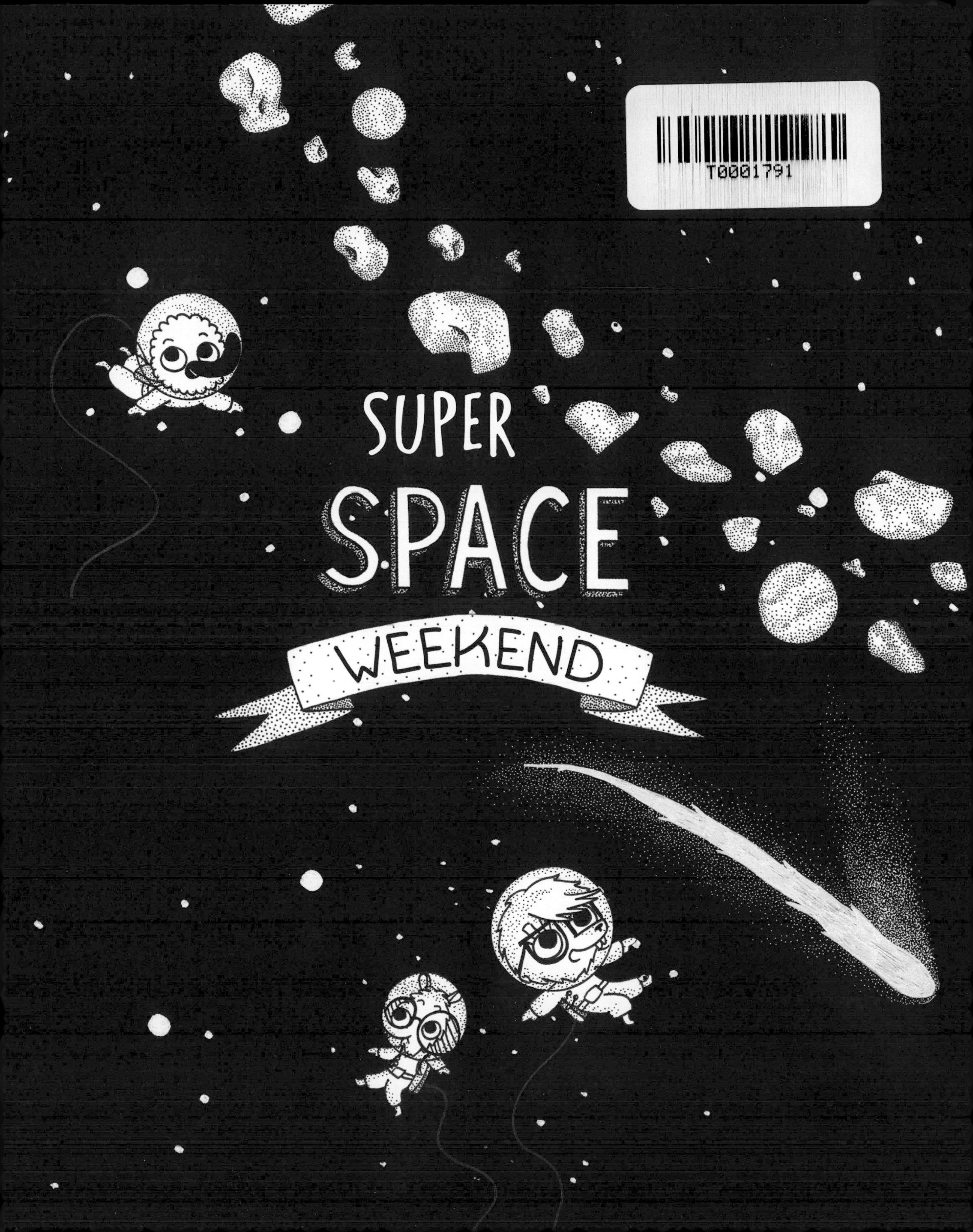
SUPER
SPACE
WEEKEND

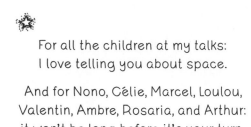

For all the children at my talks:
I love telling you about space.

And for Nono, Célie, Marcel, Loulou,
Valentin, Ambre, Rosaria, and Arthur:
it won't be long before it's your turn.

SCIENCE
ADVENTURE
CLUB

SUPER

SPACE

WEEKEND

Adventures
in Astronomy

Gaëlle Alméras
Translated by David Warriner

GREYSTONE KIDS
GREYSTONE BOOKS • VANCOUVER/BERKELEY/LONDON

Welcome to a wonderful world: our very own!

Join these three mischievous friends as they learn all about the sky above us. Squeak, Orni, and Castor each have their own personality and their own curiosity about science and the sky.

There's so much for them to learn on this super space adventure. We live in a world of wonder and beauty, filled with much more than meets the eye.

With a pair of binoculars and a scrap of red paper over your flashlight, you too can gaze into the great big universe you live in.

Young readers, this is all yours to discover—and love!

Extragalactically yours,

HÉLÈNE COURTOIS
Astrophysicist and Cosmographer

INTRODUCTION

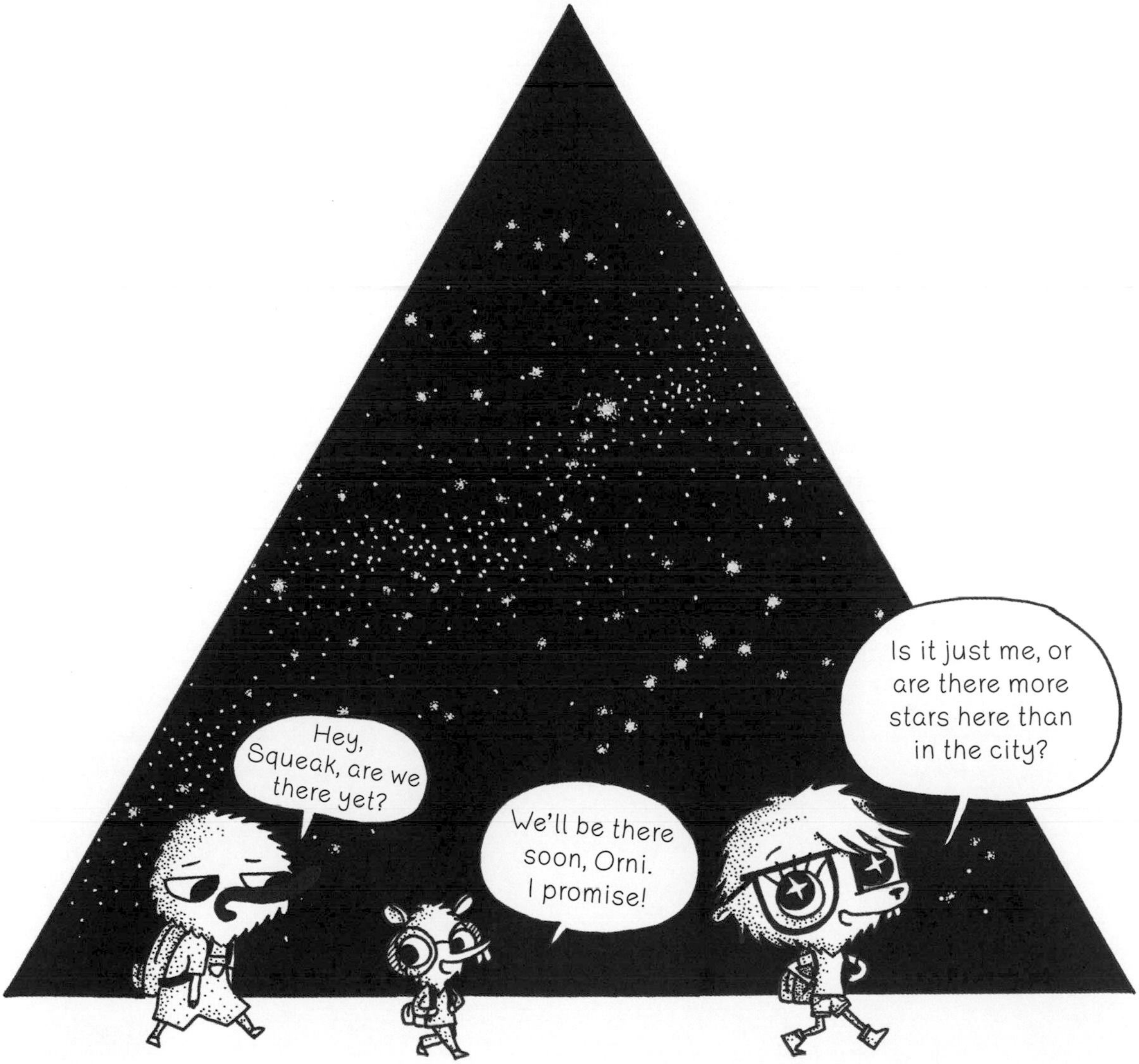
Hey, Squeak, are we there yet?
We'll be there soon, Orni. I promise!
Is it just me, or are there more stars here than in the city?

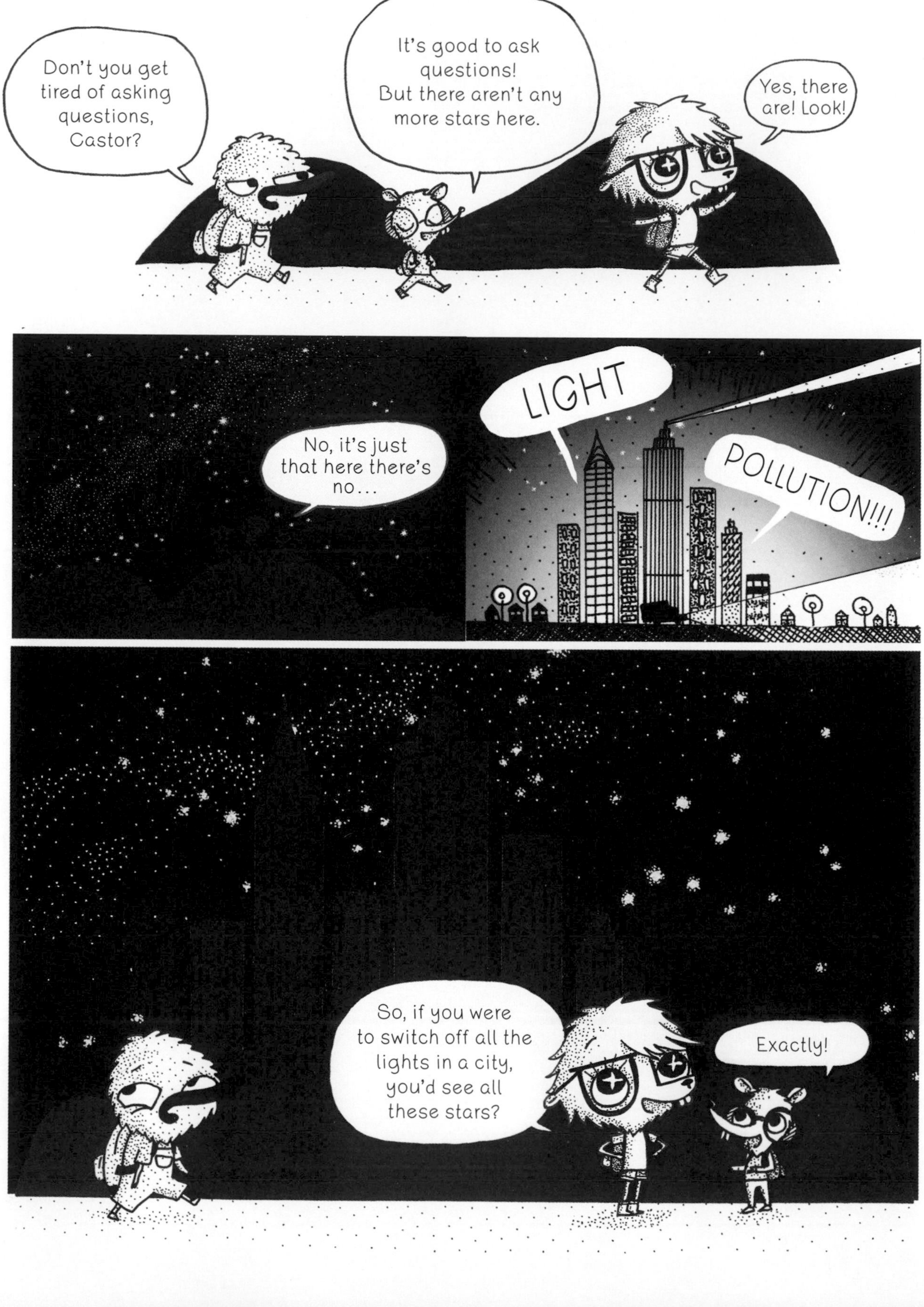
Don't you get tired of asking questions, Castor?
It's good to ask questions! But there aren't any more stars here.
Yes, there are! Look!
No, it's just that here there's no...
LIGHT
POLLUTION!!!
So, if you were to switch off all the lights in a city, you'd see all these stars?
Exactly!

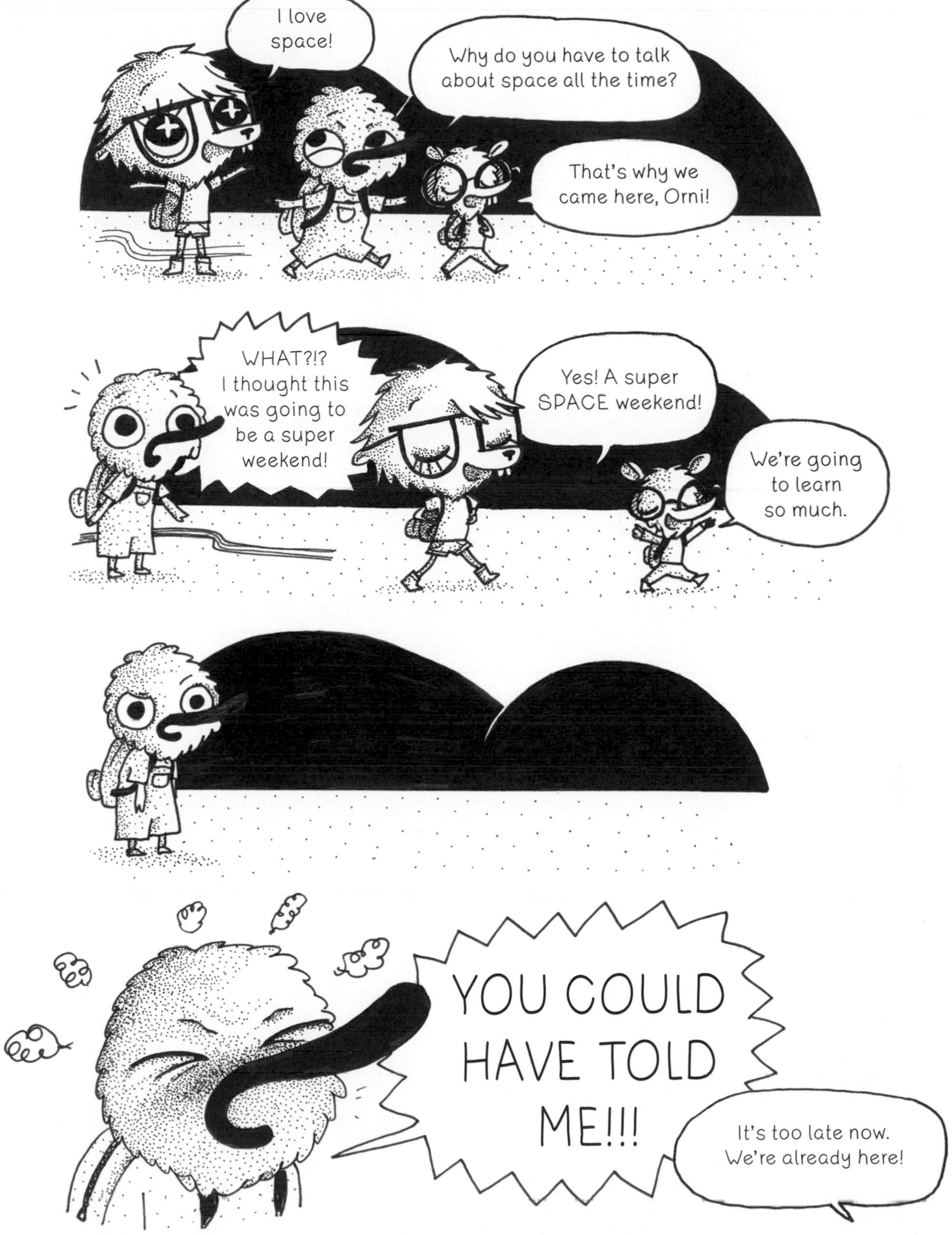
I love space!
Why do you have to talk about space all the time?
That's why we came here, Orni!
WHAT?!? I thought this was going to be a super weekend!
Yes! A super SPACE weekend!
We're going to learn so much.
YOU COULD HAVE TOLD ME!!!
It's too late now. We're already here!

Chapter 1

MAY THE STARS BE WITH YOU

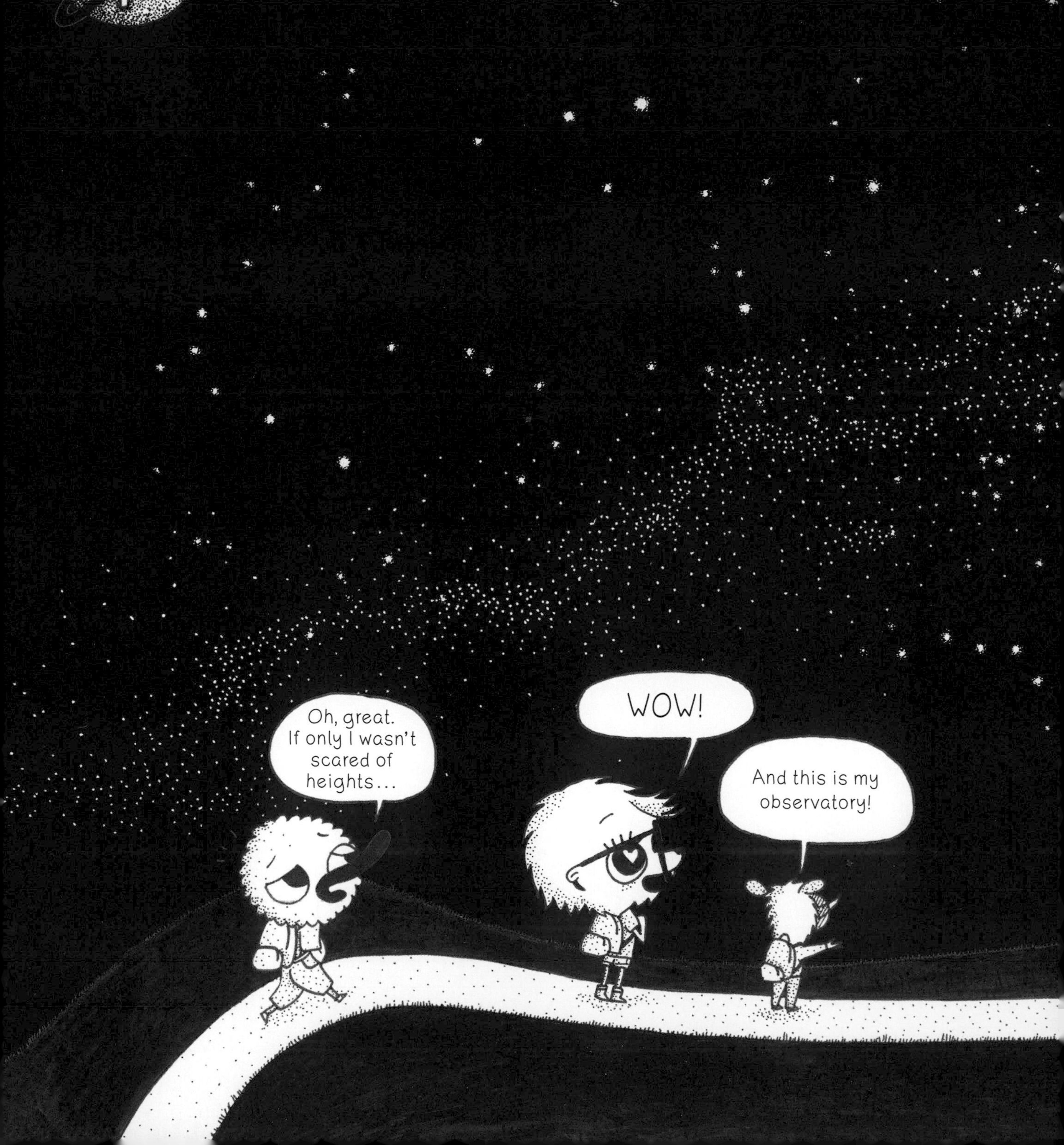
And this is my observatory!
WOW!
Oh, great. If only I wasn't scared of heights...

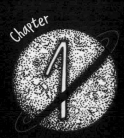

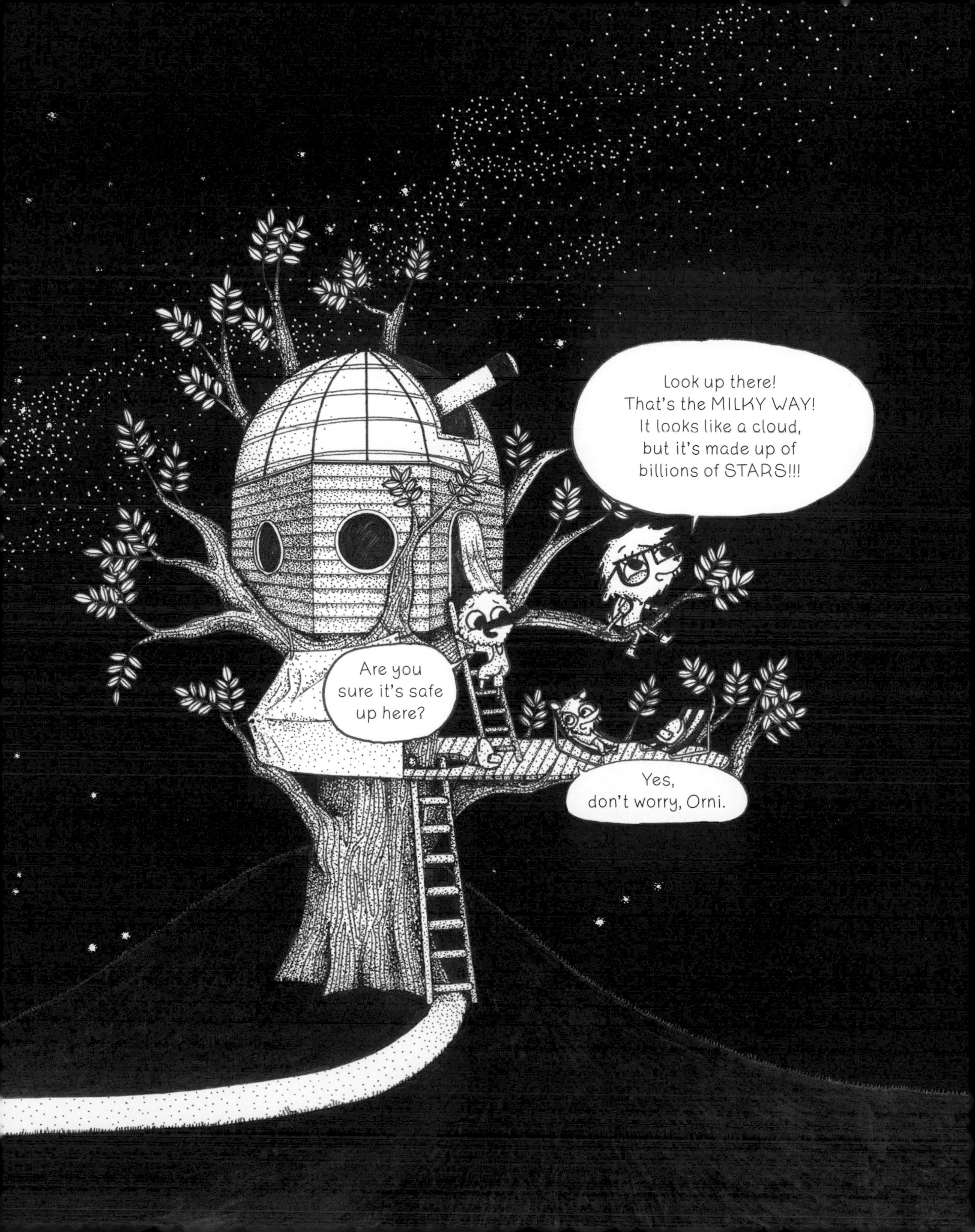
Look up there! That's the MILKY WAY! It looks like a cloud, but it's made up of billions of STARS!!!
Are you sure it's safe up here?
Yes, don't worry, Orni.

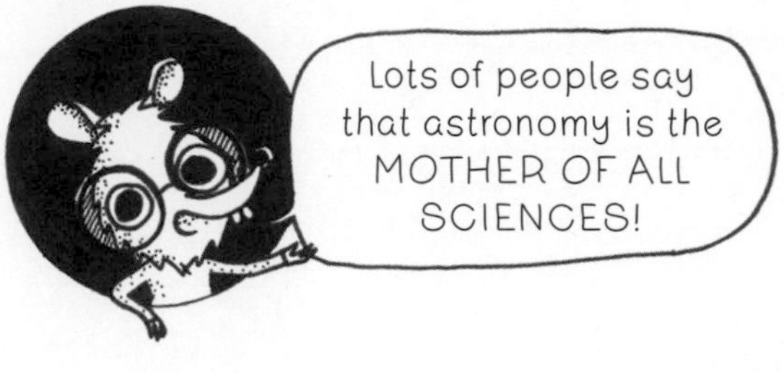
Lots of people say that astronomy is the MOTHER OF ALL SCIENCES!

It's the science of the sky, the stars, and the whole universe.

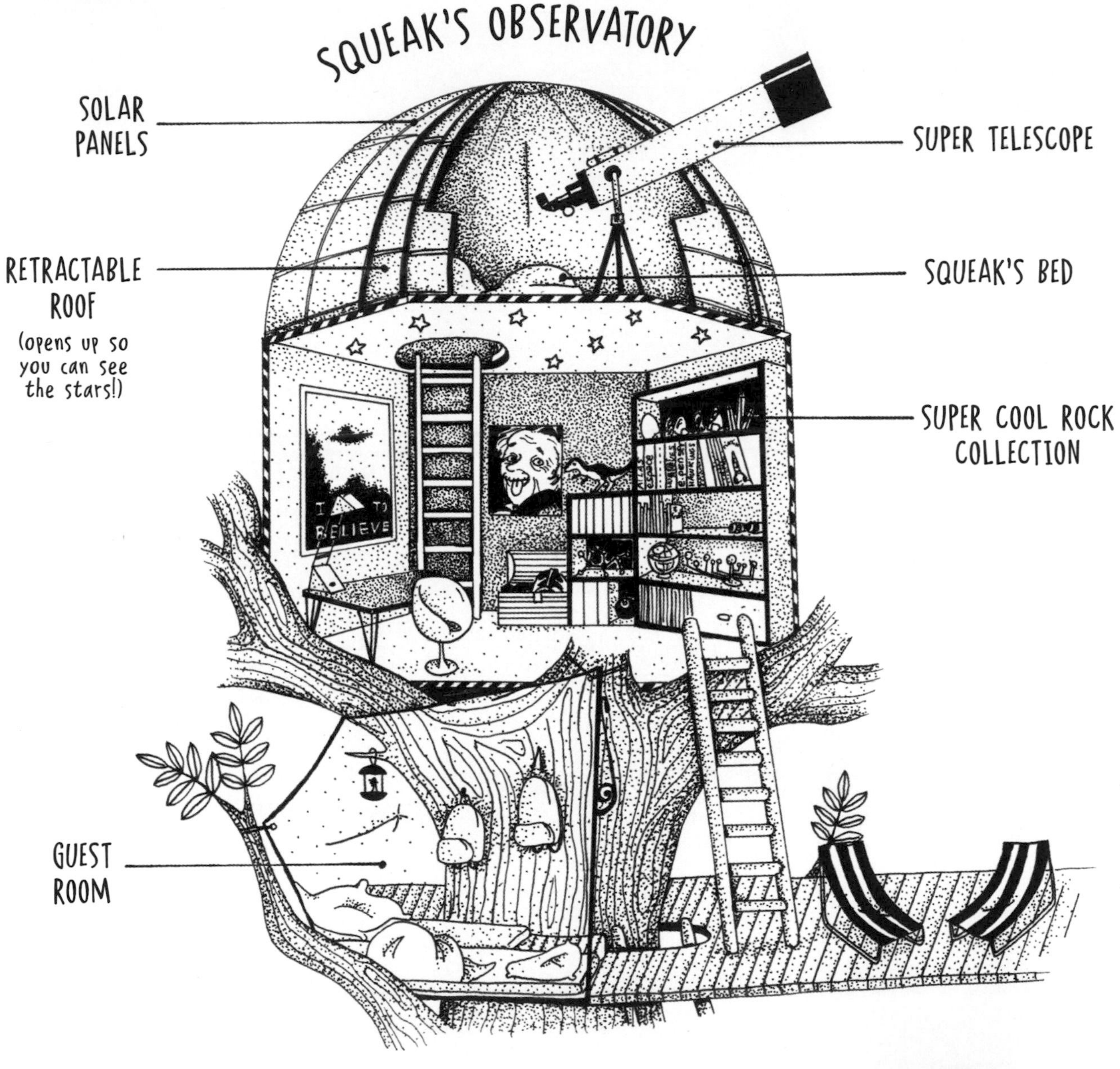
SQUEAK'S OBSERVATORY
SOLAR PANELS
SUPER TELESCOPE
RETRACTABLE ROOF
(opens up so you can see the stars!)
SQUEAK'S BED
SUPER COOL ROCK COLLECTION
GUEST ROOM

An astronomical observatory is a place with viewing instruments for looking at the night sky. They are usually located far away from city lights.

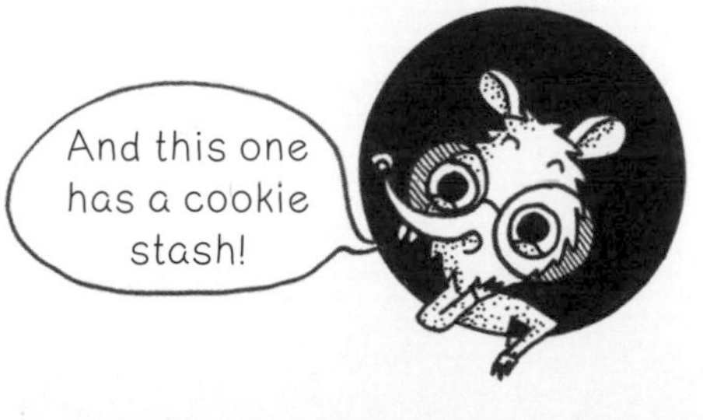
And this one has a cookie stash!

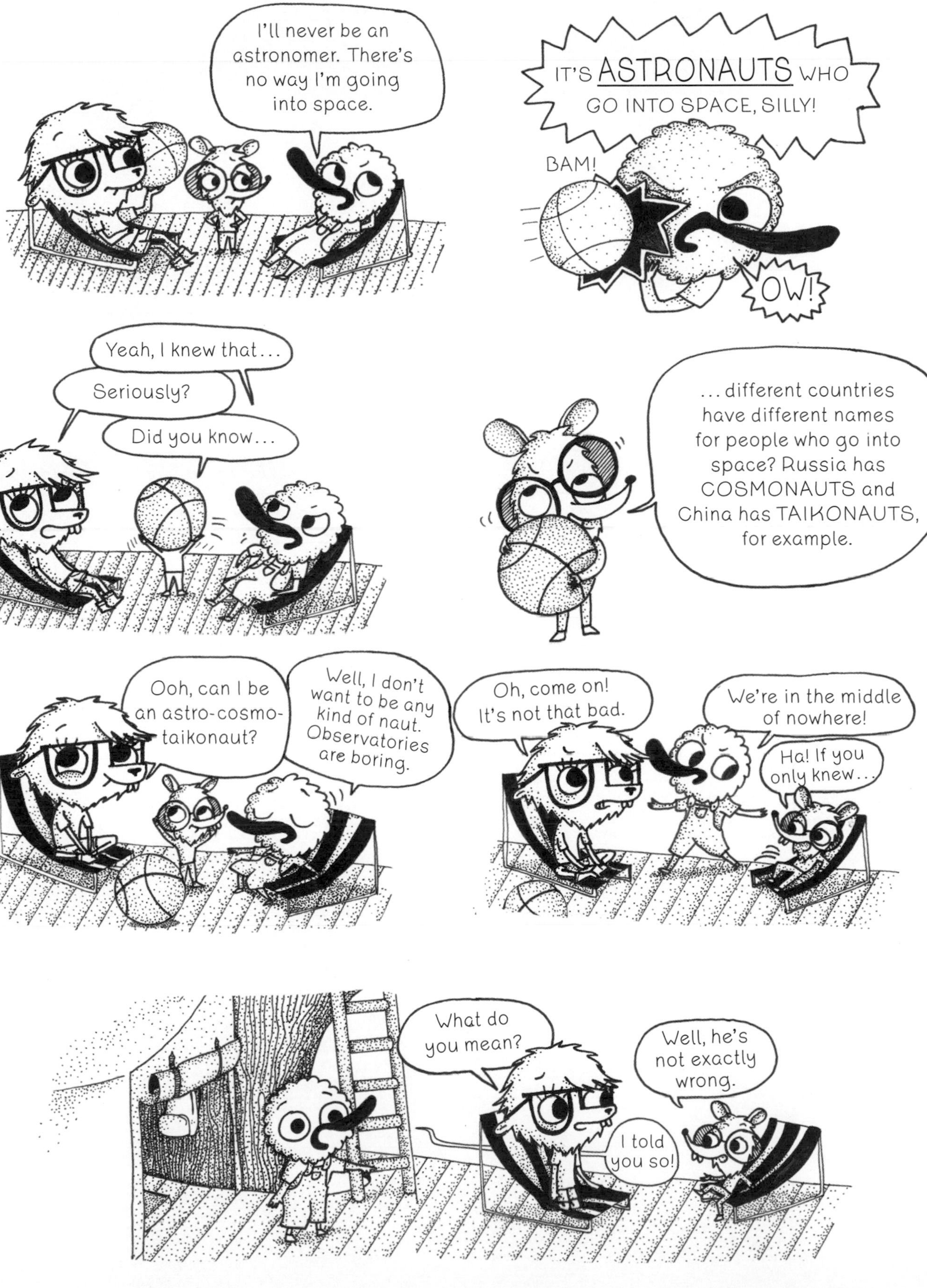
I'll never be an astronomer. There's no way I'm going into space.
IT'S ASTRONAUTS WHO GO INTO SPACE, SILLY!
BAM!
OW!
Yeah, I knew that...
Seriously?
Did you know...
...different countries have different names for people who go into space? Russia has COSMONAUTS and China has TAIKONAUTS, for example.
Ooh, can I be an astro-cosmo-taikonaut?
Well, I don't want to be any kind of naut. Observatories are boring.
Oh, come on! It's not that bad.
We're in the middle of nowhere!
Ha! If you only knew...
What do you mean?
Well, he's not exactly wrong.
I told you so!

Chapter 2

OUR PLACE IN THE COSMOS

Before we start exploring, we have to know where we are in the COSMOS. Earth is one of EIGHT PLANETS in the SOLAR SYSTEM.

And this is just one of many SOLAR SYSTEMS in OUR GALAXY!

△1 SOLAR SYSTEM

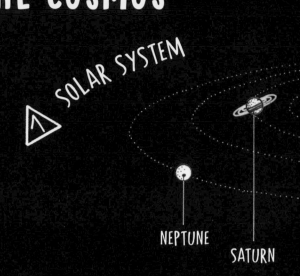

NEPTUNE

SATURN

△2 THE MILKY WAY

This is our galaxy.

That's the Sun! It looks so small.

This galaxy has a spiral shape!

There are different types of galaxies too.

← IRREGULAR galaxies

and

ELLIPTICAL galaxies →

Some scientists think that these types of galaxies were formed when two spiral galaxies collided.

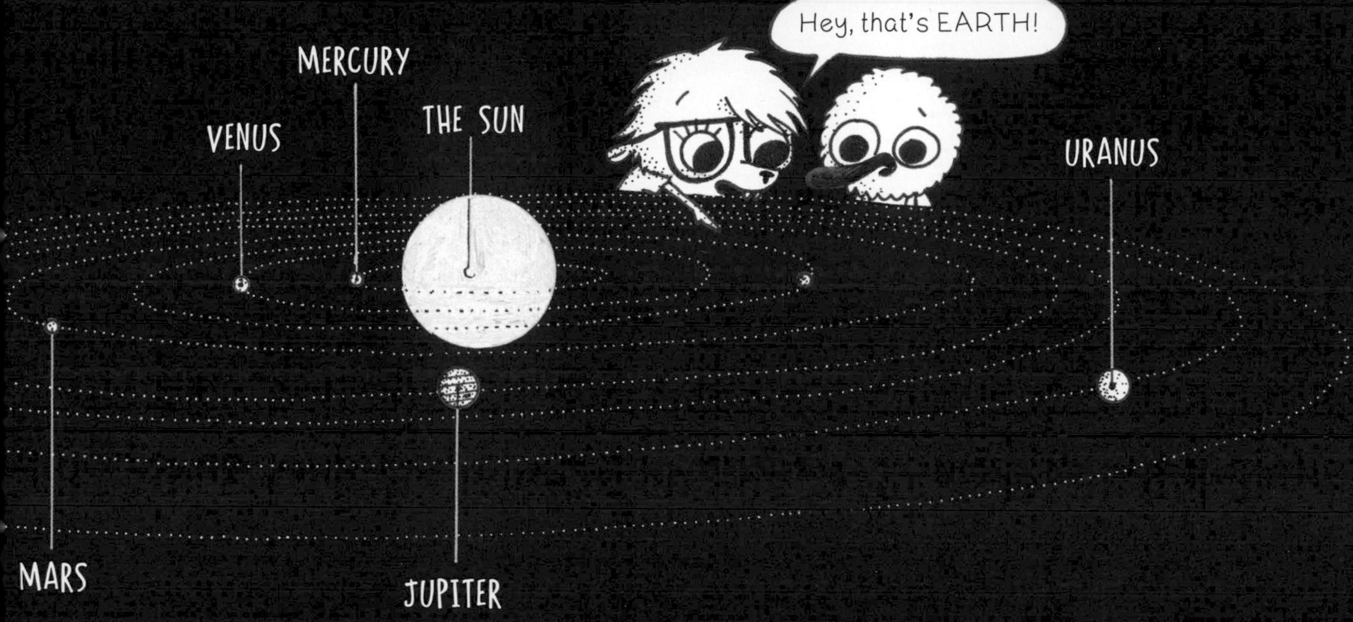
Hey, that's EARTH!
MERCURY
VENUS
THE SUN
URANUS
MARS
JUPITER

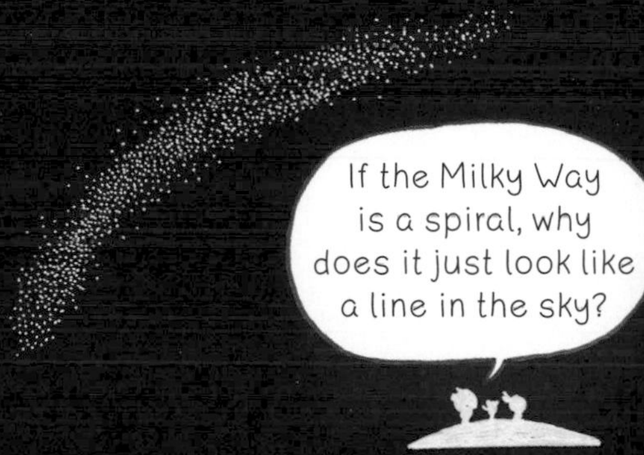
If the Milky Way is a spiral, why does it just look like a line in the sky?

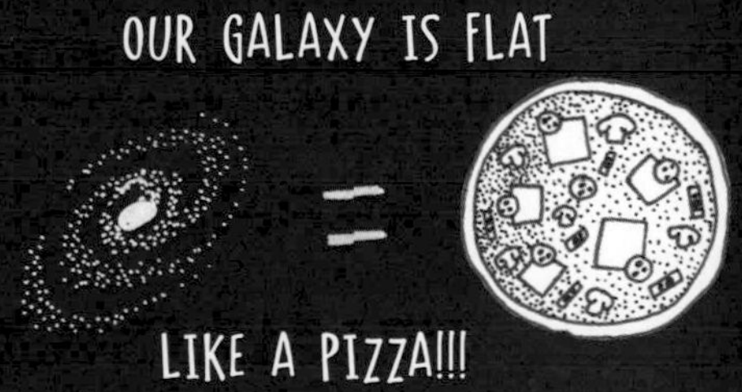
OUR GALAXY IS FLAT
=
LIKE A PIZZA!!!

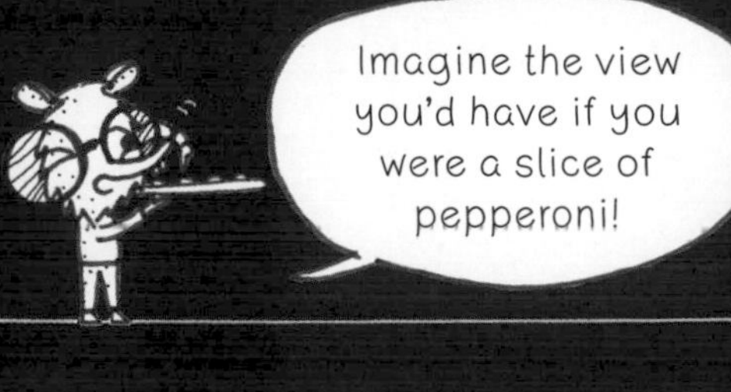
Imagine the view you'd have if you were a slice of pepperoni!

3 THE LOCAL GROUP

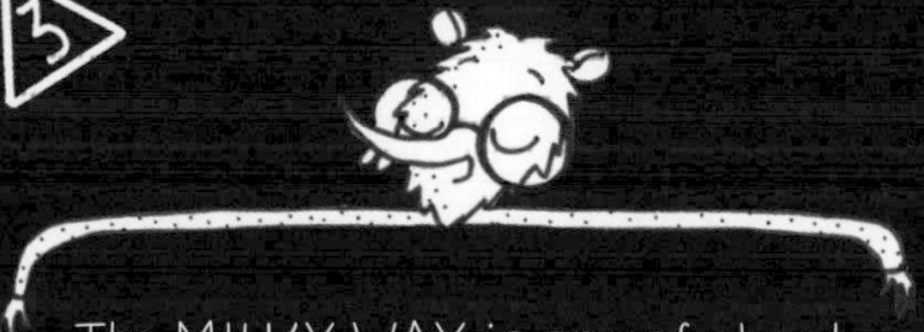

The MILKY WAY is one of about 50 galaxies in a group called the LOCAL GROUP.

Millions of years from now, it is expected to collide with the nearby ANDROMEDA GALAXY to form one gigantic GALAXY.

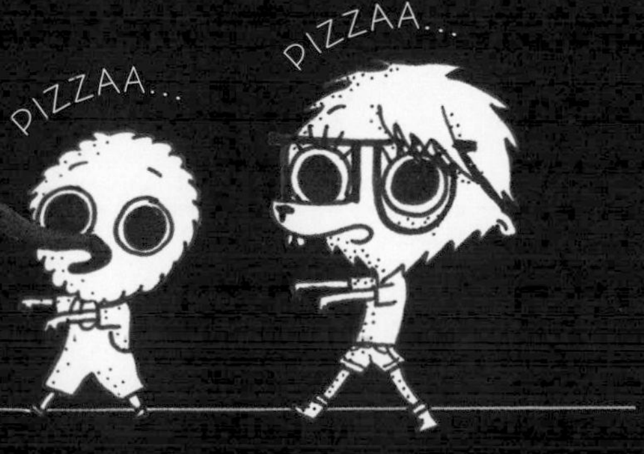
PIZZAA...
PIZZAA...

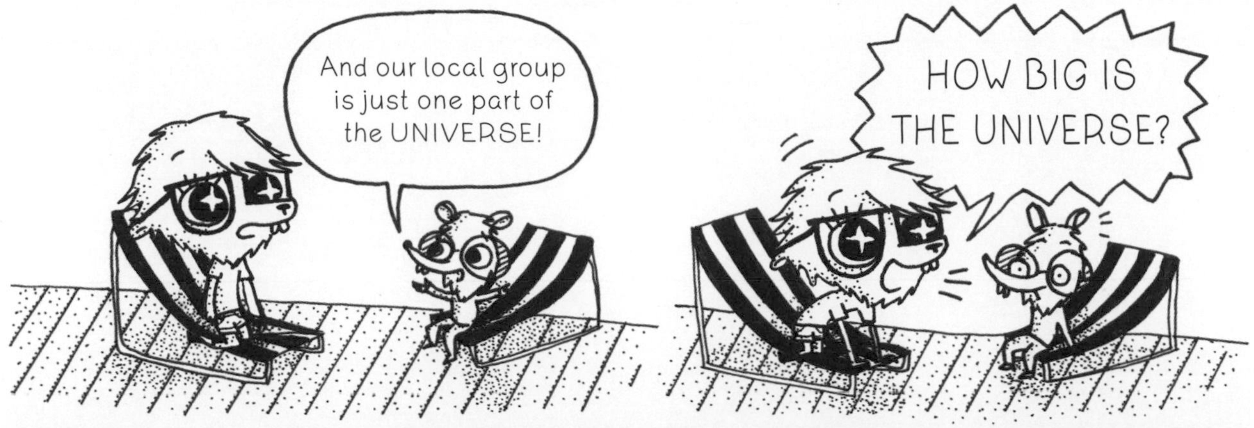
And our local group is just one part of the UNIVERSE!
HOW BIG IS THE UNIVERSE?

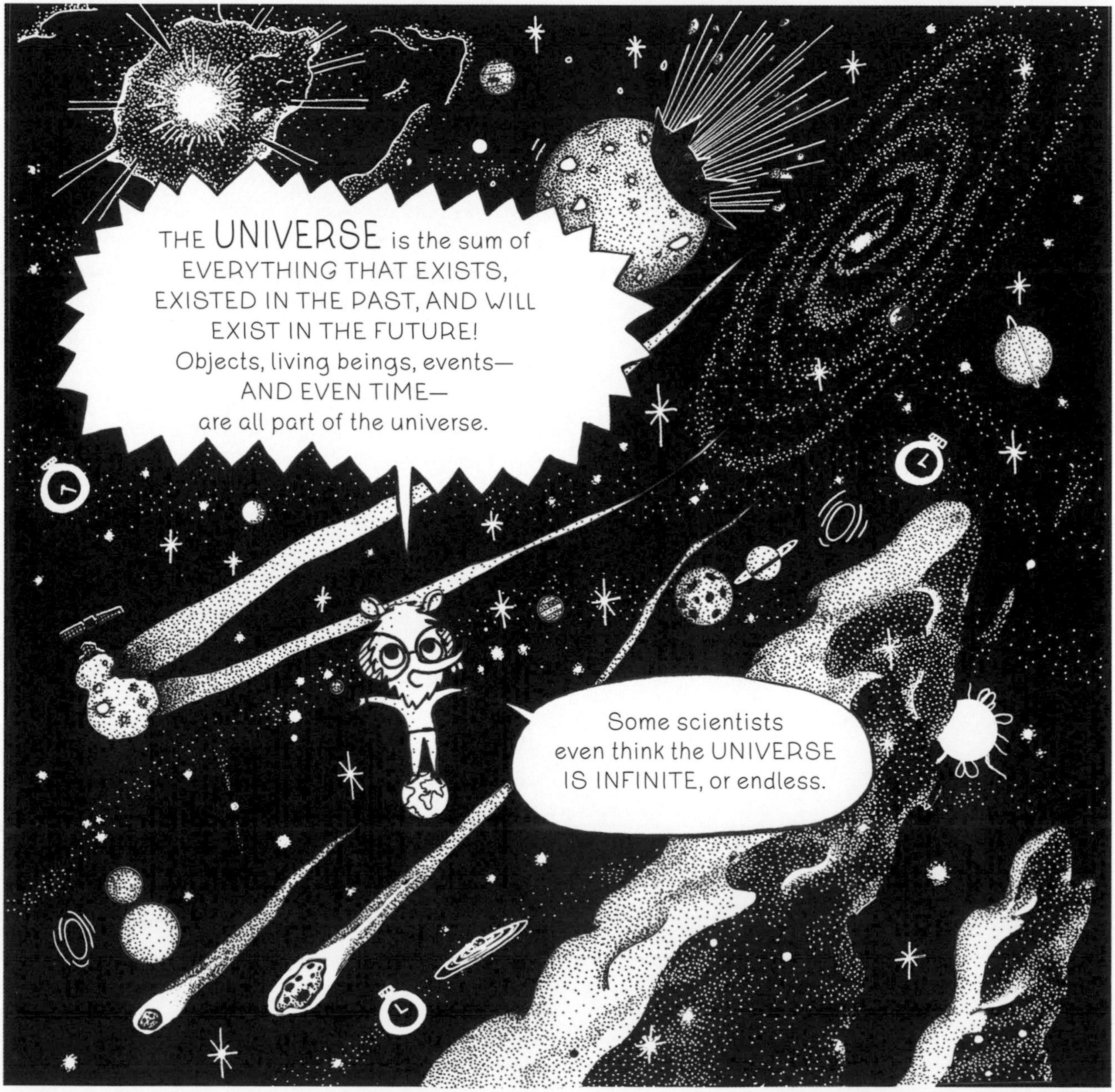
THE UNIVERSE is the sum of EVERYTHING THAT EXISTS, EXISTED IN THE PAST, AND WILL EXIST IN THE FUTURE! Objects, living beings, events— AND EVEN TIME— are all part of the universe.
Some scientists even think the UNIVERSE IS INFINITE, or endless.

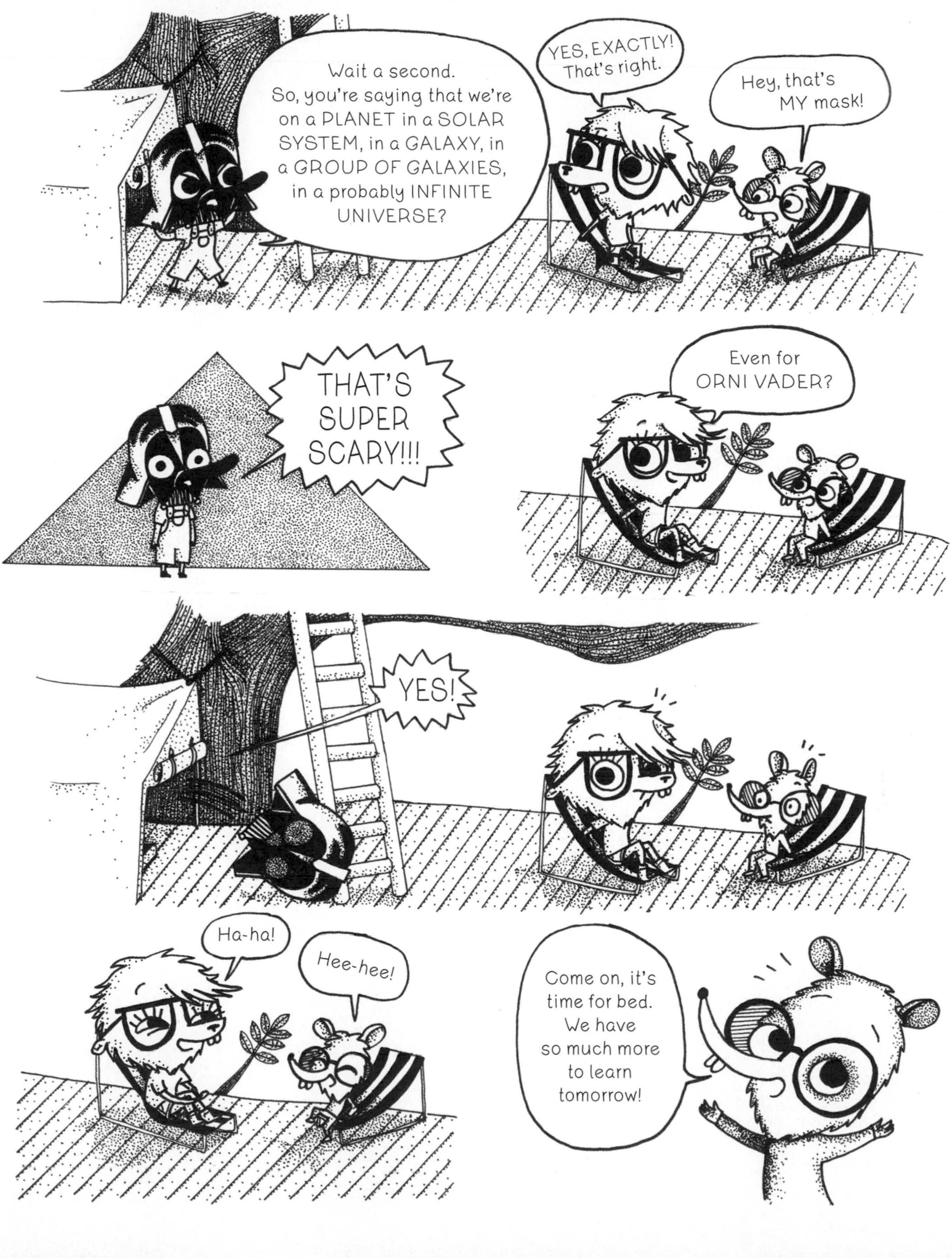
Wait a second. So, you're saying that we're on a PLANET in a SOLAR SYSTEM, in a GALAXY, in a GROUP OF GALAXIES, in a probably INFINITE UNIVERSE?
YES, EXACTLY! That's right.
Hey, that's MY mask!
THAT'S SUPER SCARY!!!
Even for ORNI VADER?
YES!
Ha-ha!
Hee-hee!
Come on, it's time for bed. We have so much more to learn tomorrow!

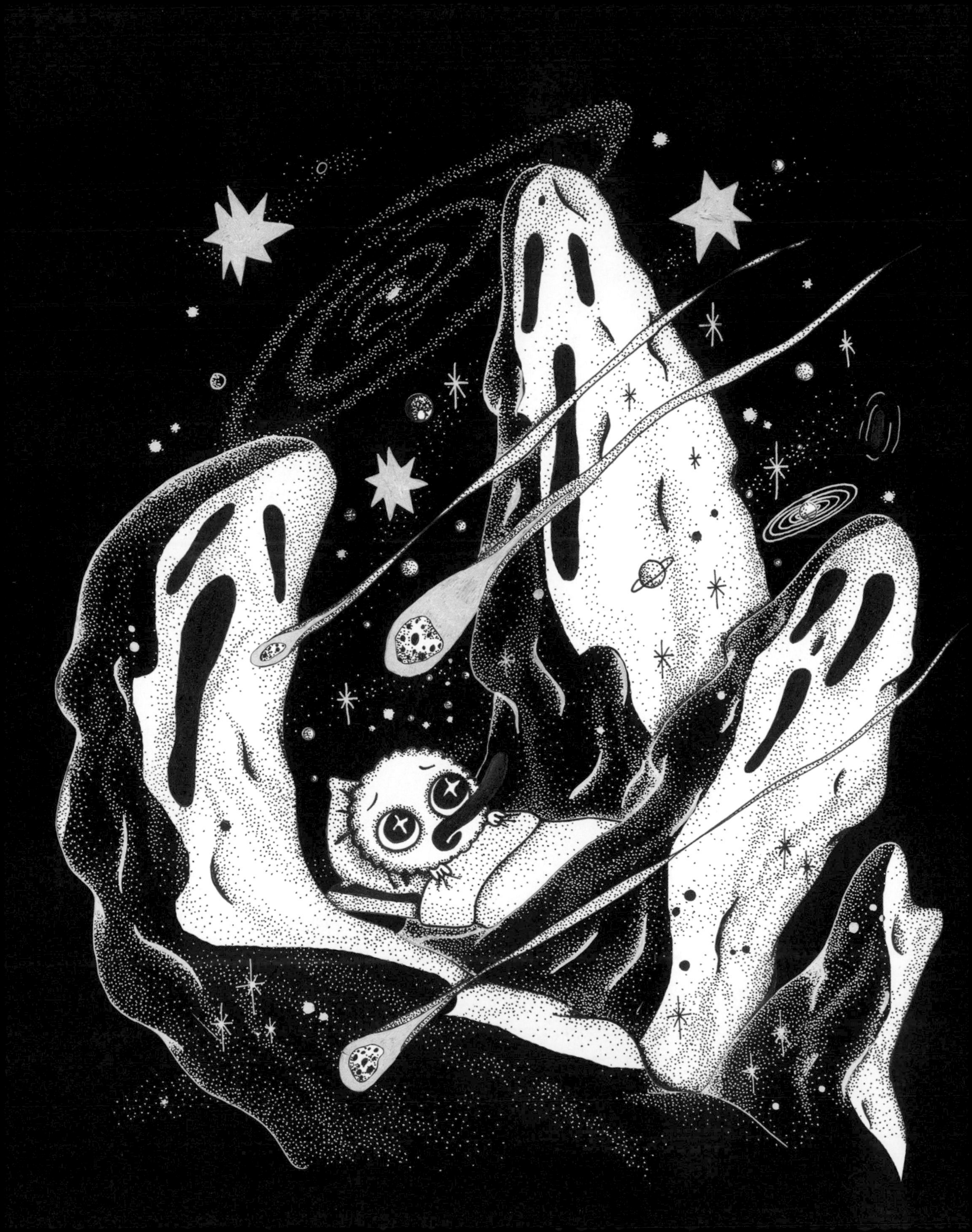

Chapter 3

CLEAN YOUR SOLAR SYSTEM

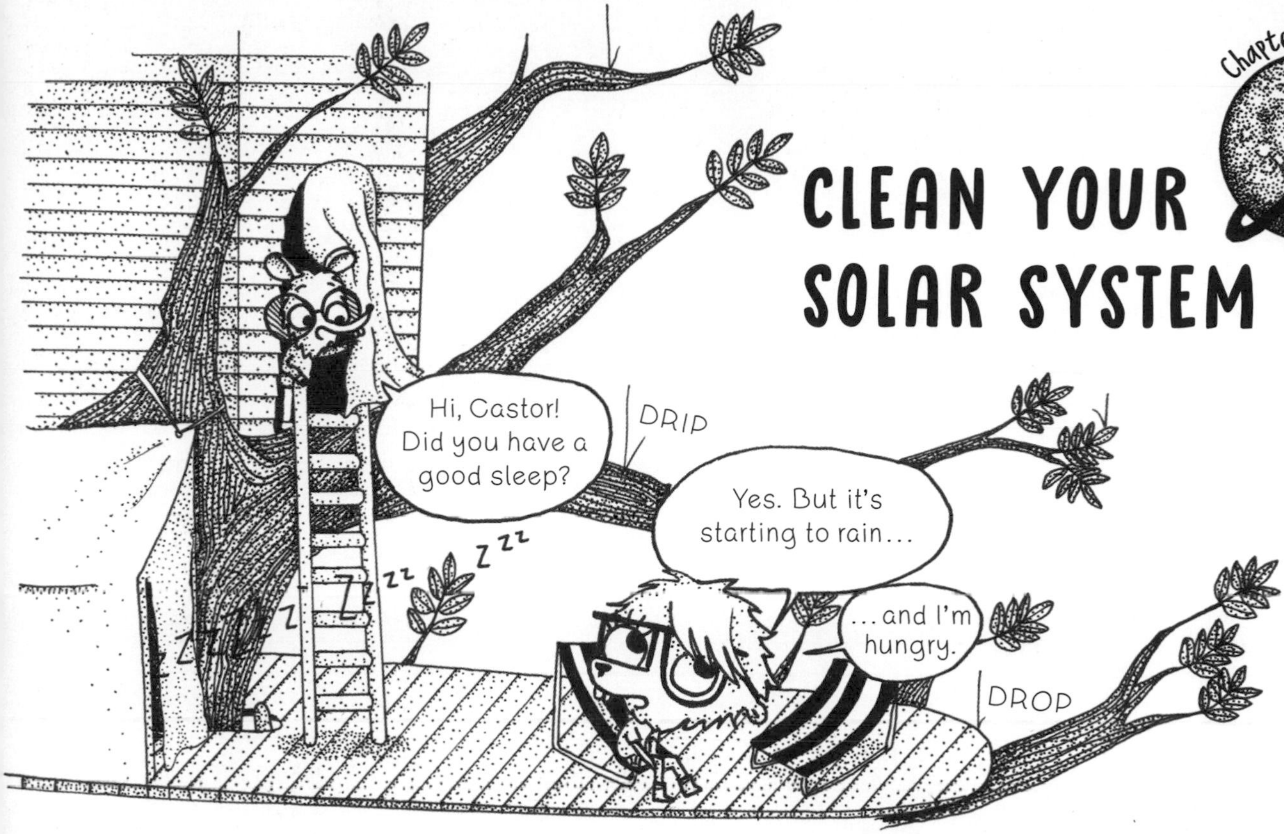
Hi, Castor! Did you have a good sleep?
DRIP
Yes. But it's starting to rain...
...and I'm hungry.
DROP

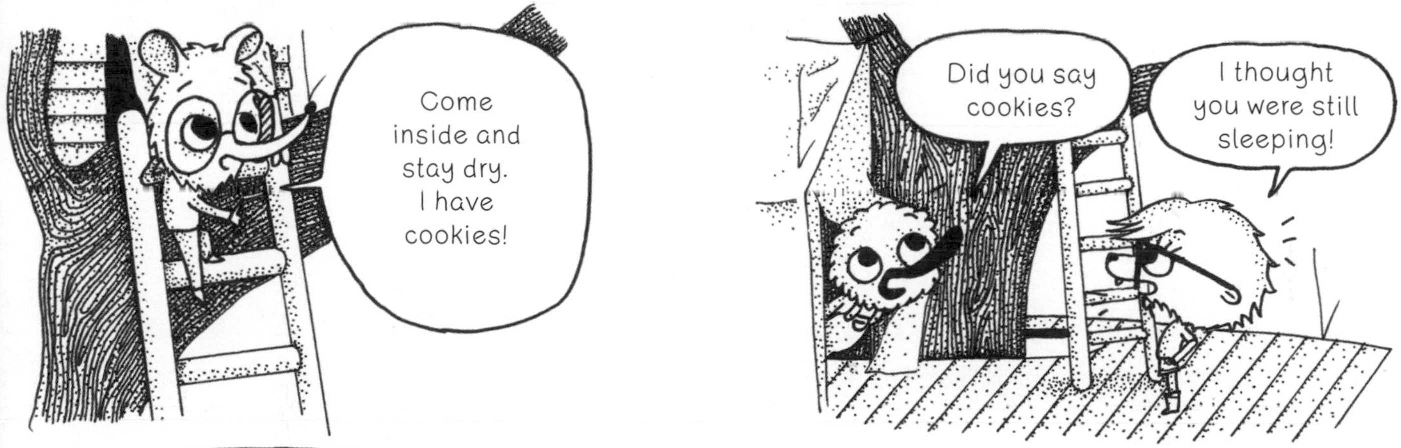
Come inside and stay dry. I have cookies!
Did you say cookies?
I thought you were still sleeping!

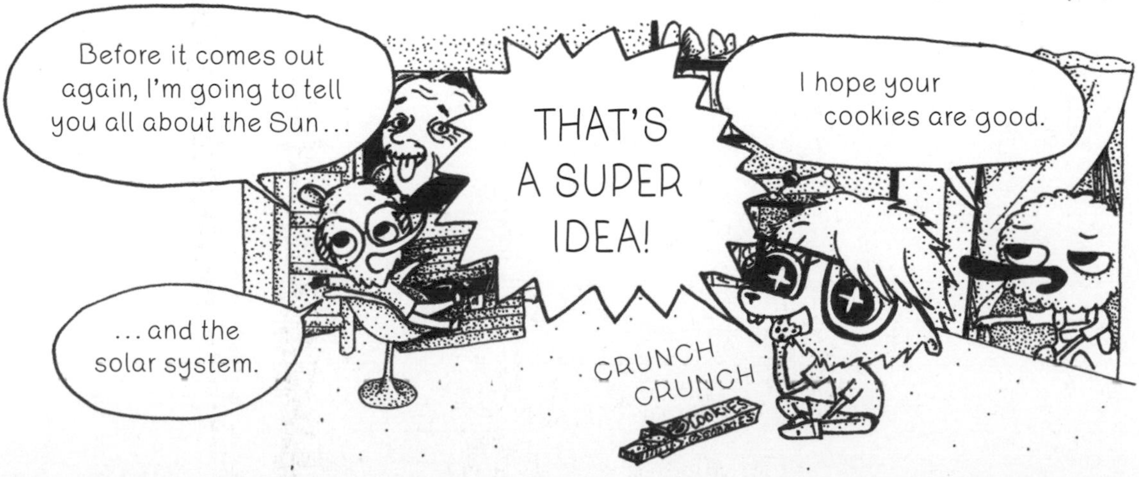
Before it comes out again, I'm going to tell you all about the Sun...
THAT'S A SUPER IDEA!
I hope your cookies are good.
...and the solar system.
CRUNCH CRUNCH

1 THE SUN

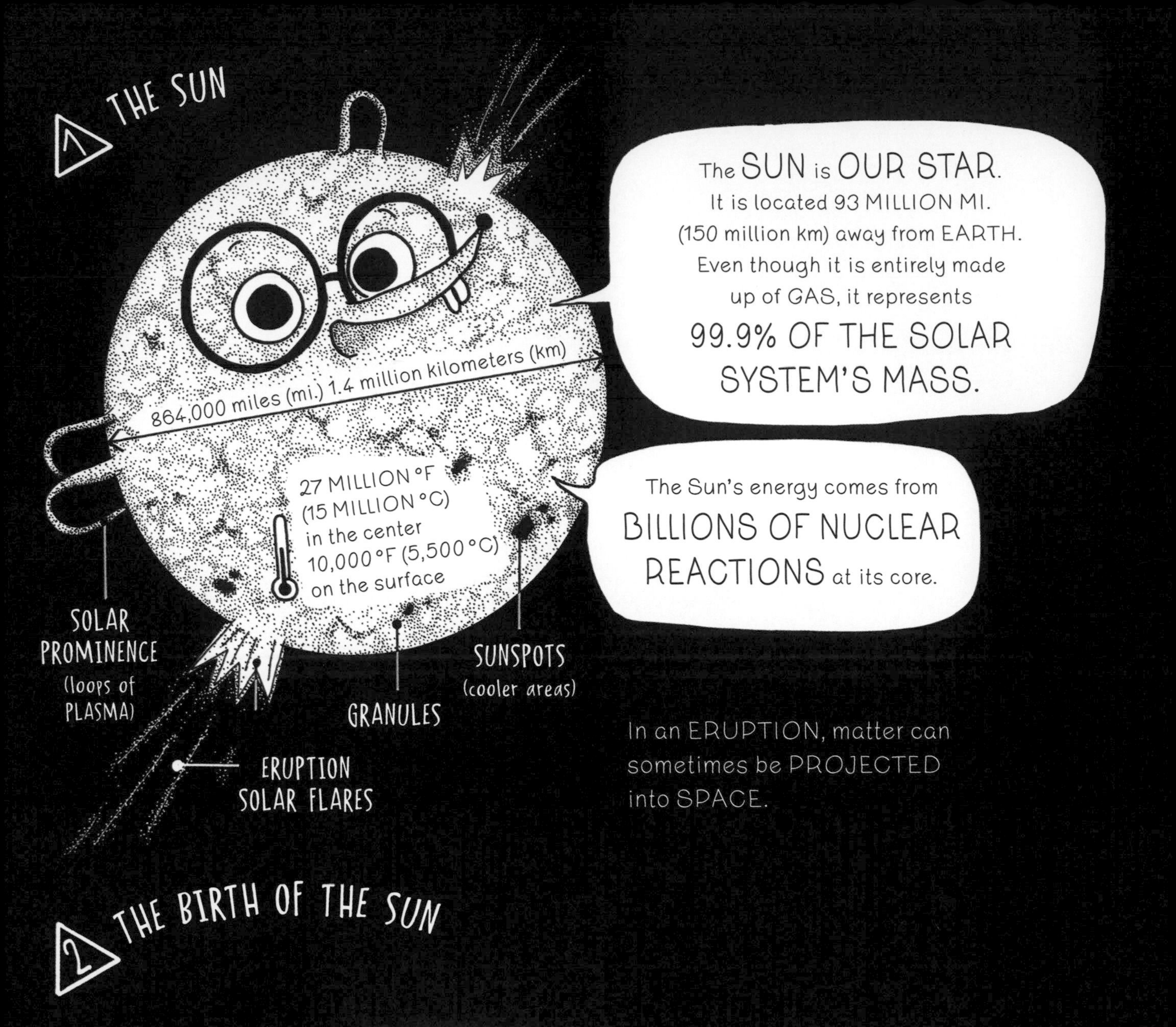
864,000 miles (mi.) 1.4 million kilometers (km)
27 MILLION °F (15 MILLION °C) in the center 10,000 °F (5,500 °C) on the surface
SOLAR PROMINENCE (loops of PLASMA)
SUNSPOTS (cooler areas)
GRANULES
ERUPTION SOLAR FLARES

The SUN is OUR STAR. It is located 93 MILLION MI. (150 million km) away from EARTH. Even though it is entirely made up of GAS, it represents 99.9% OF THE SOLAR SYSTEM'S MASS.

The Sun's energy comes from BILLIONS OF NUCLEAR REACTIONS at its core.

In an ERUPTION, matter can sometimes be PROJECTED into SPACE.

2 THE BIRTH OF THE SUN

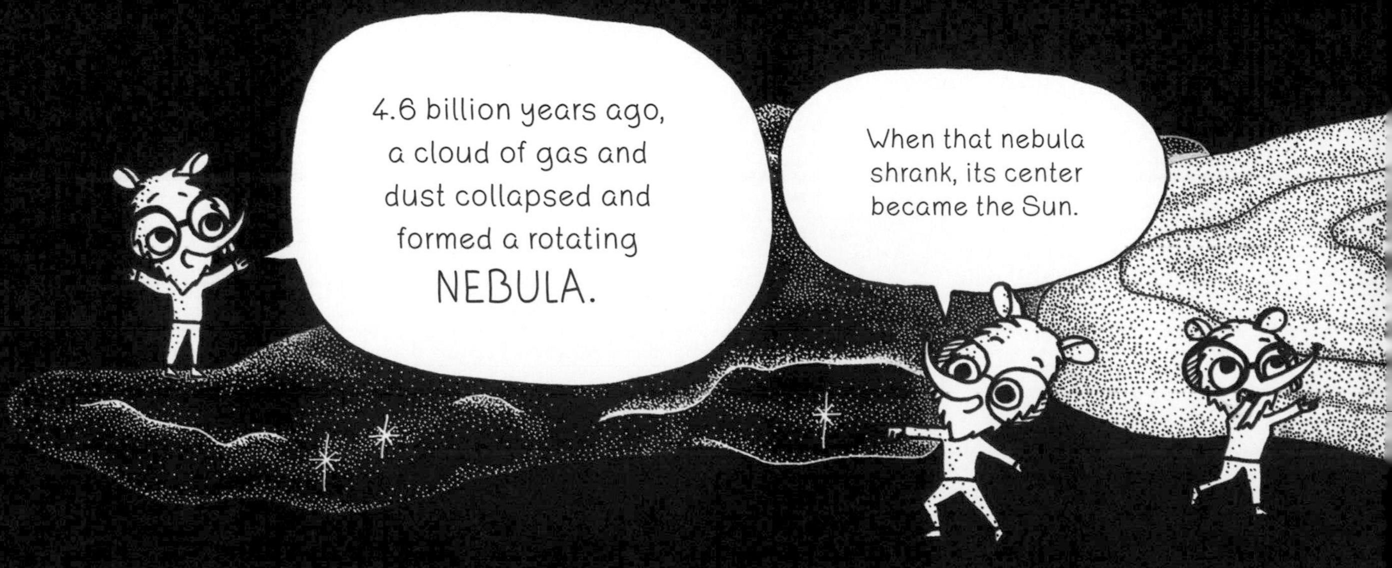
4.6 billion years ago, a cloud of gas and dust collapsed and formed a rotating NEBULA.
When that nebula shrank, its center became the Sun.

These SOLAR FLARES are NOT DANGEROUS. But they can lead to some SPECTACULAR LIGHT SHOWS here on EARTH:

THE POLAR AURORAS

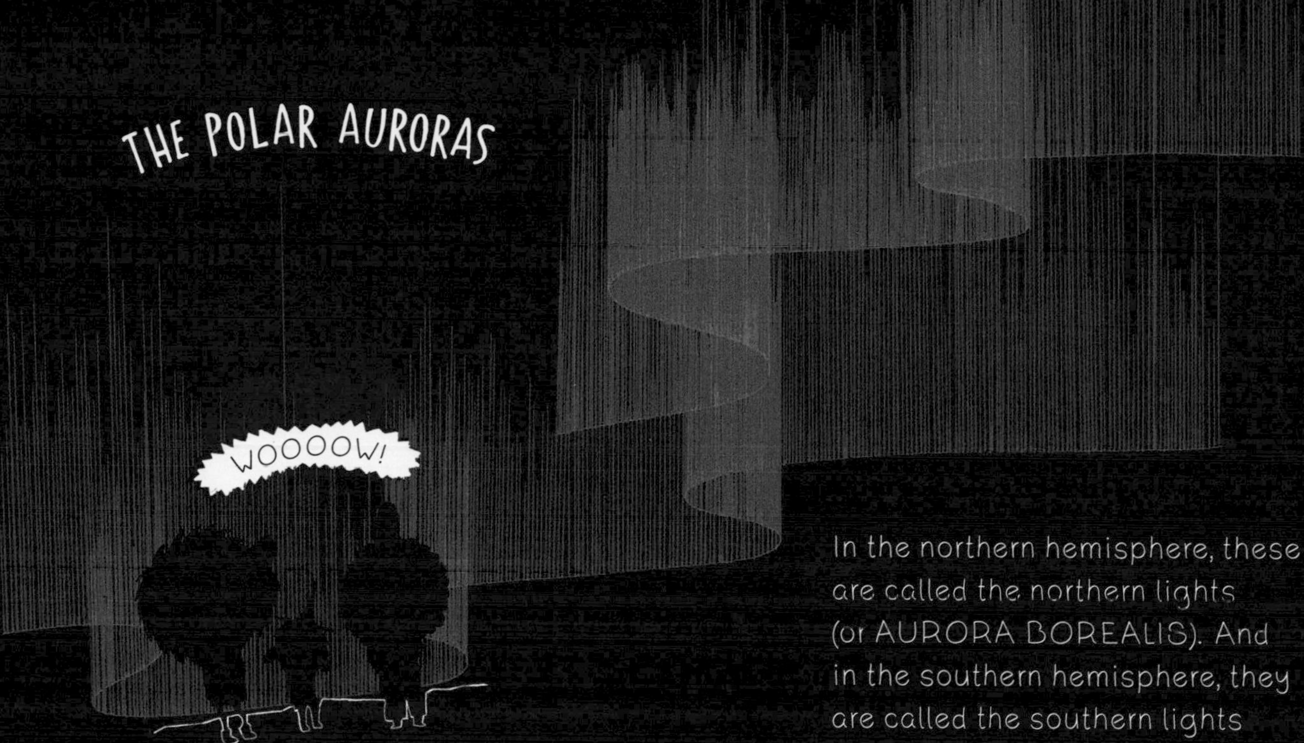
WOOOOW!

In the northern hemisphere, these are called the northern lights (or AURORA BOREALIS). And in the southern hemisphere, they are called the southern lights (or AURORA AUSTRALIS).

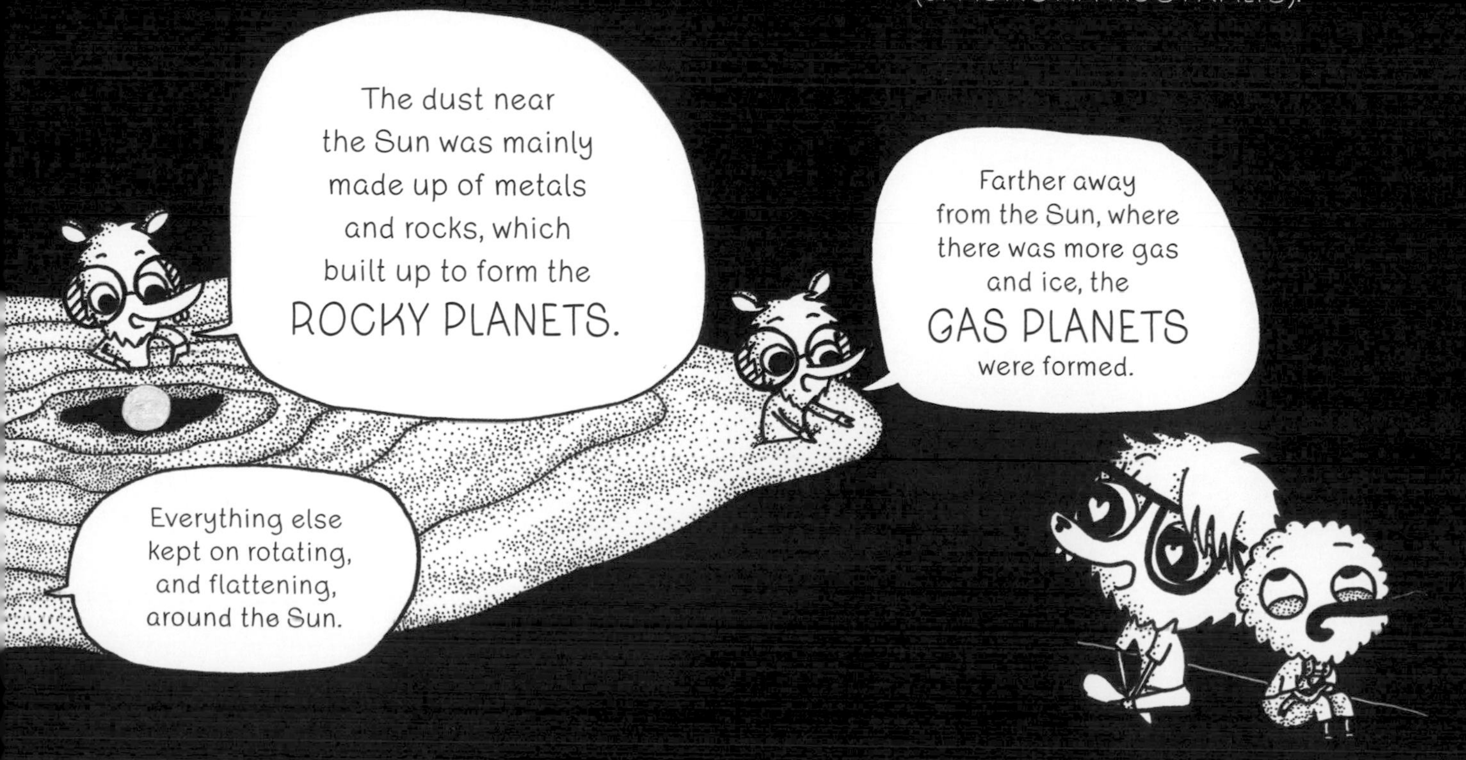
The dust near the Sun was mainly made up of metals and rocks, which built up to form the ROCKY PLANETS.
Farther away from the Sun, where there was more gas and ice, the GAS PLANETS were formed.
Everything else kept on rotating, and flattening, around the Sun.

3 THE FORMATION OF THE PLANETS

THE ROCKY PLANETS

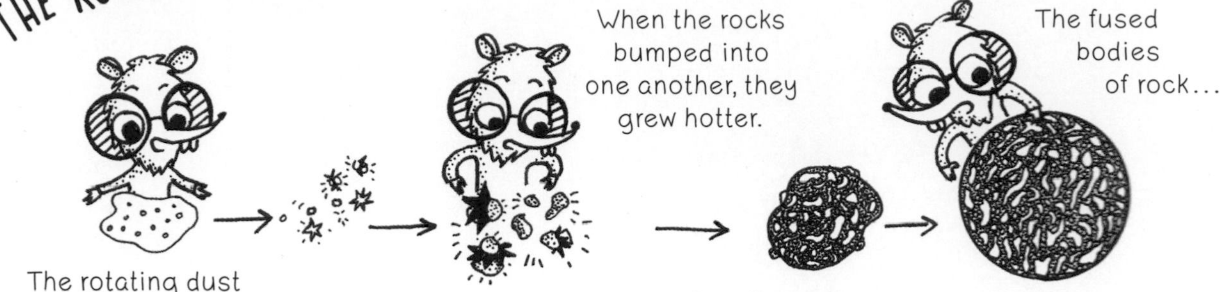
The rotating dust attracted more dust, until it formed rocks.
When the rocks bumped into one another, they grew hotter.
Then the rocks split apart, and they all fused together.
The fused bodies of rock…
… got rounder as they were rotating.

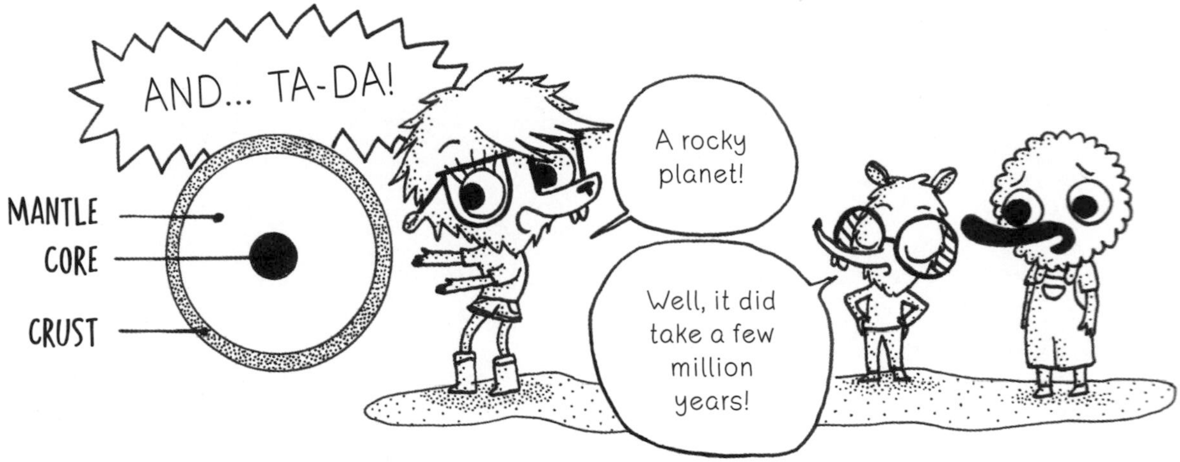
AND… TA-DA!
MANTLE
CORE
CRUST
A rocky planet!
Well, it did take a few million years!

THE GAS PLANETS

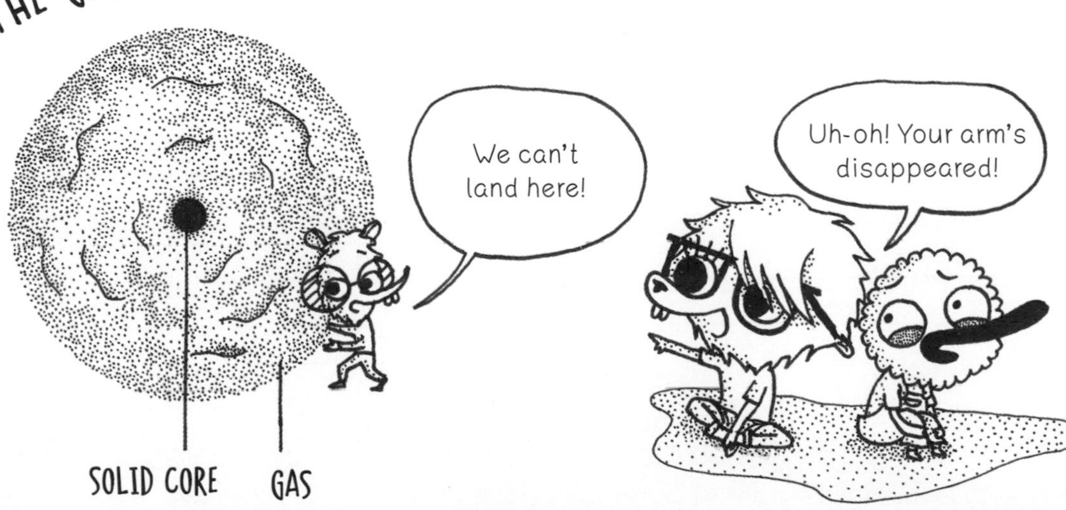
SOLID CORE
GAS
We can't land here!
Uh-oh! Your arm's disappeared!

EVERYTHING ELSE

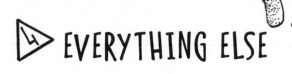

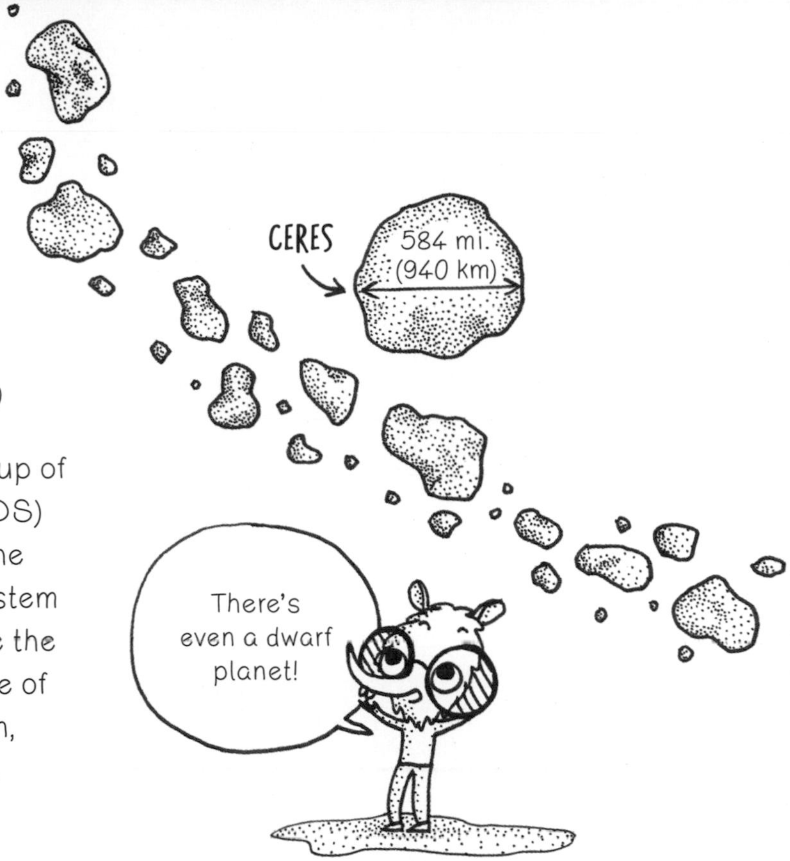
CERES
584 mi. (940 km)
There's even a dwarf planet!

THE ASTEROID BELT

(between the rocky and the gas planets)

The asteroid belt is made up of bodies of rock (ASTEROIDS) that were formed around the same time as the solar system and were not used to make the planets—probably because of their very peculiar location, between Mars and Jupiter.

THE KUIPER BELT

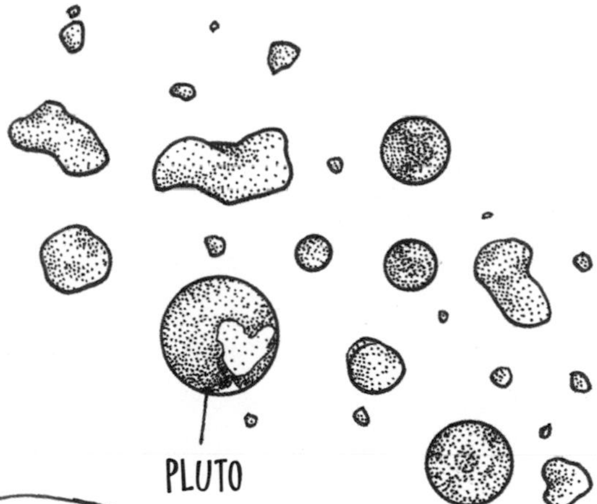
PLUTO

In the outer reaches of the solar system, there are comets and dwarf planets including MAKEMAKE, ERIS, HAUMEA, and PLUTO (since 2006)!

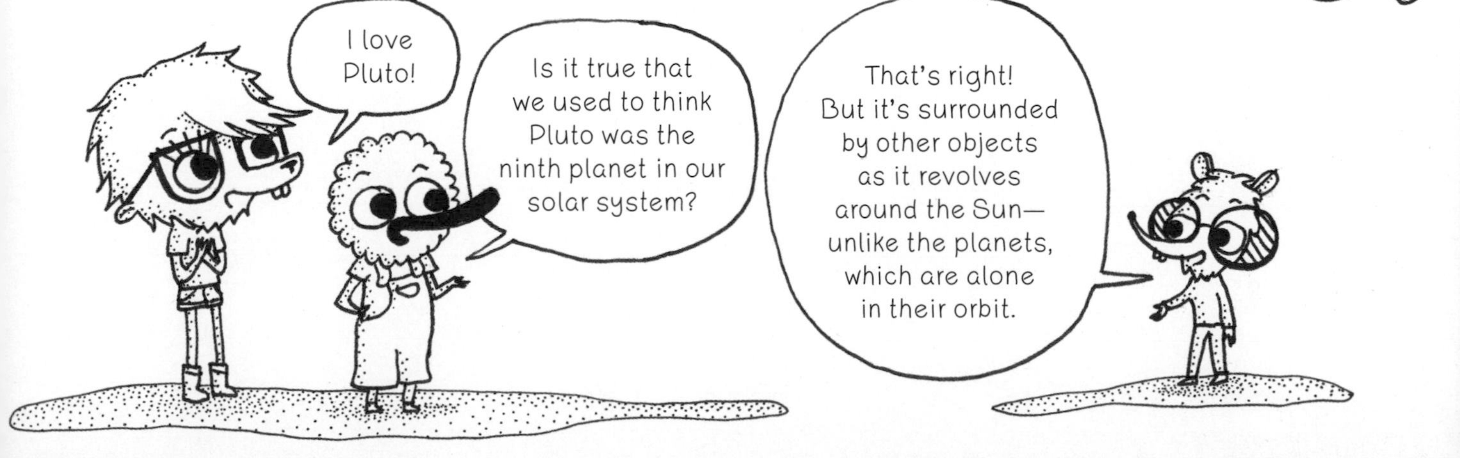
I love Pluto!
Is it true that we used to think Pluto was the ninth planet in our solar system?
That's right! But it's surrounded by other objects as it revolves around the Sun—unlike the planets, which are alone in their orbit.

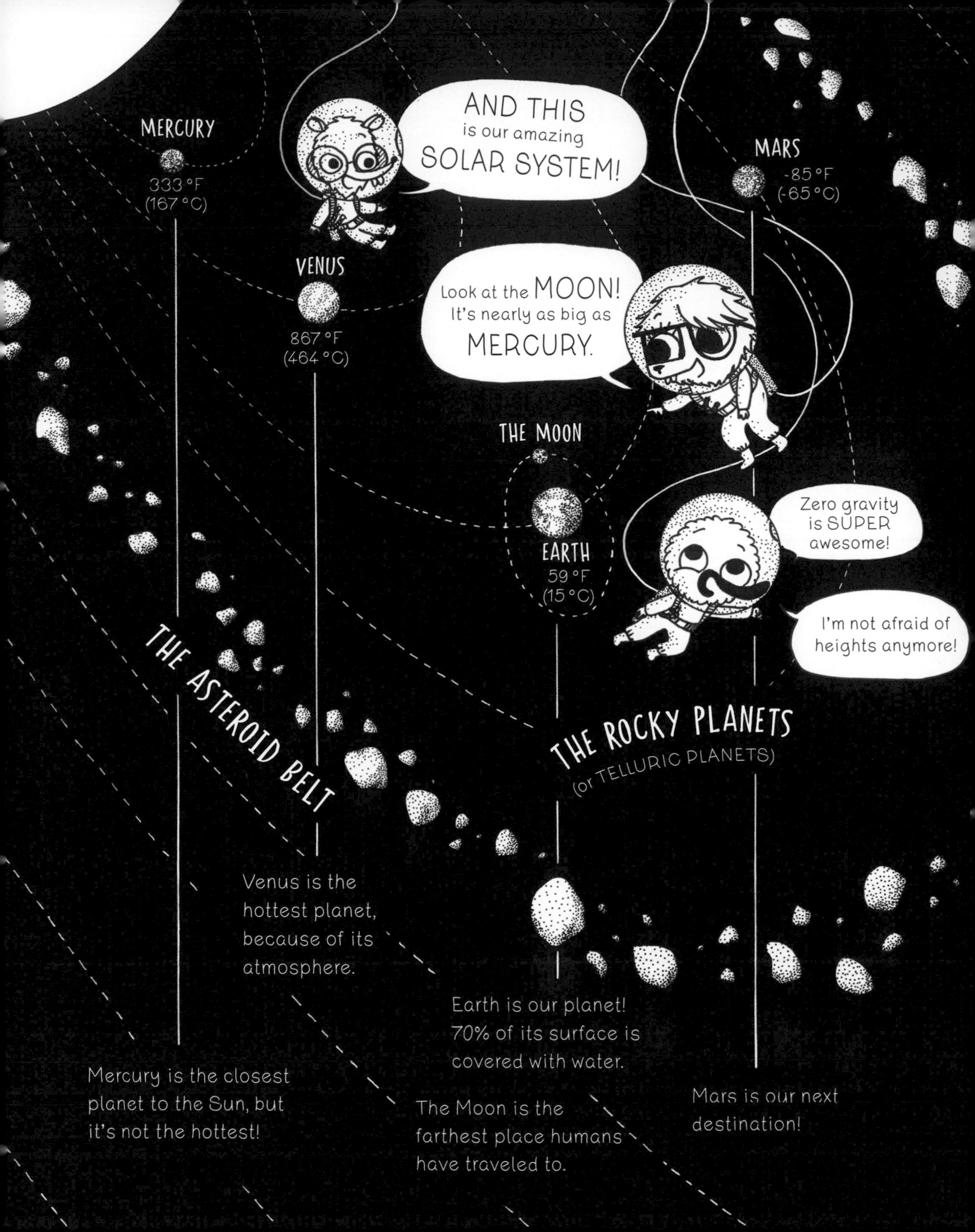
AND THIS is our amazing SOLAR SYSTEM!
MERCURY
333 °F (167 °C)
VENUS
867 °F (464 °C)
MARS
-85 °F (-65 °C)
Look at the MOON! It's nearly as big as MERCURY.
THE MOON
EARTH
59 °F (15 °C)
Zero gravity is SUPER awesome!
I'm not afraid of heights anymore!
THE ASTEROID BELT
THE ROCKY PLANETS (or TELLURIC PLANETS)
Venus is the hottest planet, because of its atmosphere.
Earth is our planet! 70% of its surface is covered with water.
Mercury is the closest planet to the Sun, but it's not the hottest!
The Moon is the farthest place humans have traveled to.
Mars is our next destination!

Jupiter is the largest planet in the solar system. It has 67 moons!

THE GAS PLANETS

JUPITER

-166 °F (-110 °C)

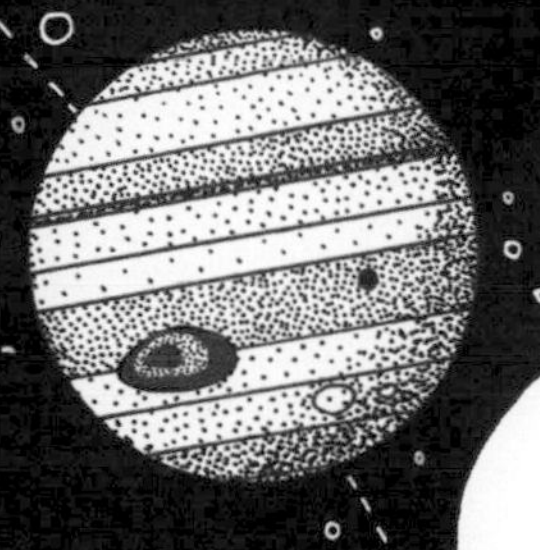

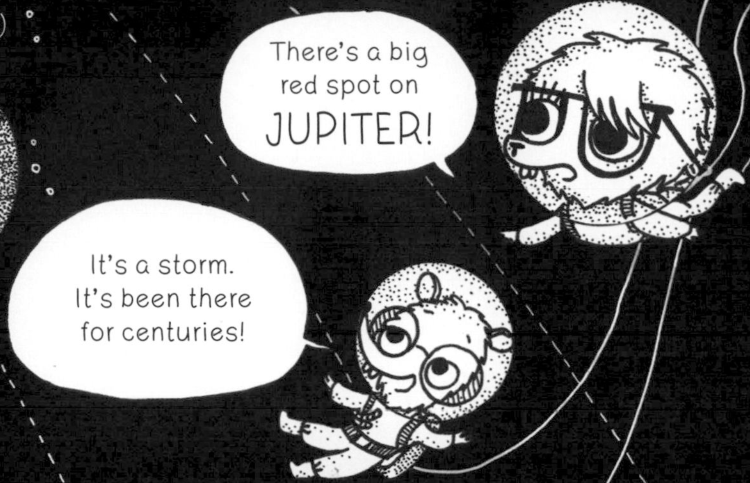
There's a big red spot on JUPITER!
It's a storm. It's been there for centuries!

NEPTUNE

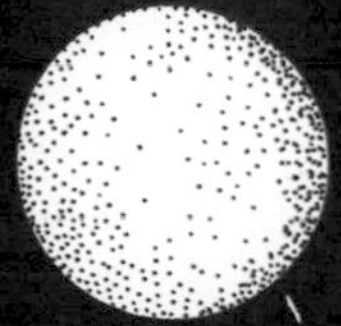

-330 °F (-200 °C)

Uranus and Neptune are nicknamed the ICE GIANTS!

Saturn is a very easy planet to recognize! Its rings are made up of rock, dust, and ice. Some of them are only 6 to 33 feet (ft.) (2 to 10 meters [m]) thick, even though they measure 224,000 mi. (360,000 km) in diameter. You can see them from Earth with a pair of binoculars!

SATURN

-220 °F (-140 °C)

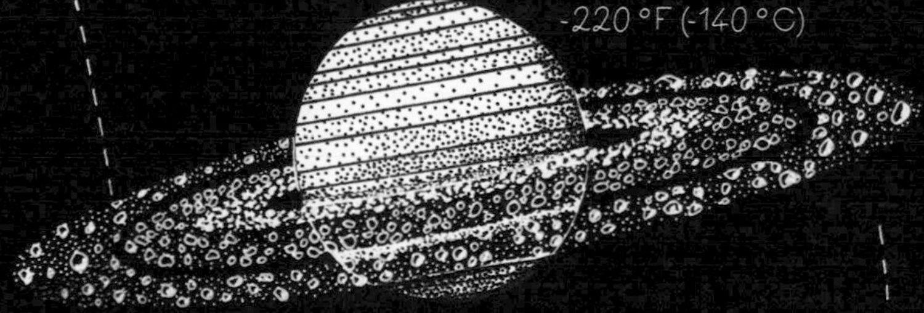

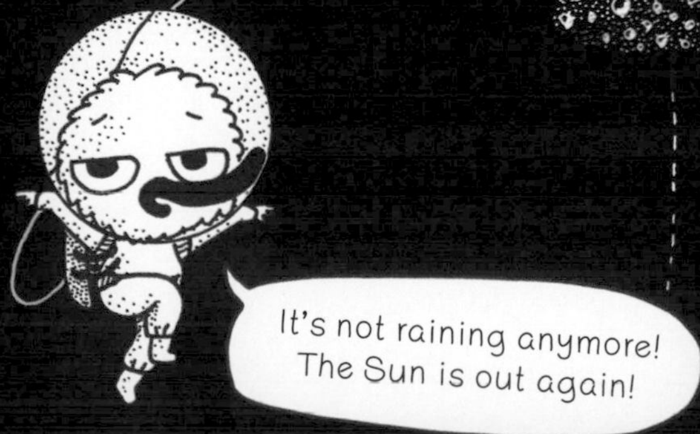
It's not raining anymore! The Sun is out again!

Uranus also has a ring, but it's much smaller.

URANUS

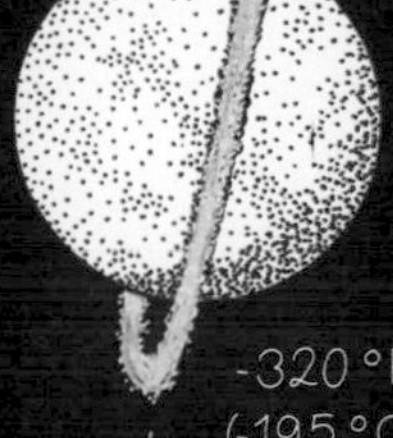

-320 °F (-195 °C)

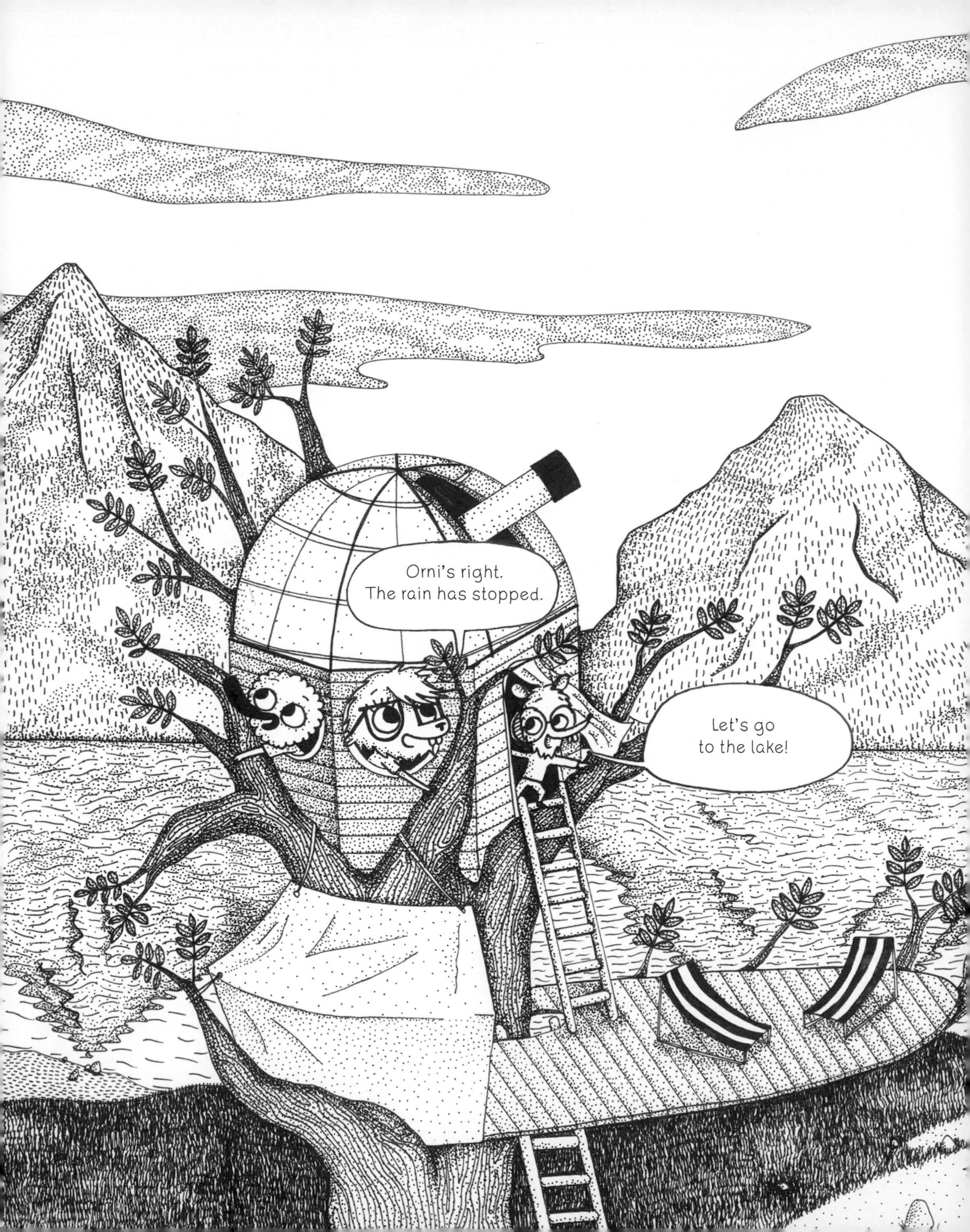
Orni's right.
The rain has stopped.
Let's go
to the lake!

Chapter 4 THE SPACE ROCK

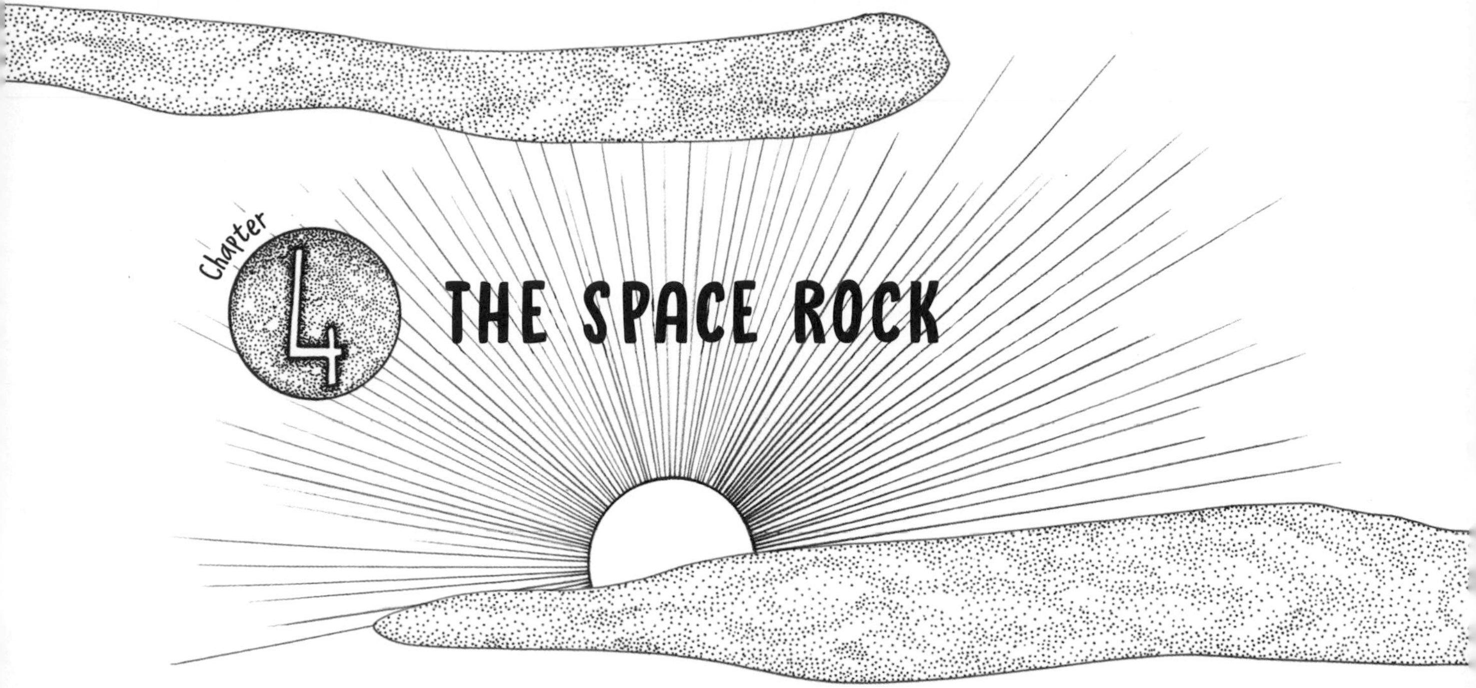

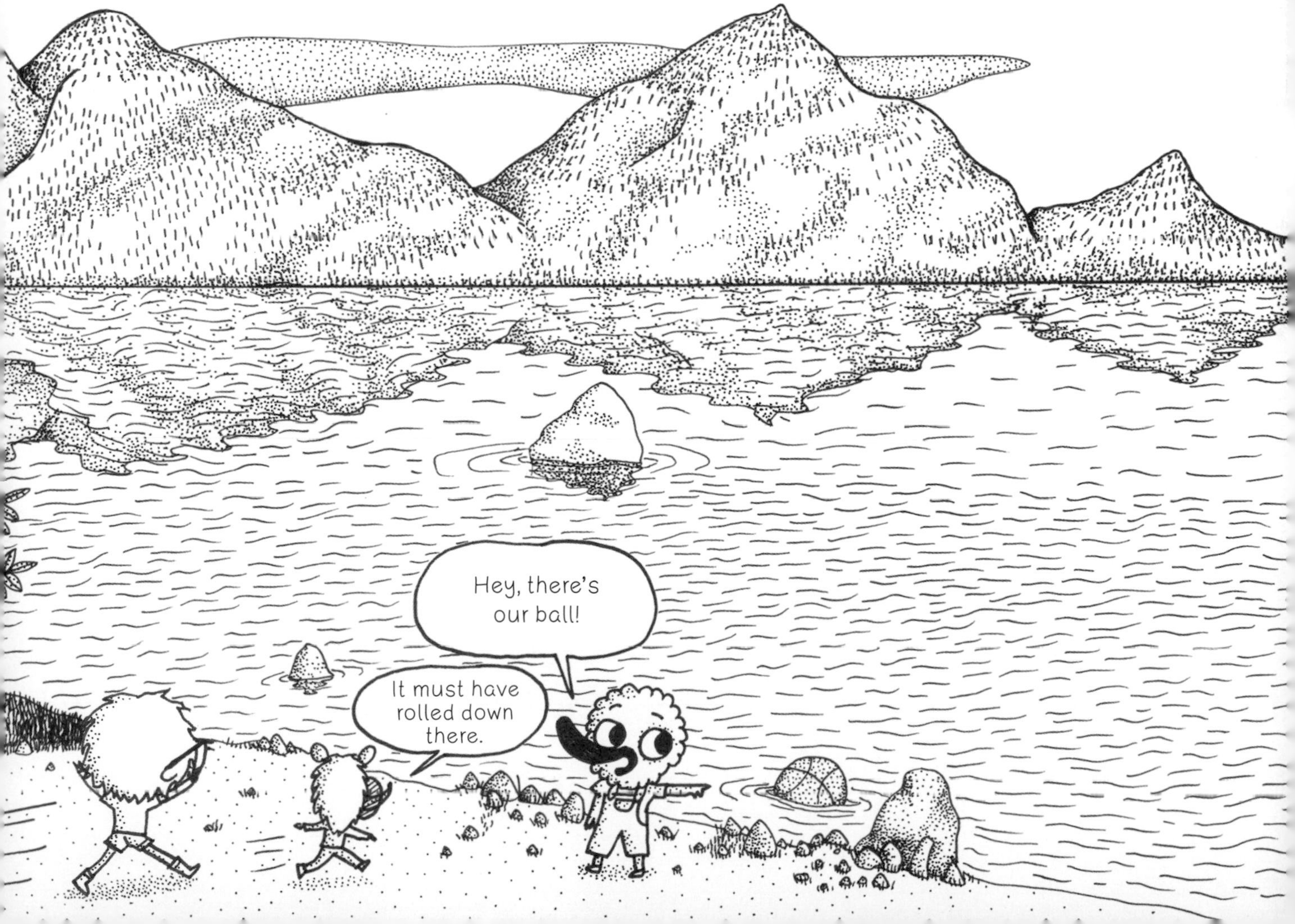
Hey, there's our ball!
It must have rolled down there.

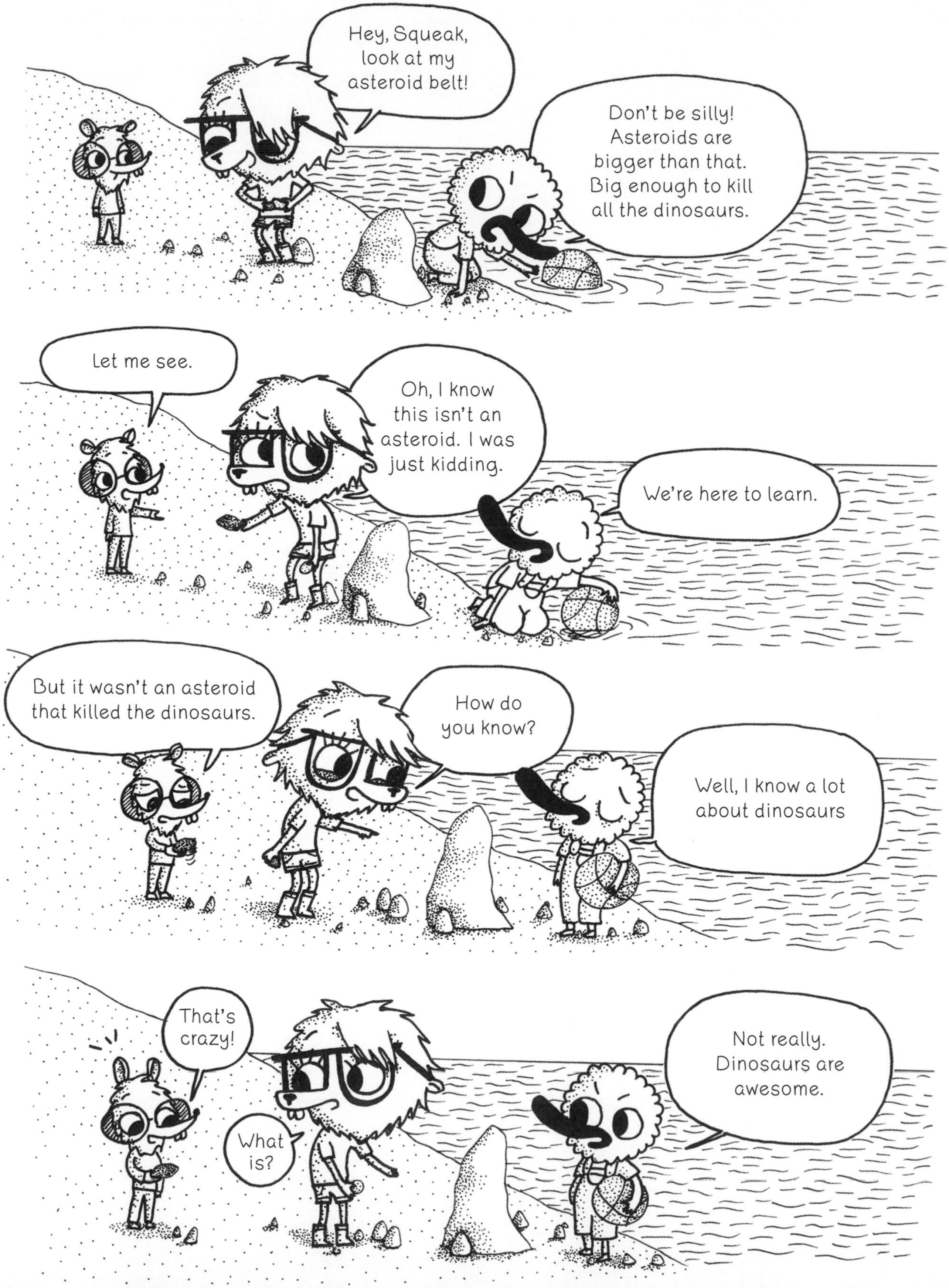
Hey, Squeak, look at my asteroid belt!
Don't be silly! Asteroids are bigger than that. Big enough to kill all the dinosaurs.
Let me see.
Oh, I know this isn't an asteroid. I was just kidding.
We're here to learn.
But it wasn't an asteroid that killed the dinosaurs.
How do you know?
Well, I know a lot about dinosaurs
That's crazy!
What is?
Not really. Dinosaurs are awesome.

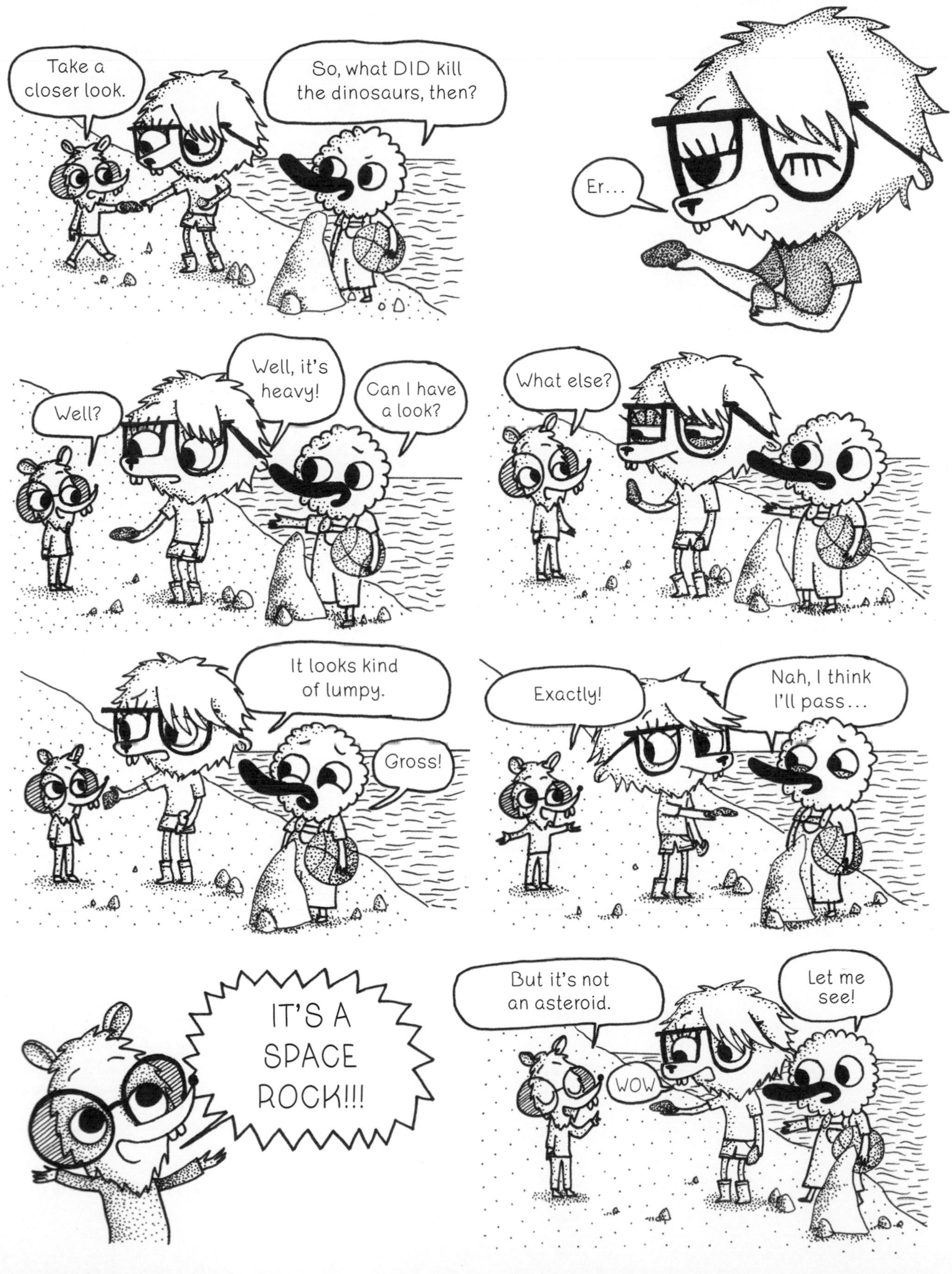
Take a closer look.
So, what DID kill the dinosaurs, then?
Er...
Well?
Well, it's heavy!
Can I have a look?
What else?
It looks kind of lumpy.
Gross!
Exactly!
Nah, I think I'll pass...
IT'S A SPACE ROCK!!!
But it's not an asteroid.
WOW
Let me see!

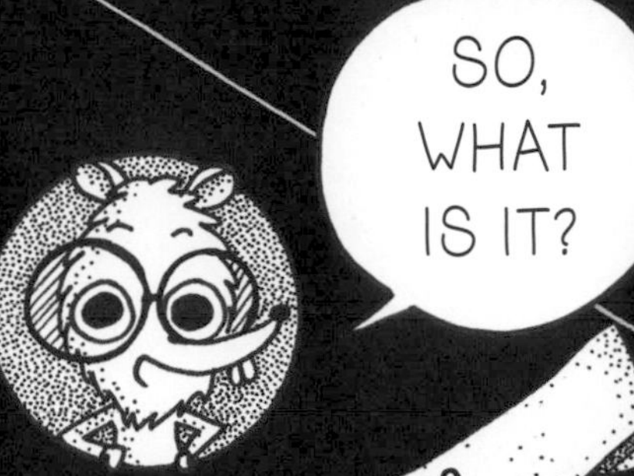
SO, WHAT IS IT?

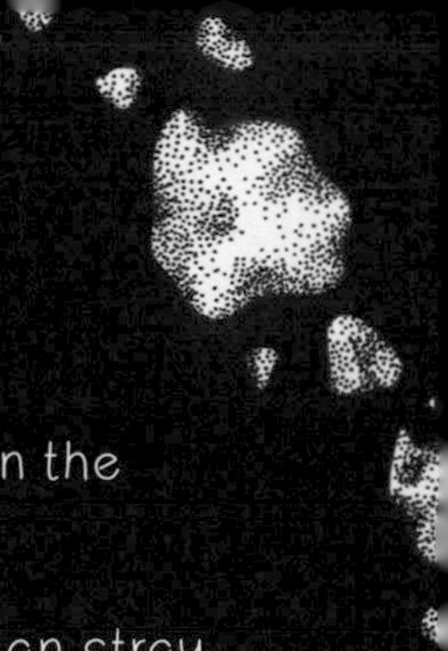

AN ASTEROID?

Asteroids are usually found in the ASTEROID BELT.

Sometimes, asteroids can stray from their path. If an asteroid gets closer than 5 million mi. (8 million km) to Earth, scientists watch it very closely!

A COMET?

Comets are made up of around 80% water. Sometimes, they're called "dirty snowballs."

When a comet is far from the Sun, the water remains solid, but as it gets closer, the water heats up and turns into a gas.

That creates two huge tails, which always point away from the Sun.

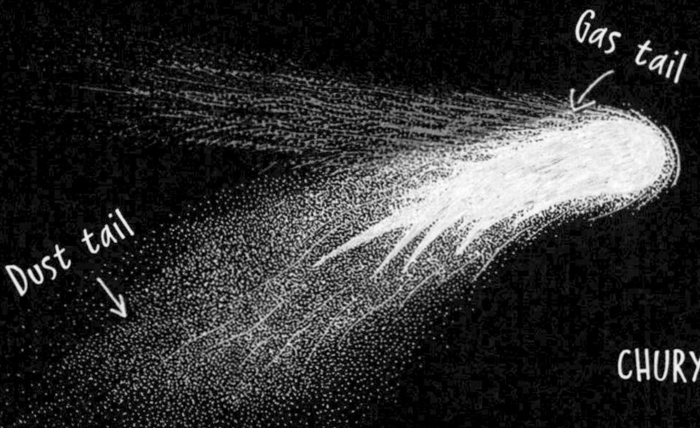
Gas tail
Dust tail

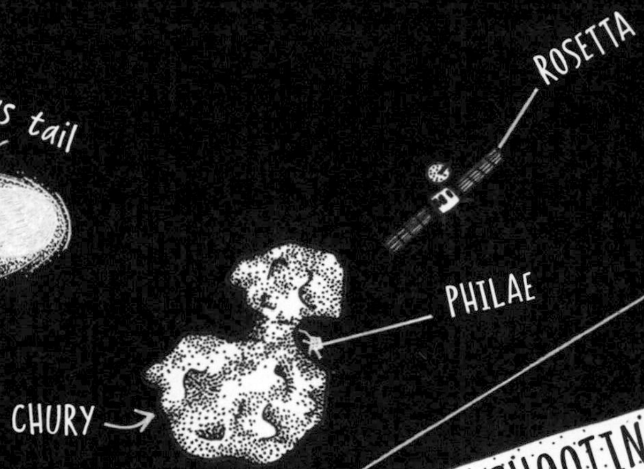
ROSETTA
PHILAE
CHURY

In 2014, the space probe Rosetta sent its lander module Philae to explore the surface of the comet CHURY!

A SHOOTING STAR?

Shooting stars are not actually stars—they're meteoroids.

Like meteorites, these are rocks that heat up when they pass through the Earth's atmosphere. But they are so small, they burn up and disappear before they reach the ground.

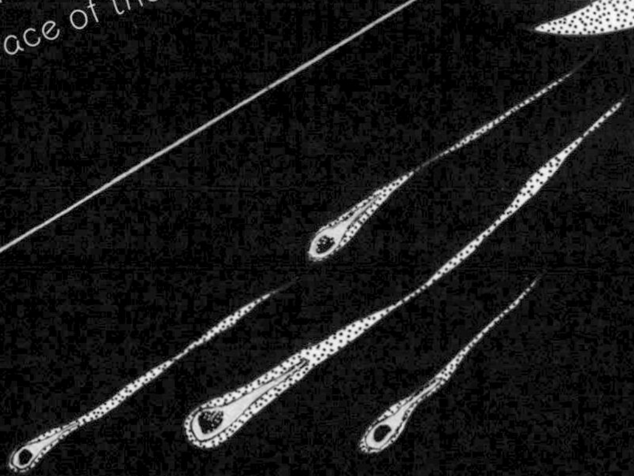

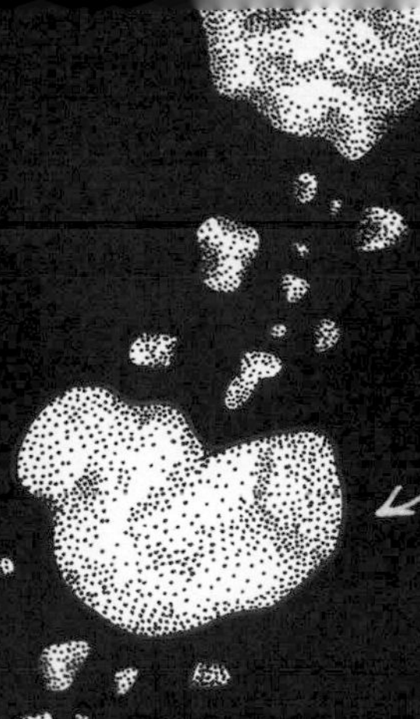

More than a million asteroids are larger than 0.6 mi. (1 km) in diameter.

They're shaped like potatoes!

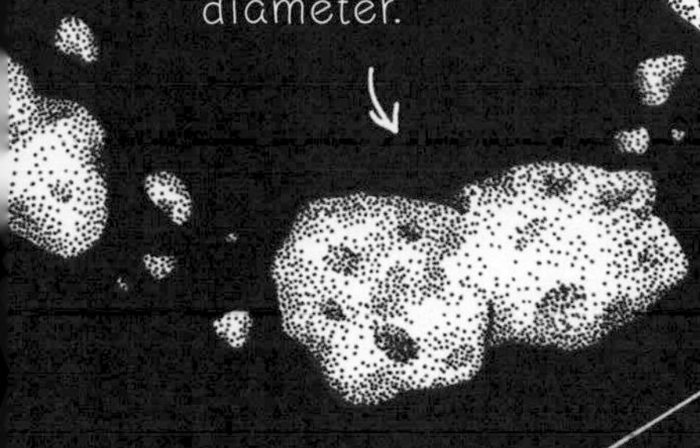

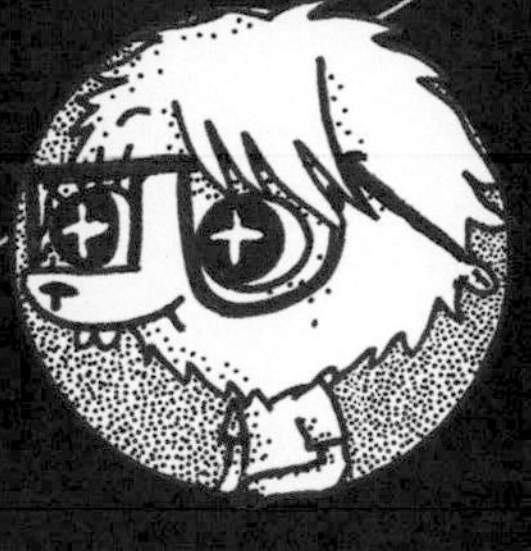

A METEORITE?

A meteorite is an object that comes from the sky and makes contact with the surface of another object, such as the Earth, the Moon, or an asteroid.

Meteorites catch fire when they enter the atmosphere. That's why they look black and pitted when they fall to Earth!

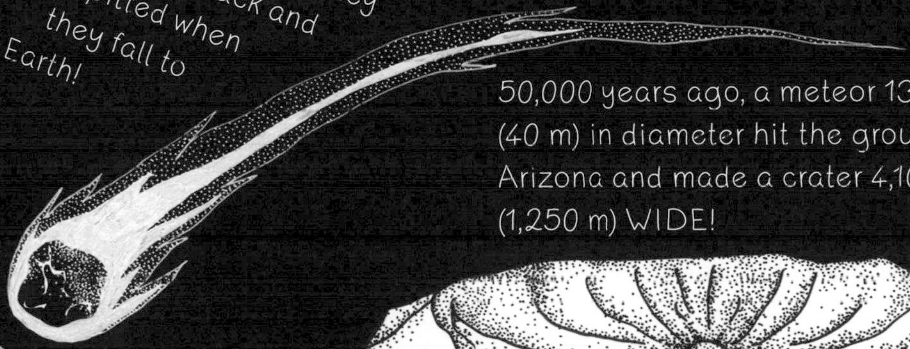

50,000 years ago, a meteor 131 ft. (40 m) in diameter hit the ground in Arizona and made a crater 4,101 ft. (1,250 m) WIDE!

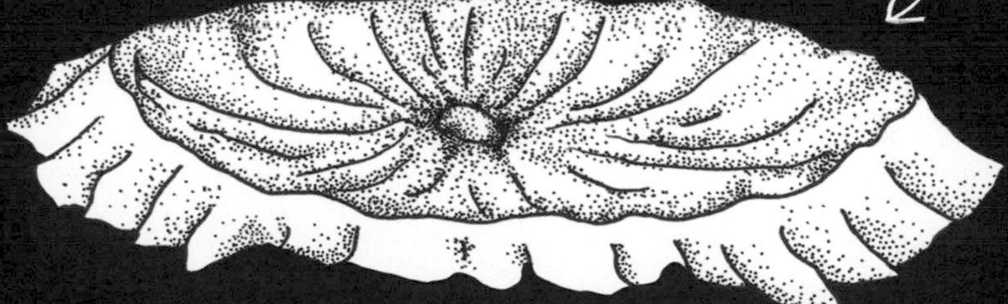

THE METEOR CRATER

August is the best time to see shooting stars. These "meteor showers" are called the Perseids, because it looks like the shooting stars are coming from the Perseus constellation.

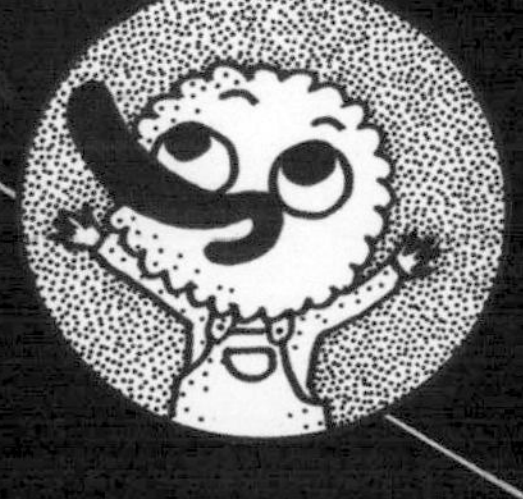
That's what killed the dinosaurs:
A METEORITE!!!

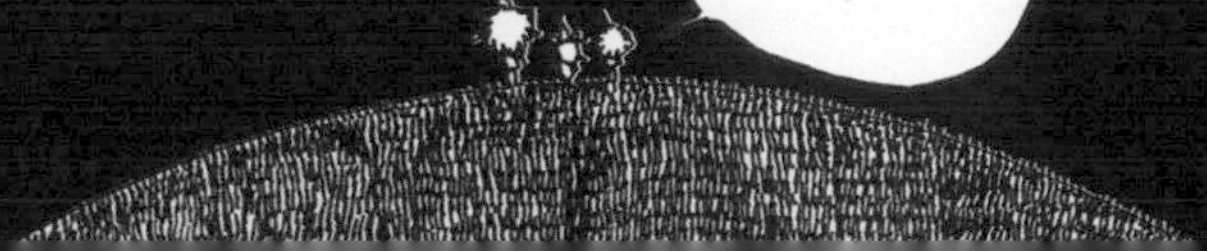
Er...
Do I have to make a wish every time?

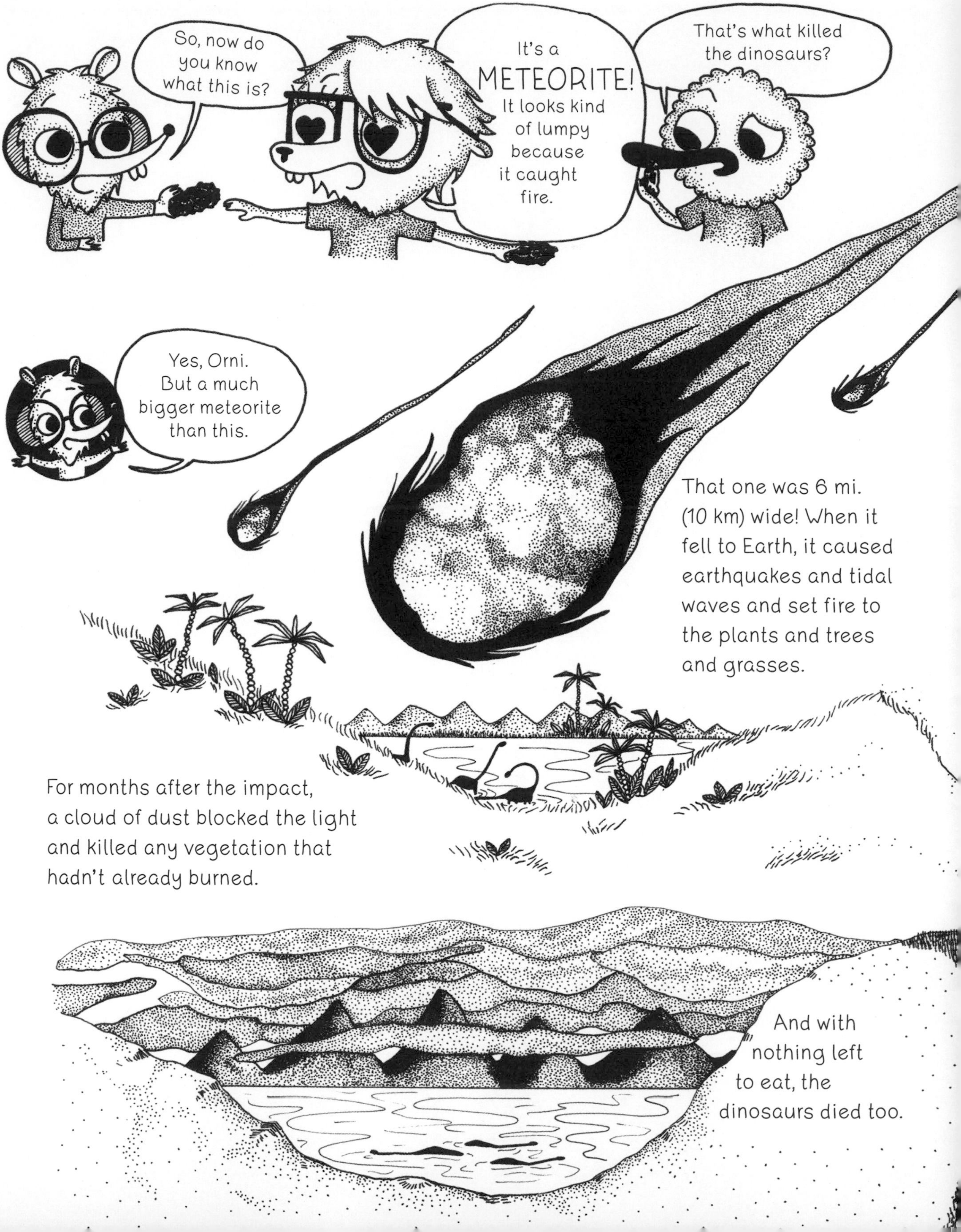
So, now do you know what this is?
It's a METEORITE! It looks kind of lumpy because it caught fire.
That's what killed the dinosaurs?
Yes, Orni. But a much bigger meteorite than this.
That one was 6 mi. (10 km) wide! When it fell to Earth, it caused earthquakes and tidal waves and set fire to the plants and trees and grasses.
For months after the impact, a cloud of dust blocked the light and killed any vegetation that hadn't already burned.
And with nothing left to eat, the dinosaurs died too.

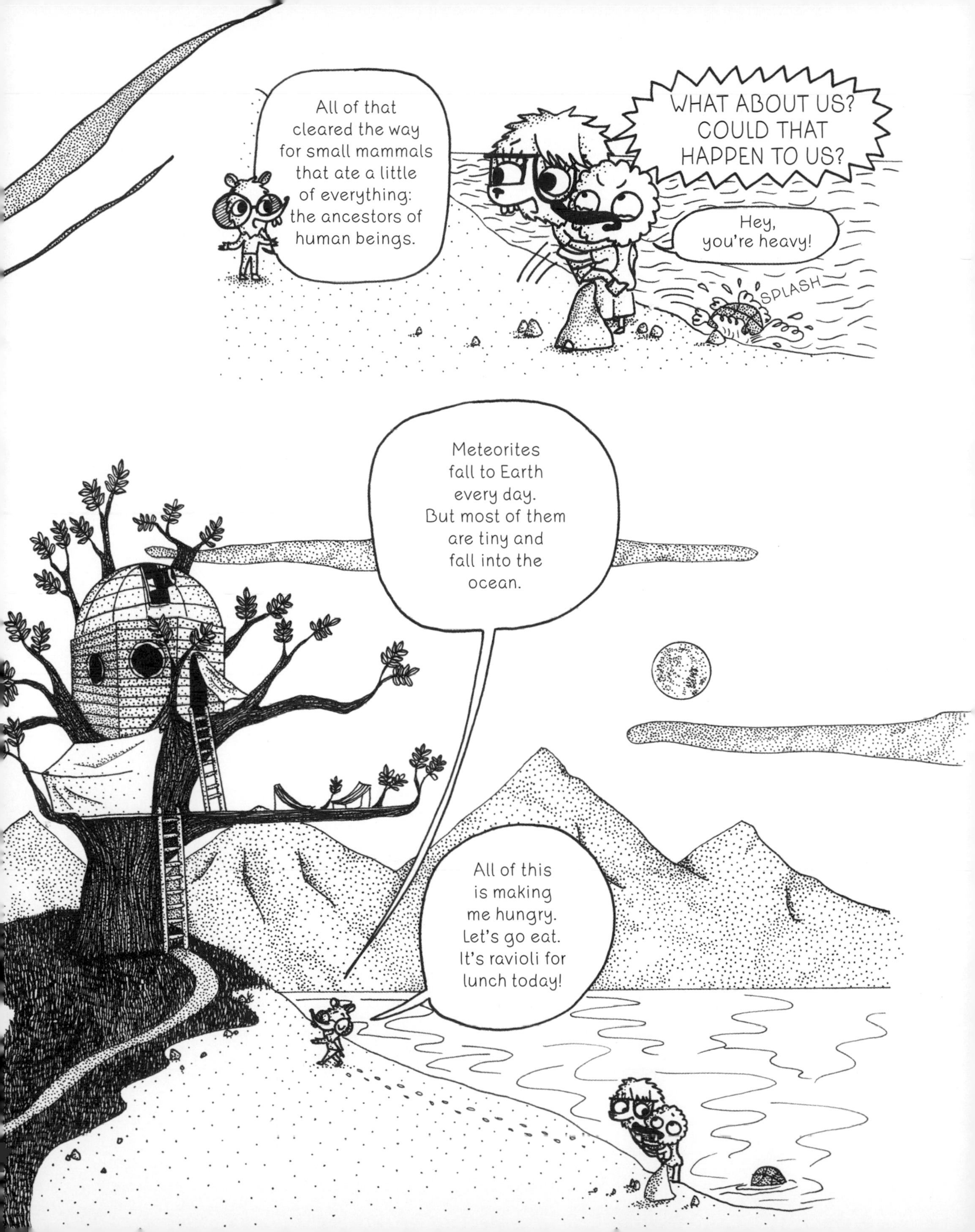
All of that cleared the way for small mammals that ate a little of everything: the ancestors of human beings.
WHAT ABOUT US? COULD THAT HAPPEN TO US?
Hey, you're heavy!
SPLASH
Meteorites fall to Earth every day. But most of them are tiny and fall into the ocean.
All of this is making me hungry. Let's go eat. It's ravioli for lunch today!

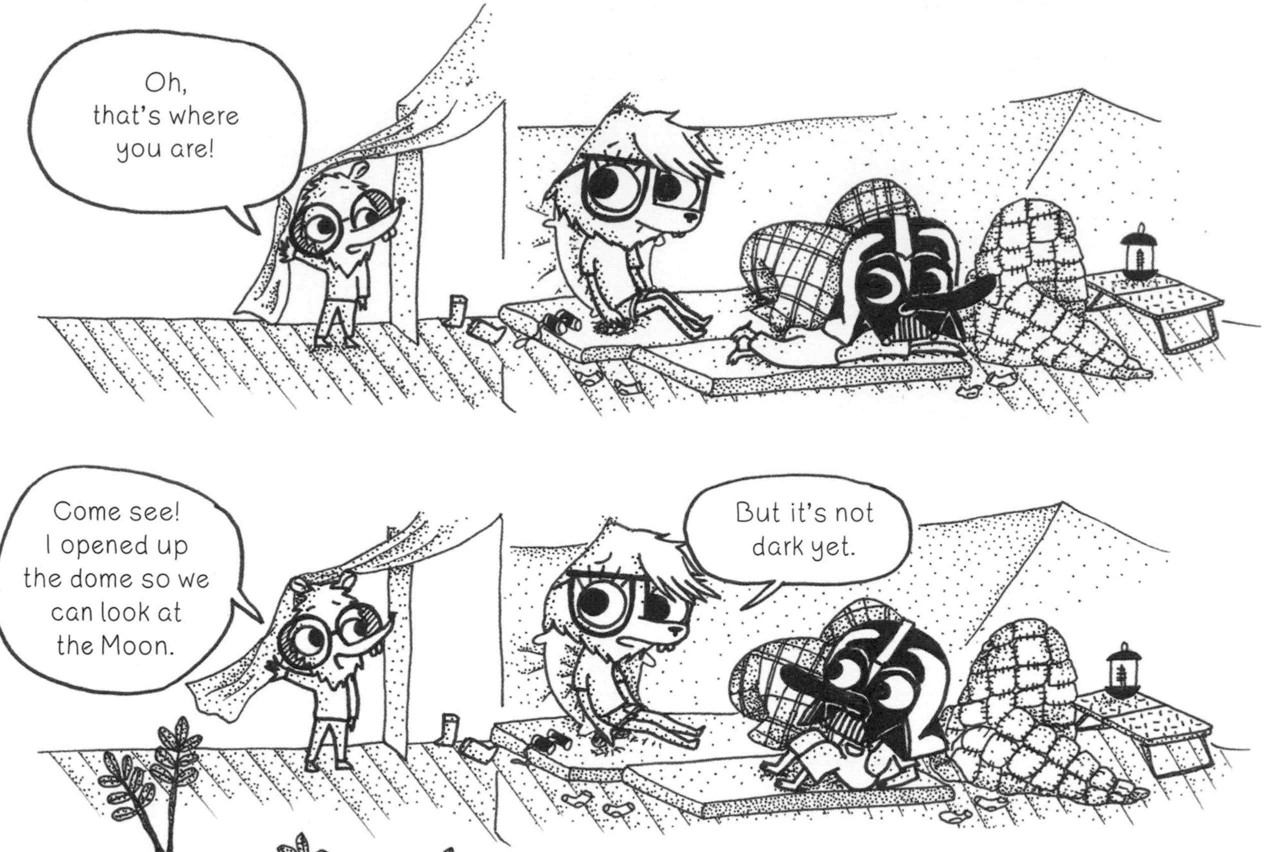
Oh, that's where you are!
Come see! I opened up the dome so we can look at the Moon.
But it's not dark yet.

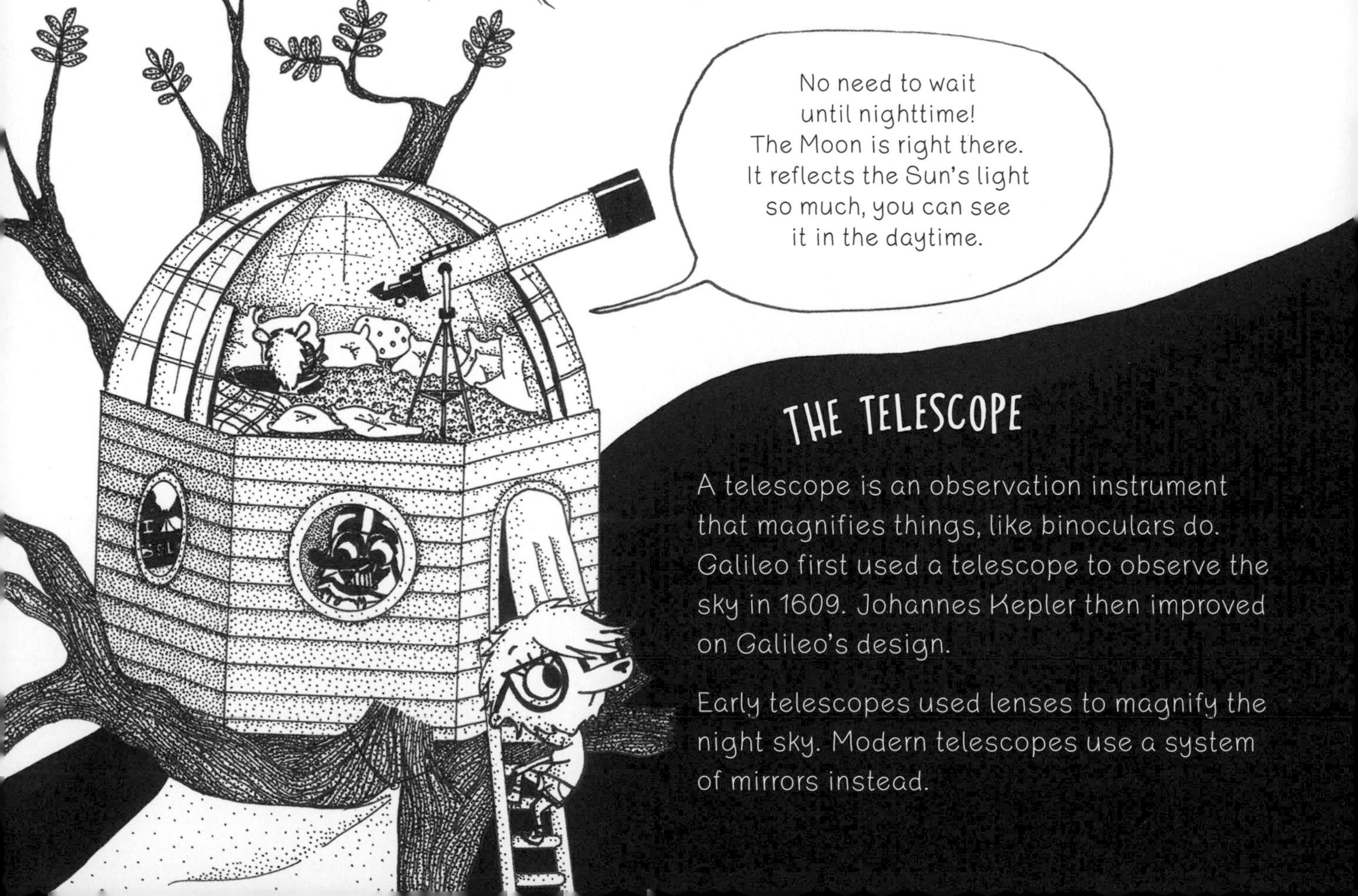
No need to wait until nighttime! The Moon is right there. It reflects the Sun's light so much, you can see it in the daytime.

THE TELESCOPE

A telescope is an observation instrument that magnifies things, like binoculars do. Galileo first used a telescope to observe the sky in 1609. Johannes Kepler then improved on Galileo's design.

Early telescopes used lenses to magnify the night sky. Modern telescopes use a system of mirrors instead.

Chapter 5

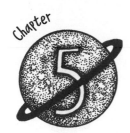

OVER THE MOON

The Moon is the Earth's only natural satellite. It takes 28 days for it to travel all the way around.

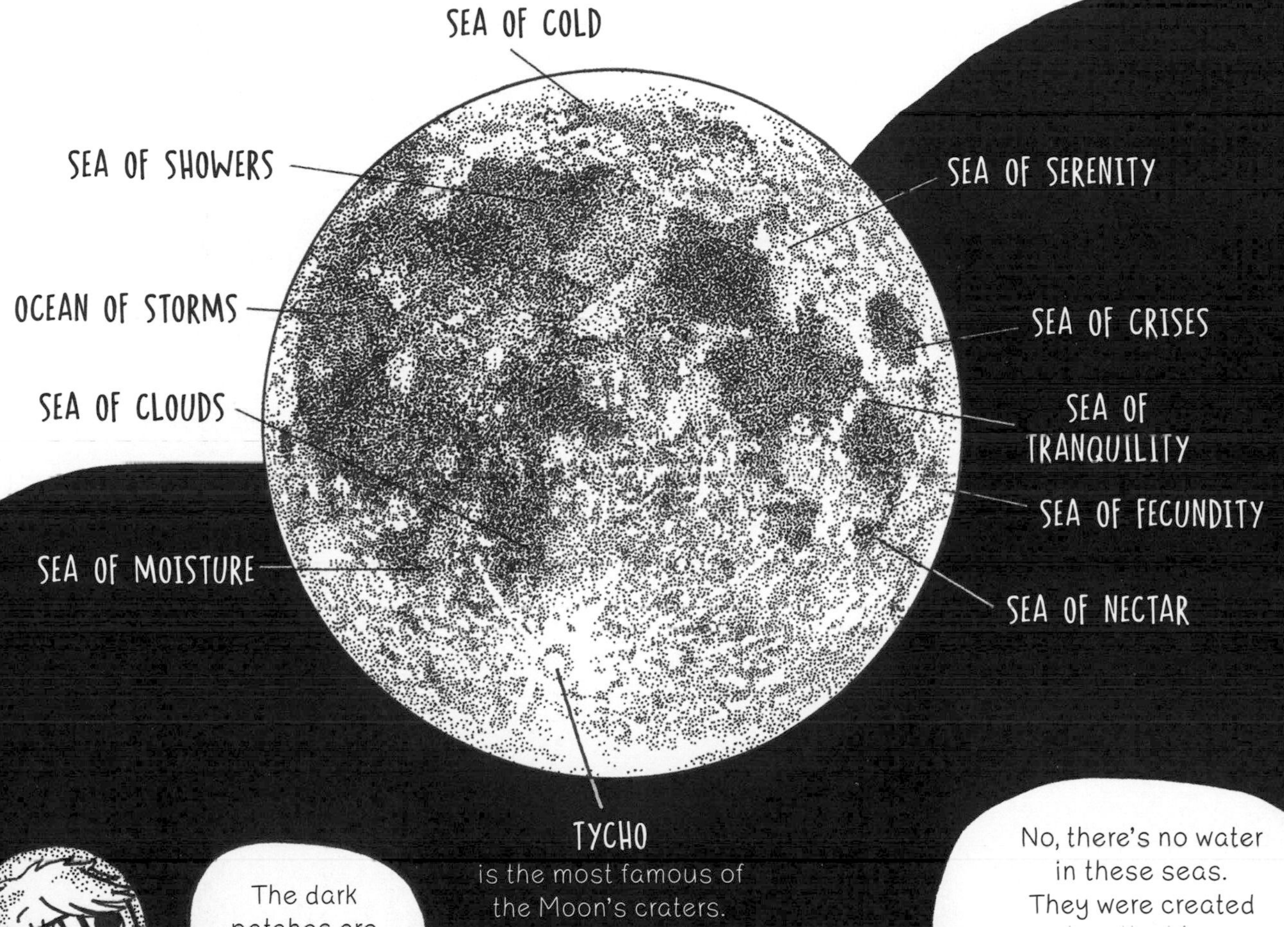
SEA OF COLD
SEA OF SHOWERS
SEA OF SERENITY
OCEAN OF STORMS
SEA OF CRISES
SEA OF CLOUDS
SEA OF TRANQUILITY
SEA OF FECUNDITY
SEA OF MOISTURE
SEA OF NECTAR
TYCHO
is the most famous of the Moon's craters.

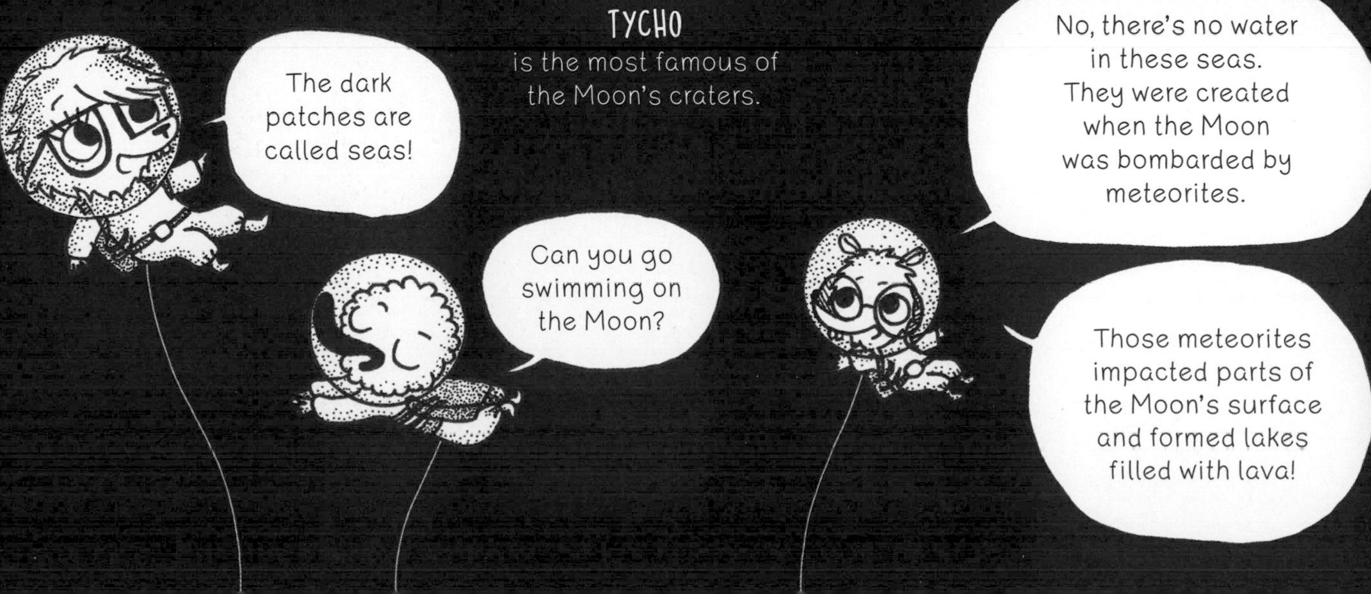
The dark patches are called seas!
Can you go swimming on the Moon?
No, there's no water in these seas. They were created when the Moon was bombarded by meteorites.
Those meteorites impacted parts of the Moon's surface and formed lakes filled with lava!

THE BIRTH OF THE MOON

When the solar system began, there were more planets orbiting around the Sun.

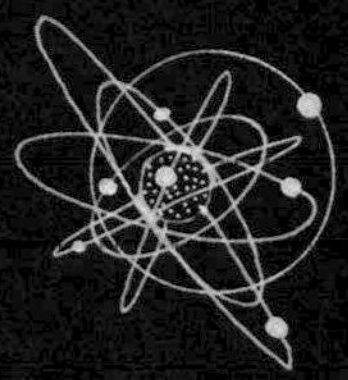

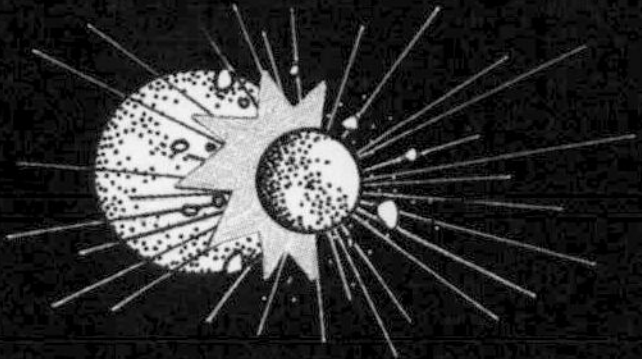

One of them, THEIA, crashed into the Earth. This created a huge dust cloud.

The dust clumped together as it revolved around the Earth.

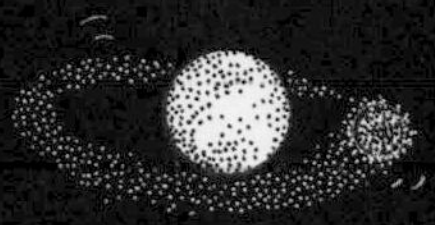

And the Moon was born!

THE PHASES OF THE MOON

The Moon rotates on its axis, and it also rotates around the Earth, which in turn rotates around the Sun.

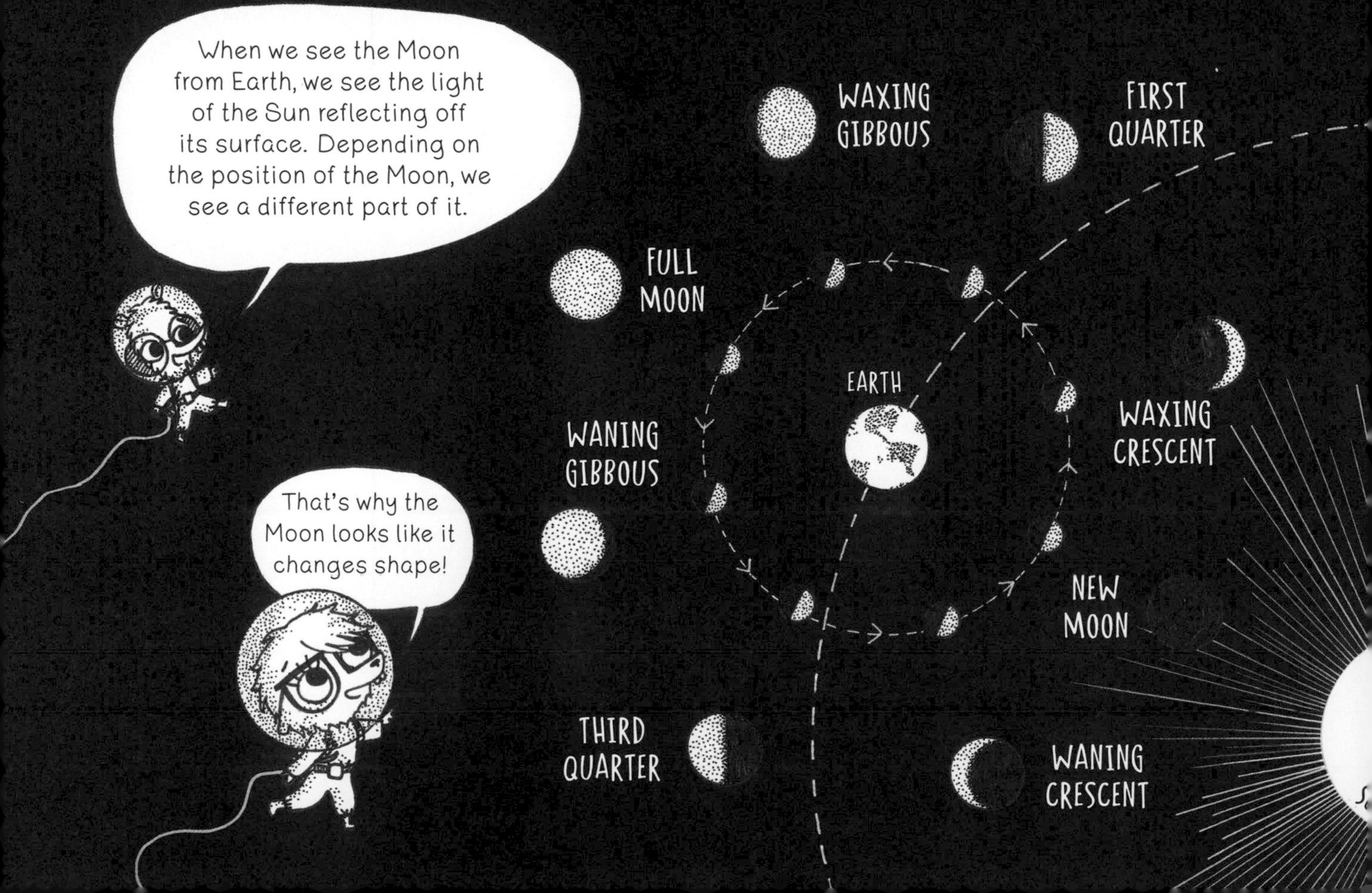
When we see the Moon from Earth, we see the light of the Sun reflecting off its surface. Depending on the position of the Moon, we see a different part of it.
That's why the Moon looks like it changes shape!
WAXING GIBBOUS
FIRST QUARTER
FULL MOON
EARTH
WAXING CRESCENT
WANING GIBBOUS
NEW MOON
THIRD QUARTER
WANING CRESCENT

THE FAR SIDE OF THE MOON

The Moon takes 28 days to revolve around the Earth, and it also takes 28 days to revolve on its own axis. Because these movements are in sync, we always see light reflected from the same side of the Moon. That's why the far side of the Moon is sometimes called the "dark side."

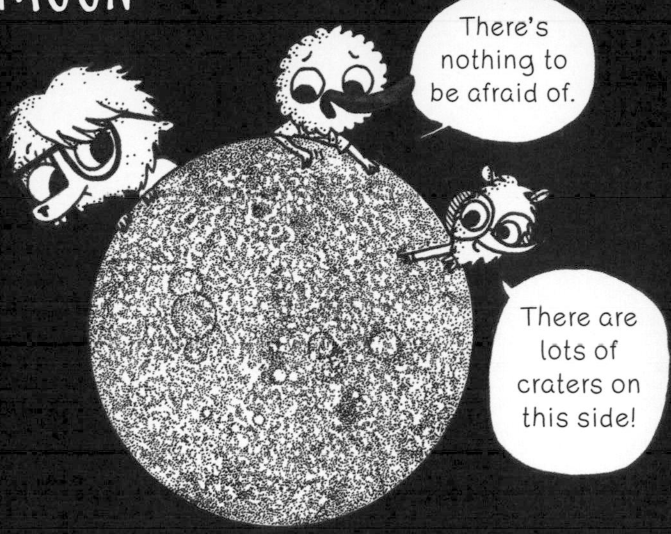
There's nothing to be afraid of.
There are lots of craters on this side!

SOLAR ECLIPSES

An eclipse happens when the Moon passes right in front of the Sun during a New Moon. The shadow of the Moon turns daylight into darkness over a small part of the Earth. This is called a TOTAL ECLIPSE.

You have to use special glasses to look at an eclipse.

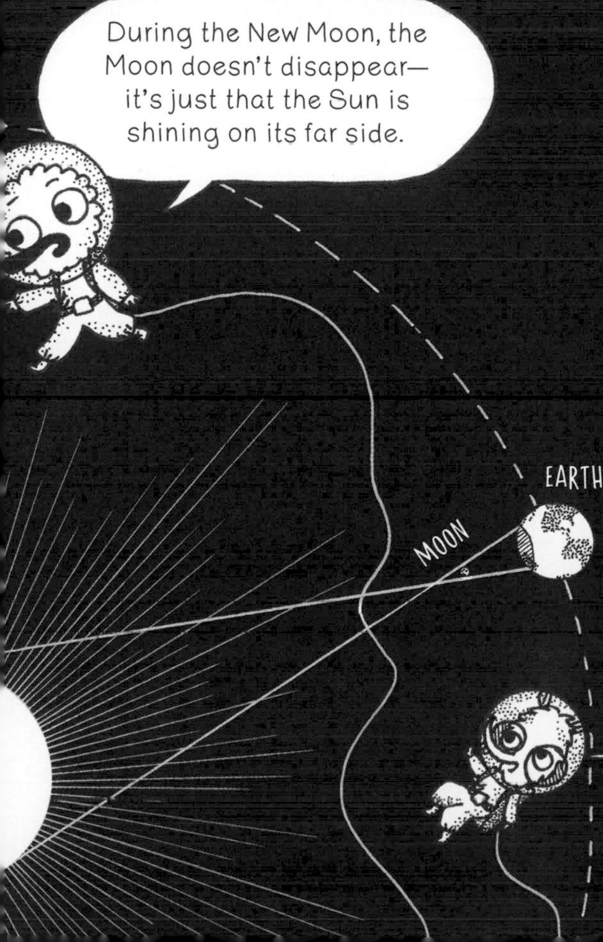
During the New Moon, the Moon doesn't disappear— it's just that the Sun is shining on its far side.
EARTH
MOON

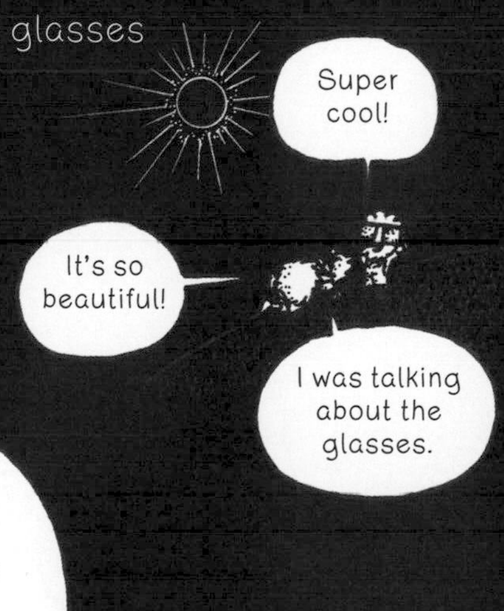
Super cool!
It's so beautiful!
I was talking about the glasses.

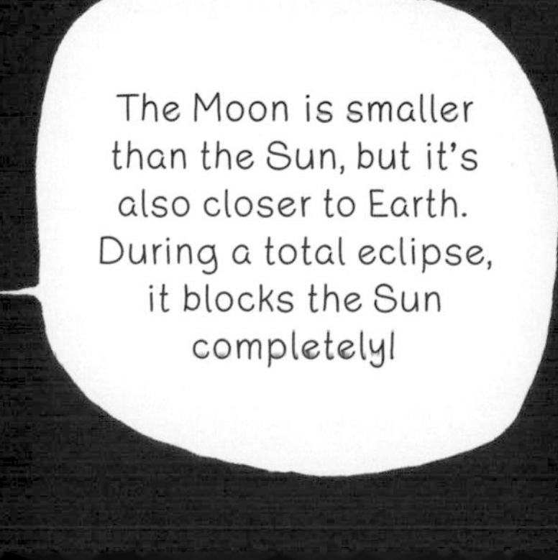
The Moon is smaller than the Sun, but it's also closer to Earth. During a total eclipse, it blocks the Sun completely!

WALKING ON THE MOON!

The Moon is 238,855 mi. (384,400 km) away from Earth. In 1969, it took 3 days for the crew of Apollo 11 to travel there. Neil Armstrong was the first astronaut to walk on the surface. Between 1969 and 1972, 12 people were lucky enough to walk on the Moon. All of them were American, and none of them were women. No one has returned to the Moon since then.

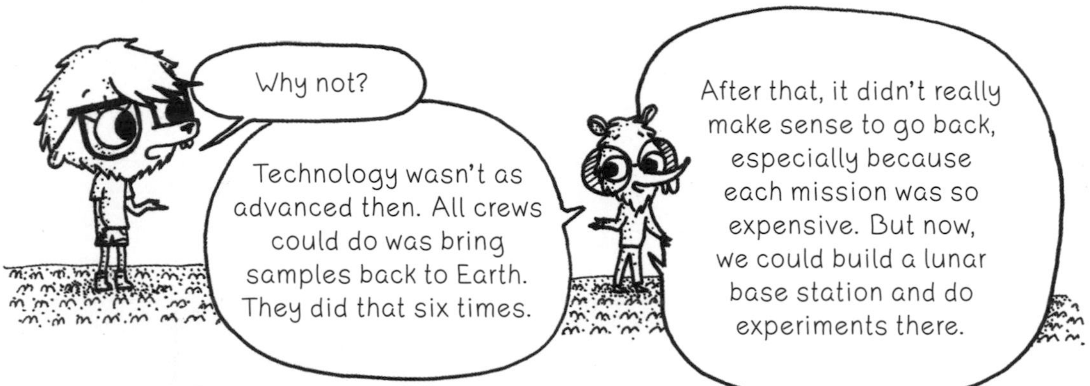

Why not?
Technology wasn't as advanced then. All crews could do was bring samples back to Earth. They did that six times.
After that, it didn't really make sense to go back, especially because each mission was so expensive. But now, we could build a lunar base station and do experiments there.

AND WE WILL GO BACK!

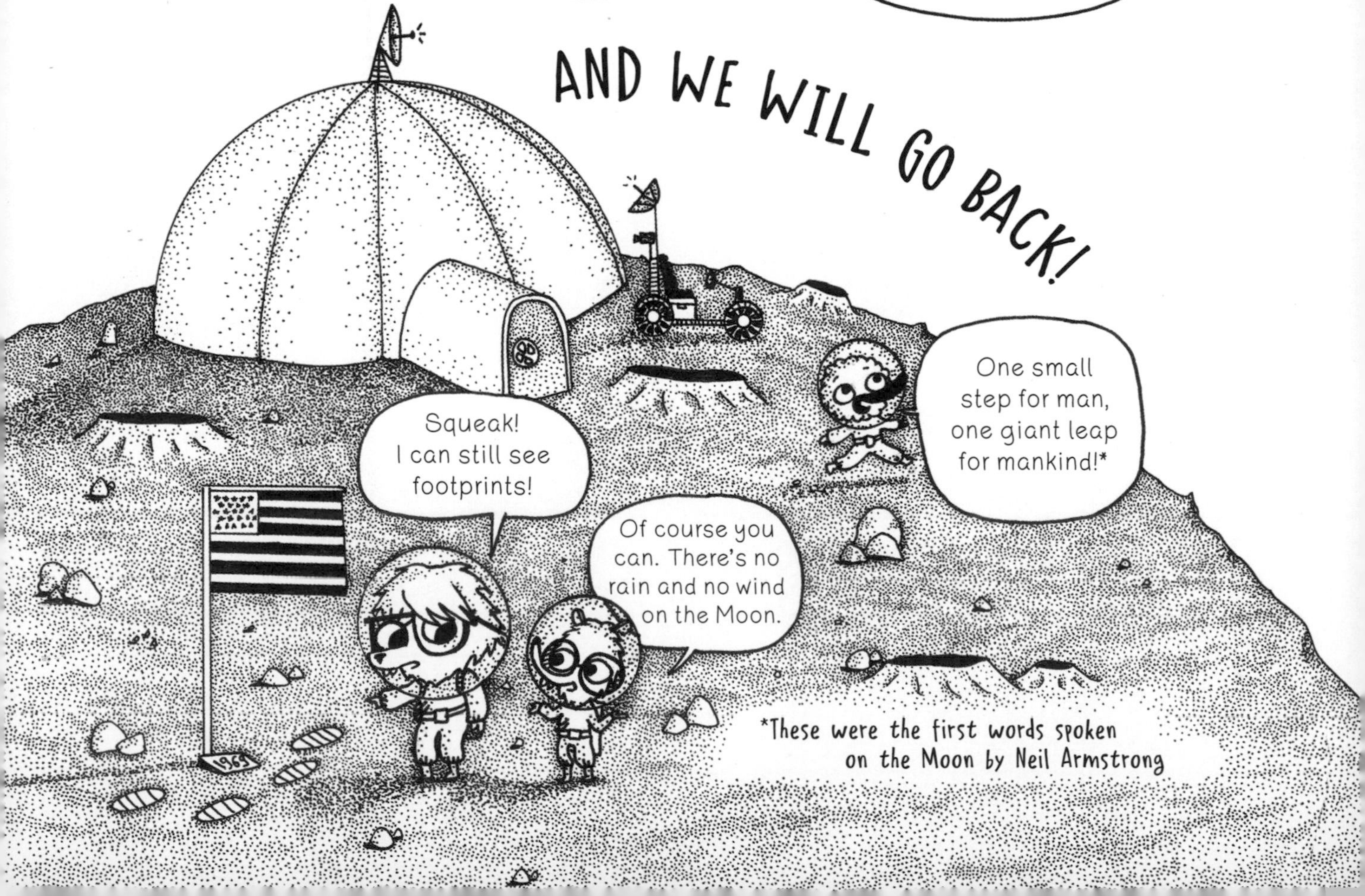

One small step for man, one giant leap for mankind!*
Squeak! I can still see footprints!
Of course you can. There's no rain and no wind on the Moon.
1969
*These were the first words spoken on the Moon by Neil Armstrong

So, why have no women gone into space?

Yeah, why?

I said no women had gone to the Moon, not into space!

SUPER SPACE WOMEN

Since the beginning of space travel, more than 70 women have traveled into space!

VALENTINA TERESHKOVA

First female cosmonaut

(2 years after her fellow Russian, YURI GAGARIN, the first man in space)

1963

1983

SALLY RIDE

First American woman in space

CLAUDIE HAIGNERÉ

First French woman in space

1996

1992

ROBERTA BONDAR

First Canadian woman in space

And maybe one day... Castor, the first woman to walk on the Moon!

CASTOR

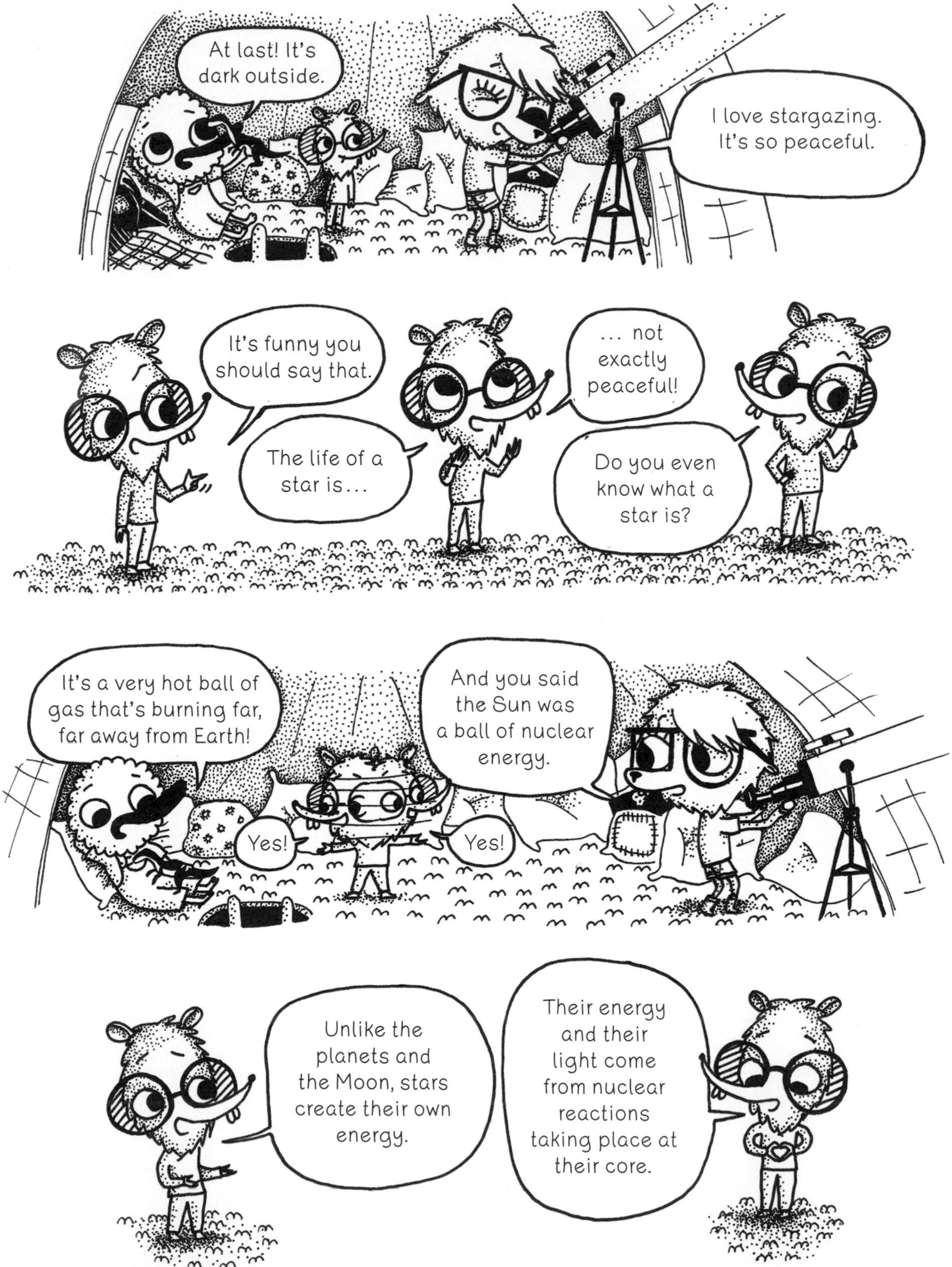
At last! It's dark outside.
I love stargazing. It's so peaceful.
It's funny you should say that.
The life of a star is...
... not exactly peaceful!
Do you even know what a star is?
It's a very hot ball of gas that's burning far, far away from Earth!
Yes!
Yes!
And you said the Sun was a ball of nuclear energy.
Unlike the planets and the Moon, stars create their own energy.
Their energy and their light come from nuclear reactions taking place at their core.

Chapter 6 THE LIFE OF A STAR

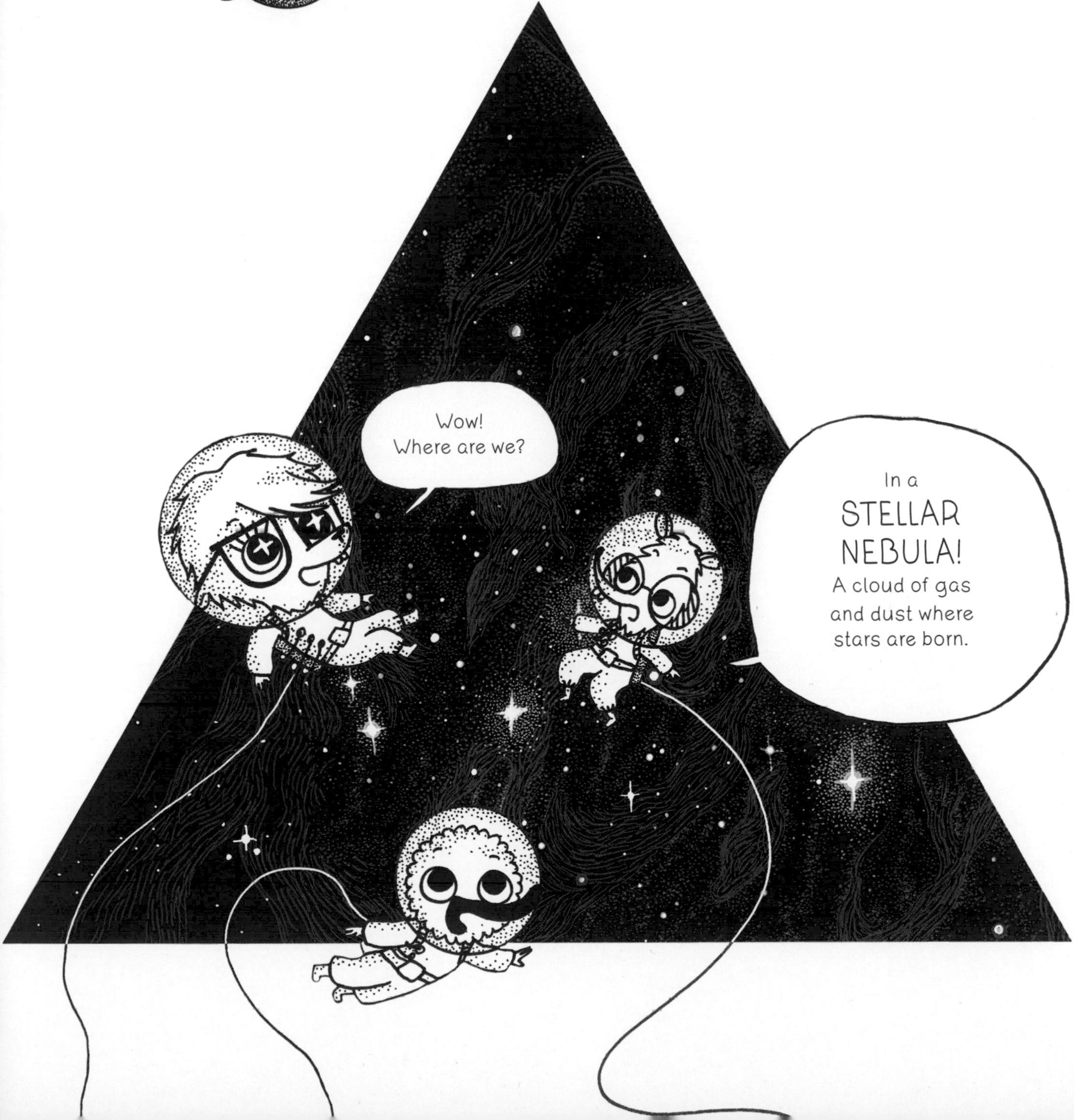
Wow!
Where are we?
In a STELLAR NEBULA!
A cloud of gas and dust where stars are born.

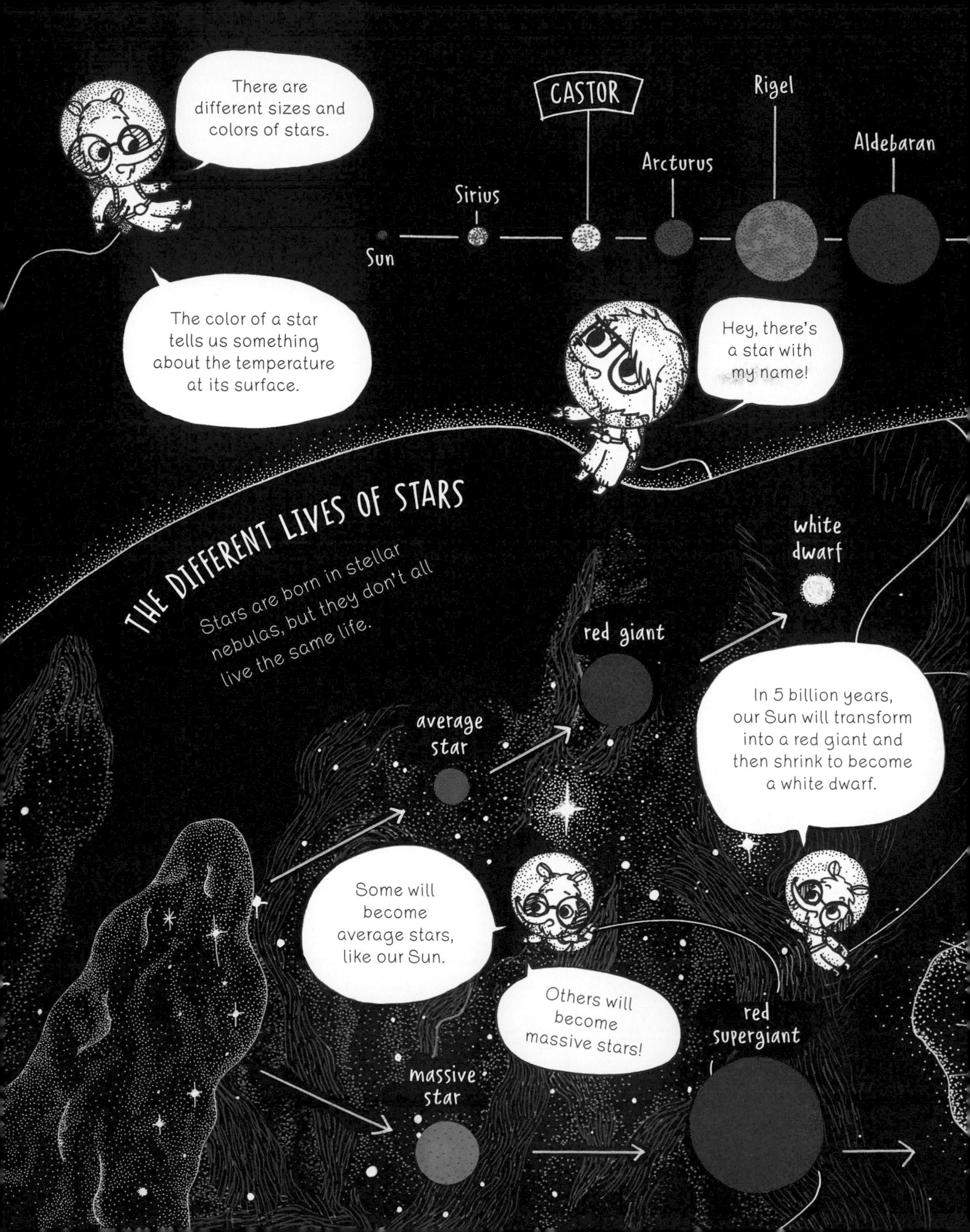
There are different sizes and colors of stars.
Sun
Sirius
CASTOR
Arcturus
Rigel
Aldebaran
The color of a star tells us something about the temperature at its surface.
Hey, there's a star with my name!
THE DIFFERENT LIVES OF STARS
Stars are born in stellar nebulas, but they don't all live the same life.
white dwarf
red giant
average star
In 5 billion years, our Sun will transform into a red giant and then shrink to become a white dwarf.
Some will become average stars, like our Sun.
Others will become massive stars!
red supergiant
massive star

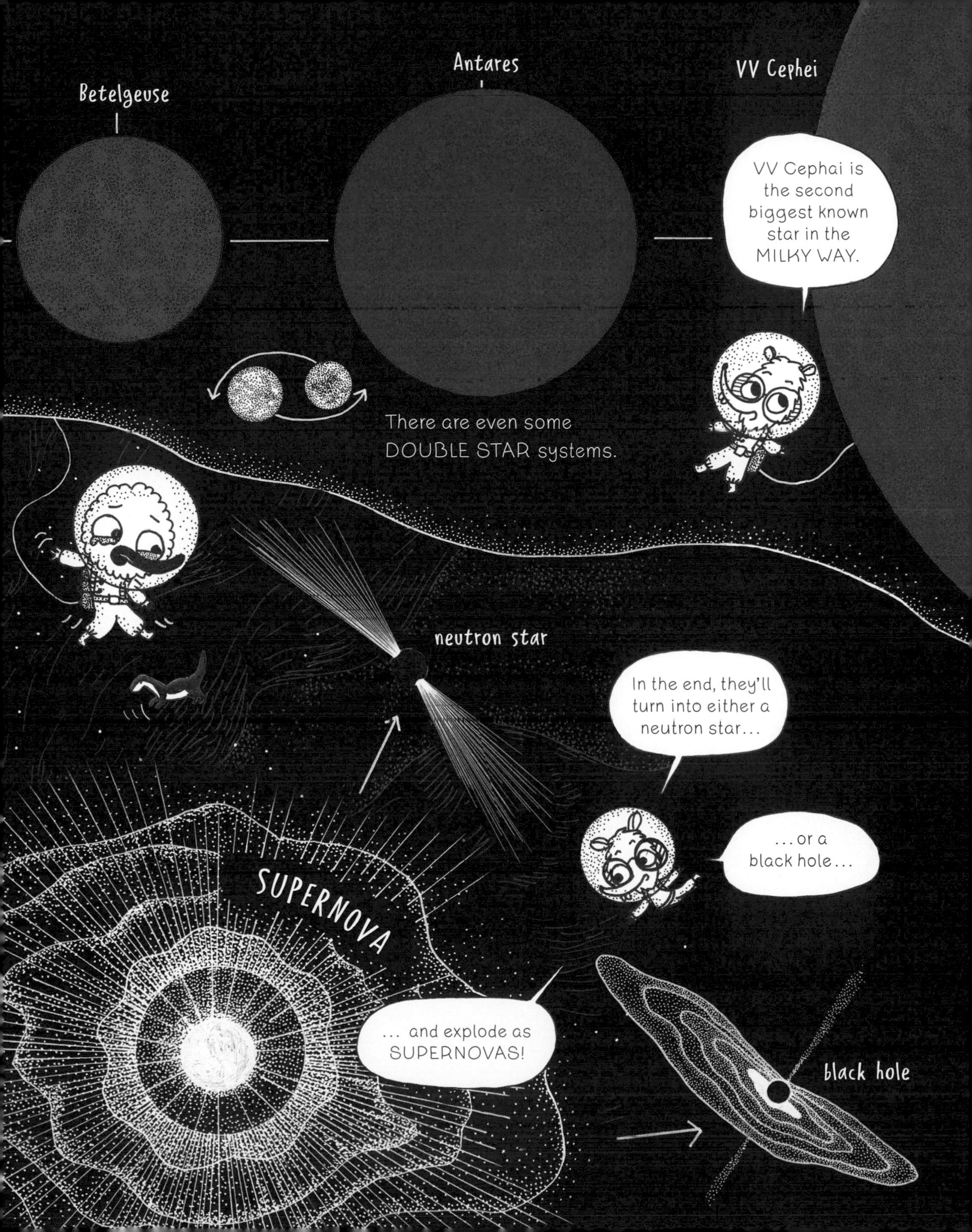
Betelgeuse
Antares
VV Cephei
VV Cephai is the second biggest known star in the MILKY WAY.
There are even some DOUBLE STAR systems.
neutron star
In the end, they'll turn into either a neutron star...
...or a black hole...
SUPERNOVA
... and explode as SUPERNOVAS!
black hole

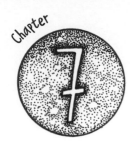

THE SUPER MAP OF THE SKY

From Earth, the stars look so small, like they're sparkling lights sticking to a big black sheet in THE NIGHT SKY!

On that sheet, they always look like they're in the same place beside one another.

When we look up, it's easy to think the stars are turning around us. This movement of the stars in the night sky is called APPARENT MOTION.

How do I know which star I'm looking at?

I must have a map of the night sky somewhere in here...

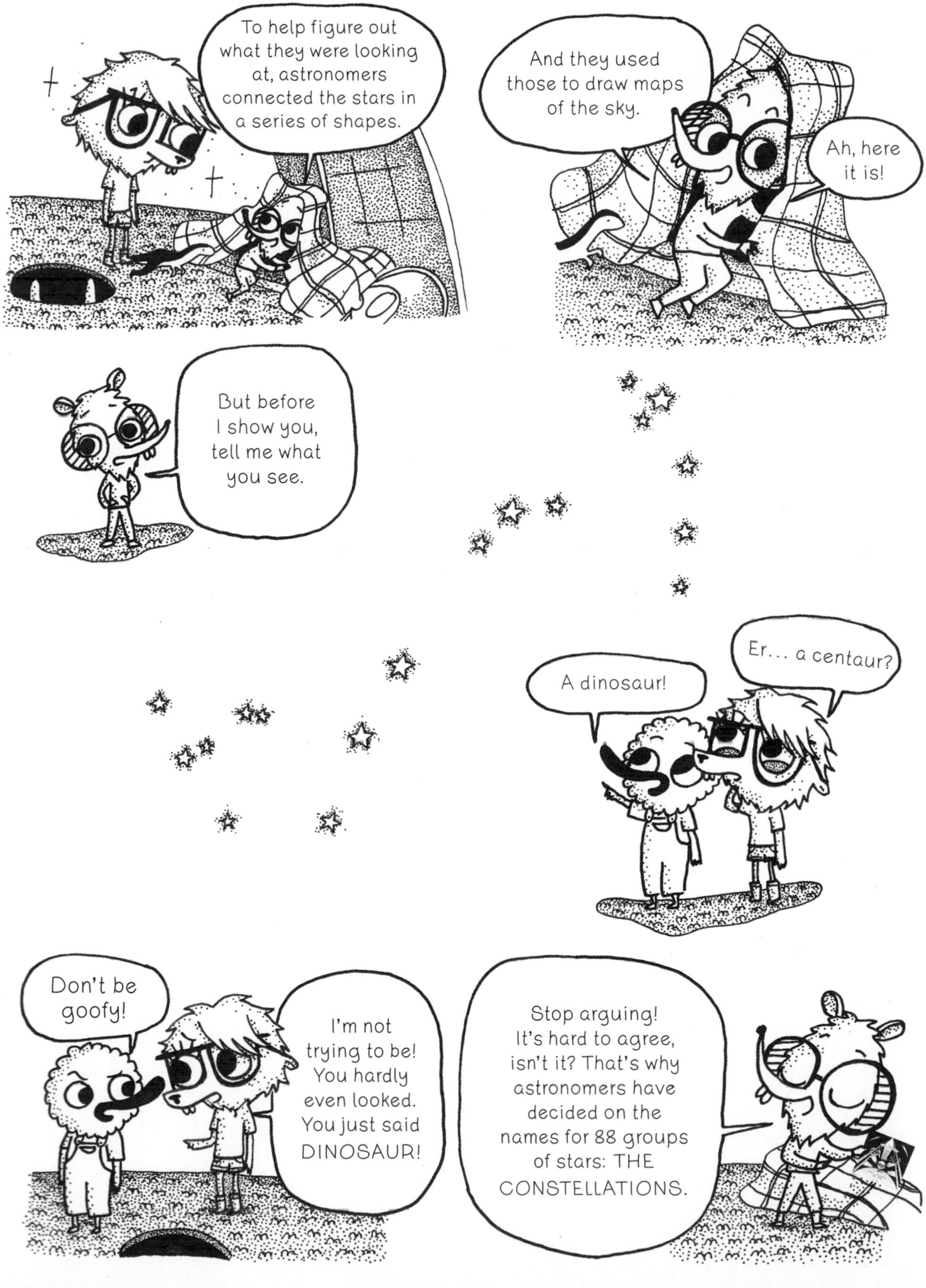
To help figure out what they were looking at, astronomers connected the stars in a series of shapes.
And they used those to draw maps of the sky.
Ah, here it is!
But before I show you, tell me what you see.
A dinosaur!
Er... a centaur?
Don't be goofy!
I'm not trying to be! You hardly even looked. You just said DINOSAUR!
Stop arguing! It's hard to agree, isn't it? That's why astronomers have decided on the names for 88 groups of stars: THE CONSTELLATIONS.

THE CONSTELLATIONS

There are 88 constellations in total, but you can't see all of them at the same time from the same place.

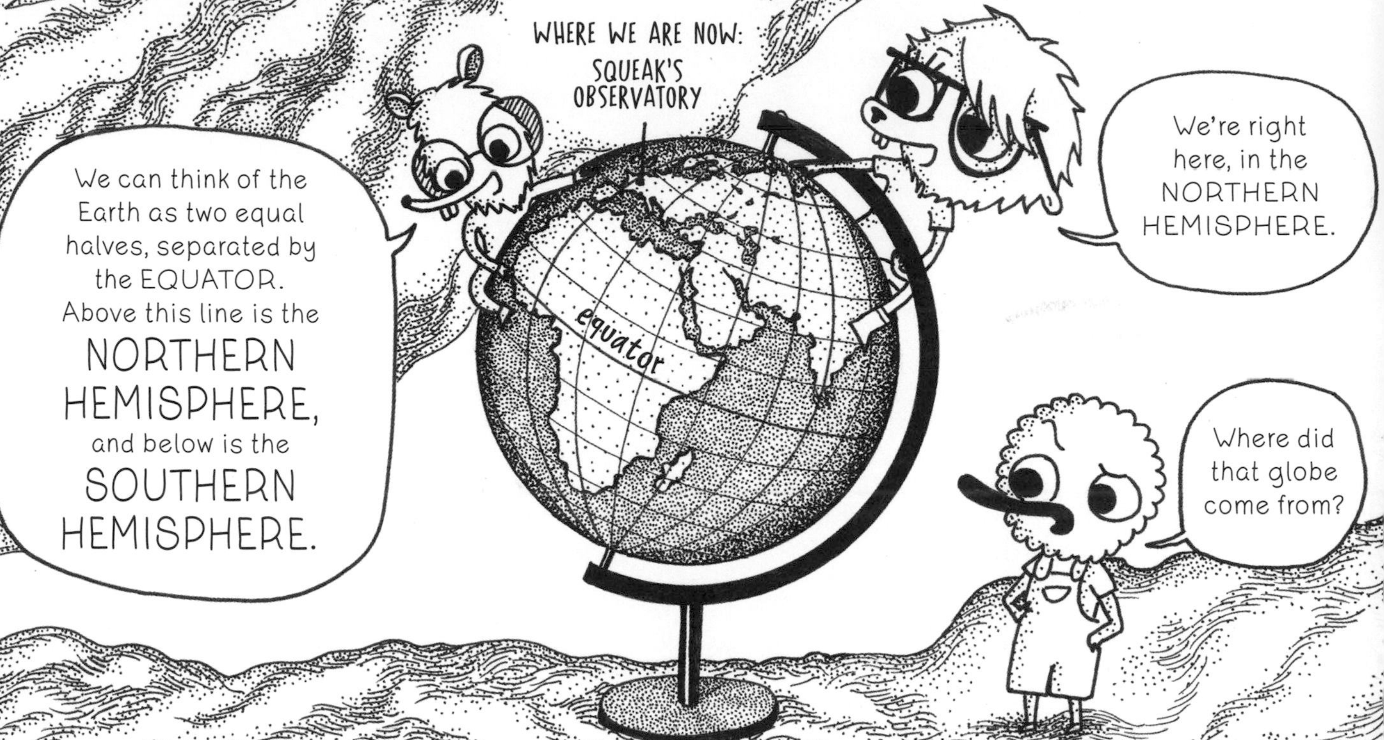

WHERE WE ARE NOW: SQUEAK'S OBSERVATORY
We can think of the Earth as two equal halves, separated by the EQUATOR. Above this line is the NORTHERN HEMISPHERE, and below is the SOUTHERN HEMISPHERE.
equator
We're right here, in the NORTHERN HEMISPHERE.
Where did that globe come from?

The stars in a constellation are not really next to one another.

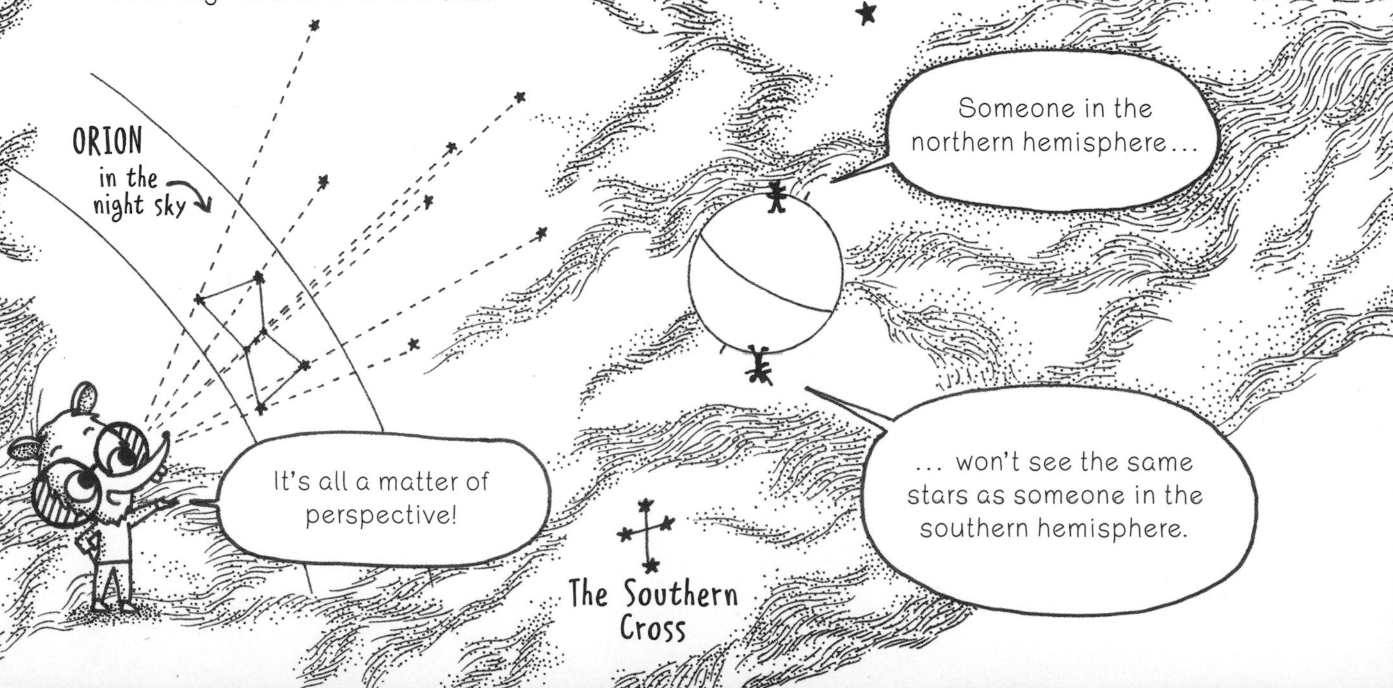

Polaris
ORION in the night sky
Someone in the northern hemisphere...
... won't see the same stars as someone in the southern hemisphere.
It's all a matter of perspective!
The Southern Cross

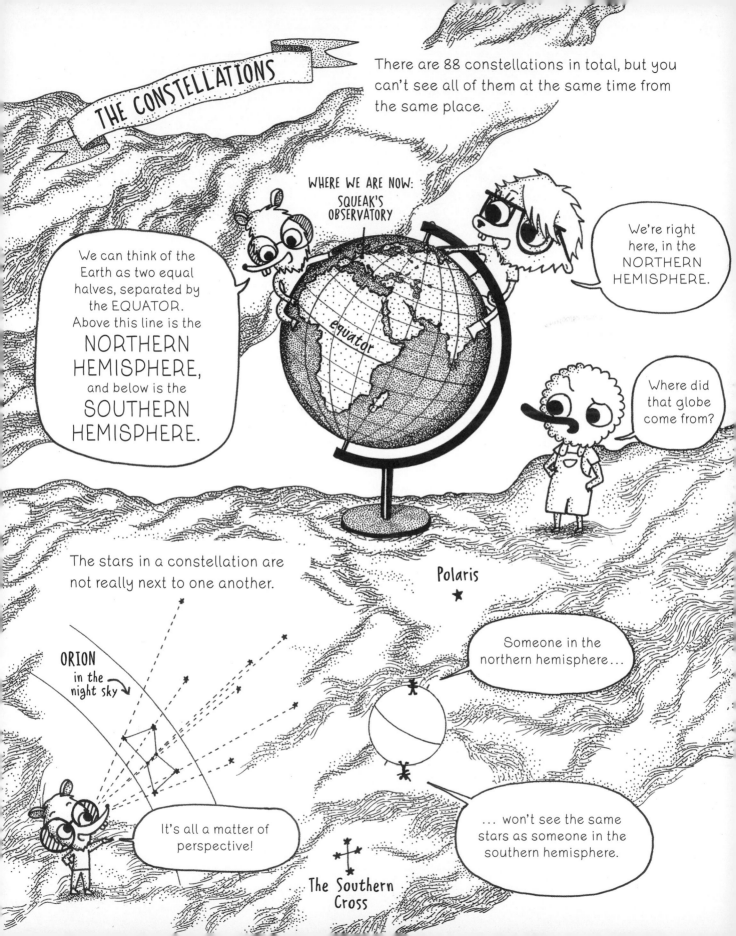

Here's the

MAP OF THE NIGHT SKY

in the northern hemisphere.

The names of the constellations were sometimes inspired by people, animals, or things of legend.

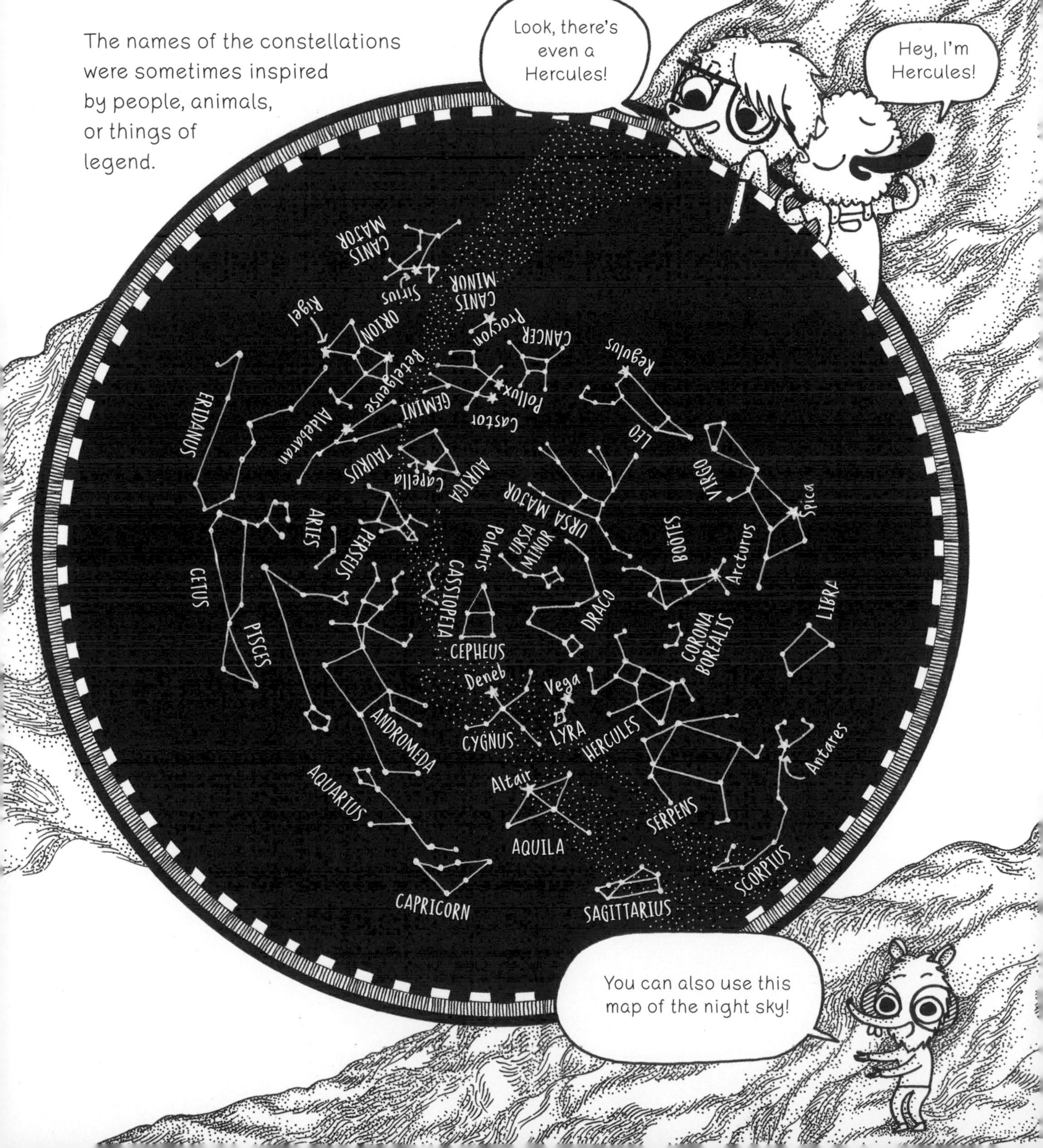

Look, there's even a Hercules!
Hey, I'm Hercules!
CANIS MAJOR
Sirius
CANIS MINOR
Procyon
Rigel
ORION
CANCER
Regulus
Betelgeuse
GEMINI
Pollux
Castor
ERIDANUS
Aldebaran
LEO
TAURUS
Capella
AURIGA
VIRGO
URSA MAJOR
ARIES
PERSEUS
Polaris
URSA MINOR
BOÖTES
Spica
CETUS
CASSIOPEIA
Arcturus
PISCES
CEPHEUS
DRACO
CORONA BOREALIS
LIBRA
Deneb
Vega
ANDROMEDA
CYGNUS
LYRA
HERCULES
Antares
AQUARIUS
Altair
SERPENS
AQUILA
SCORPIUS
CAPRICORN
SAGITTARIUS
You can also use this map of the night sky!

Chapter 8 TO THE NORTH

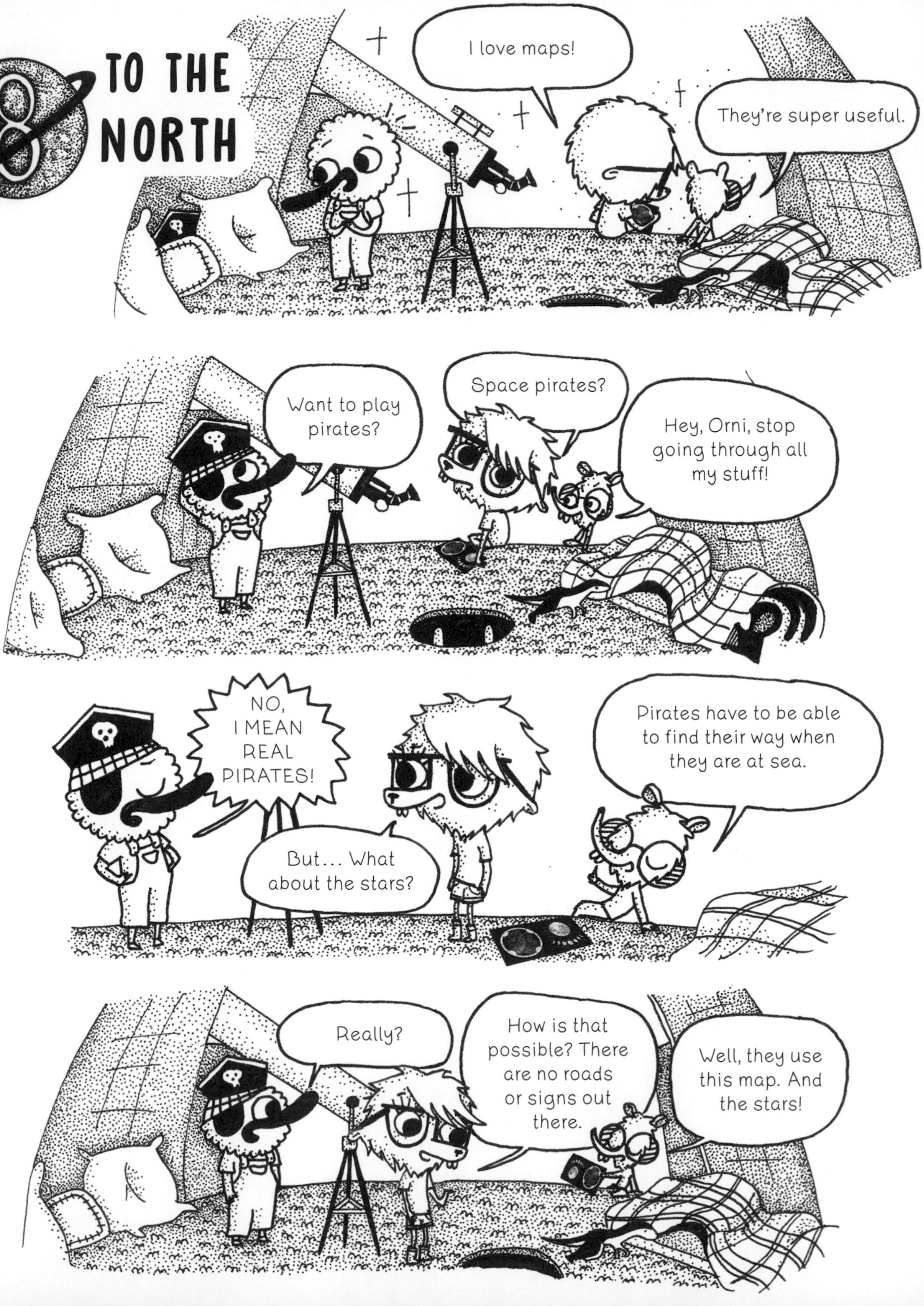

I love maps!
They're super useful.
Want to play pirates?
Space pirates?
Hey, Orni, stop going through all my stuff!
NO, I MEAN REAL PIRATES!
But... What about the stars?
Pirates have to be able to find their way when they are at sea.
Really?
How is that possible? There are no roads or signs out there.
Well, they use this map. And the stars!

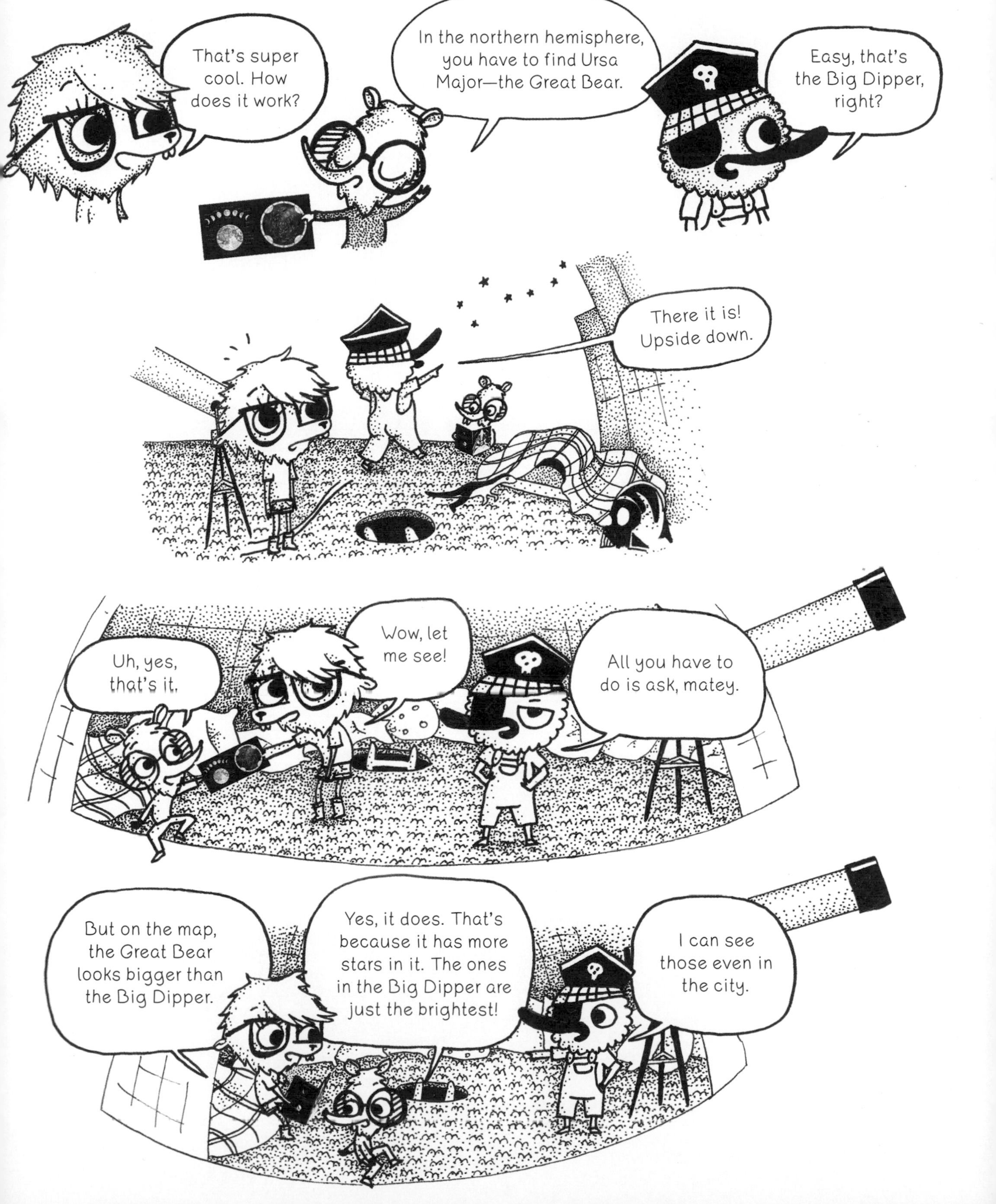
That's super cool. How does it work?
In the northern hemisphere, you have to find Ursa Major—the Great Bear.
Easy, that's the Big Dipper, right?
There it is! Upside down.
Uh, yes, that's it.
Wow, let me see!
All you have to do is ask, matey.
But on the map, the Great Bear looks bigger than the Big Dipper.
Yes, it does. That's because it has more stars in it. The ones in the Big Dipper are just the brightest!
I can see those even in the city.

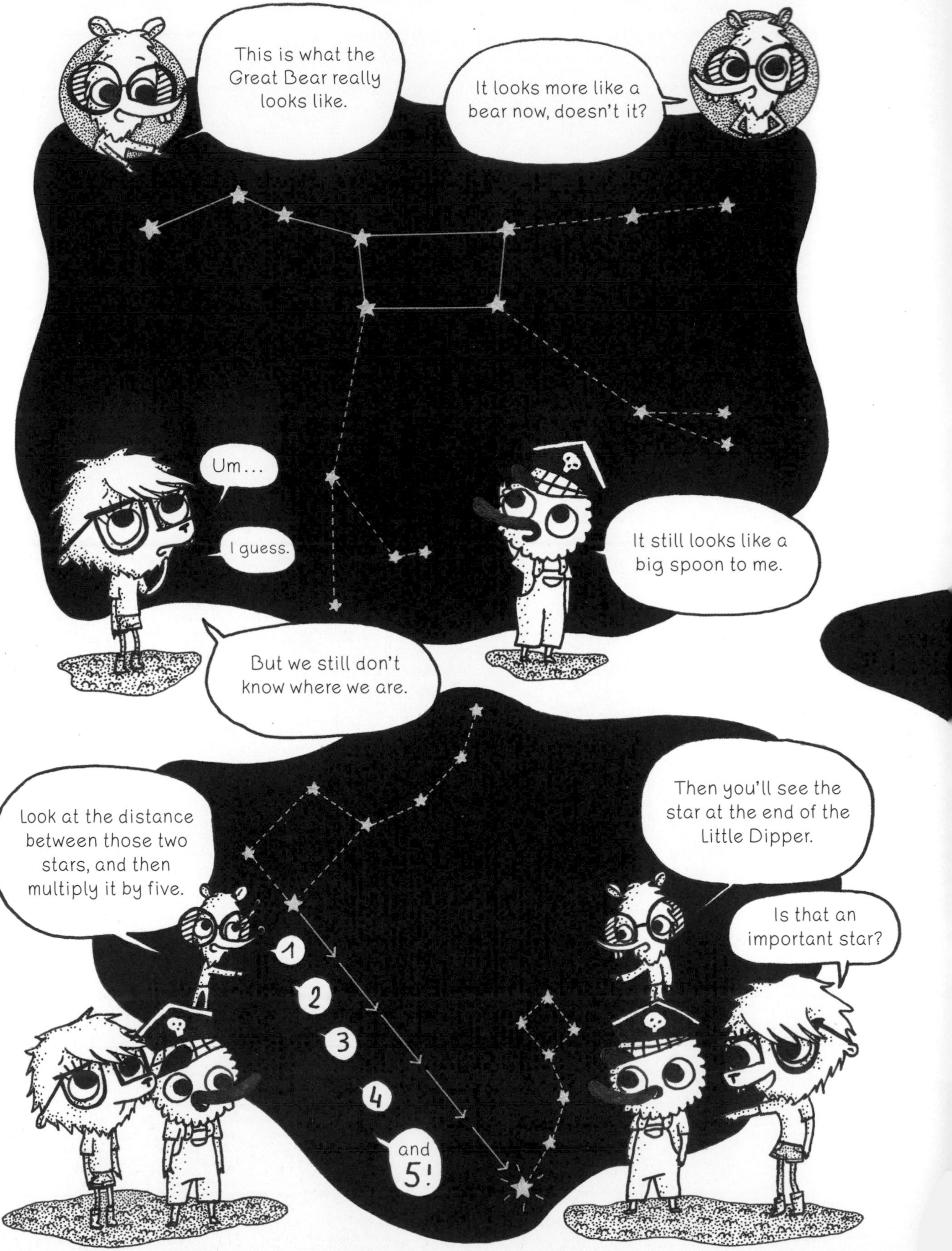
This is what the Great Bear really looks like.
It looks more like a bear now, doesn't it?
Um...
I guess.
It still looks like a big spoon to me.
But we still don't know where we are.
Look at the distance between those two stars, and then multiply it by five.
1
2
3
4
and 5!
Then you'll see the star at the end of the Little Dipper.
Is that an important star?

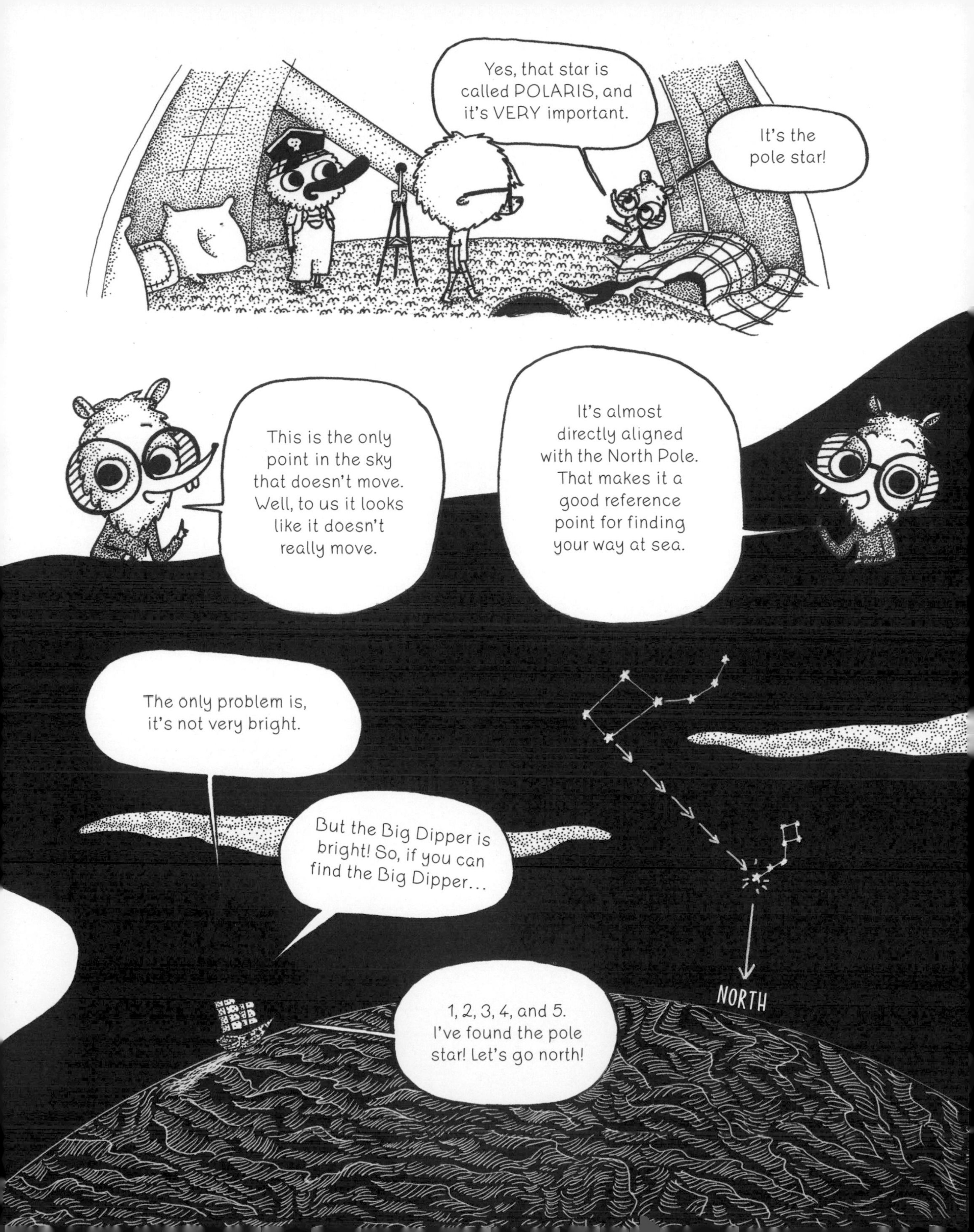

Yes, that star is called POLARIS, and it's VERY important.
It's the pole star!
This is the only point in the sky that doesn't move. Well, to us it looks like it doesn't really move.
It's almost directly aligned with the North Pole. That makes it a good reference point for finding your way at sea.
The only problem is, it's not very bright.
But the Big Dipper is bright! So, if you can find the Big Dipper...
NORTH
1, 2, 3, 4, and 5. I've found the pole star! Let's go north!

THE POLE STAR

If we could speed up time, this is how we might see the stars moving through the night.

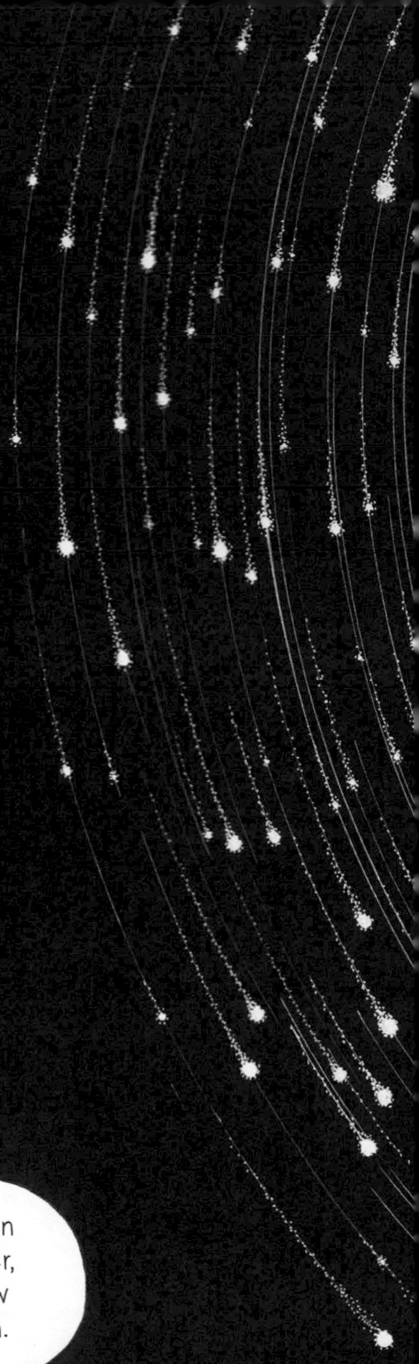

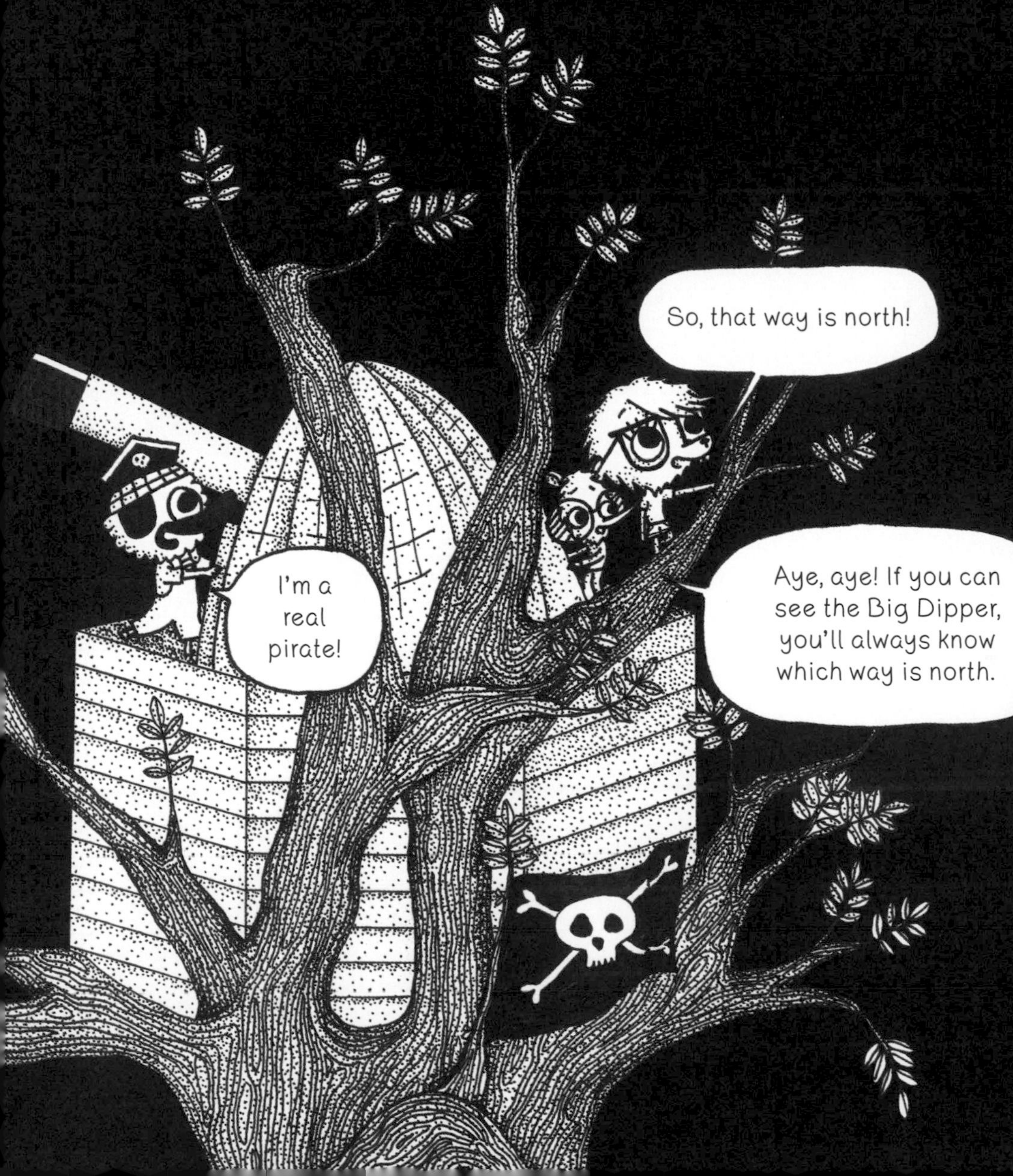

So, that way is north!
I'm a real pirate!
Aye, aye! If you can see the Big Dipper, you'll always know which way is north.

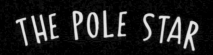

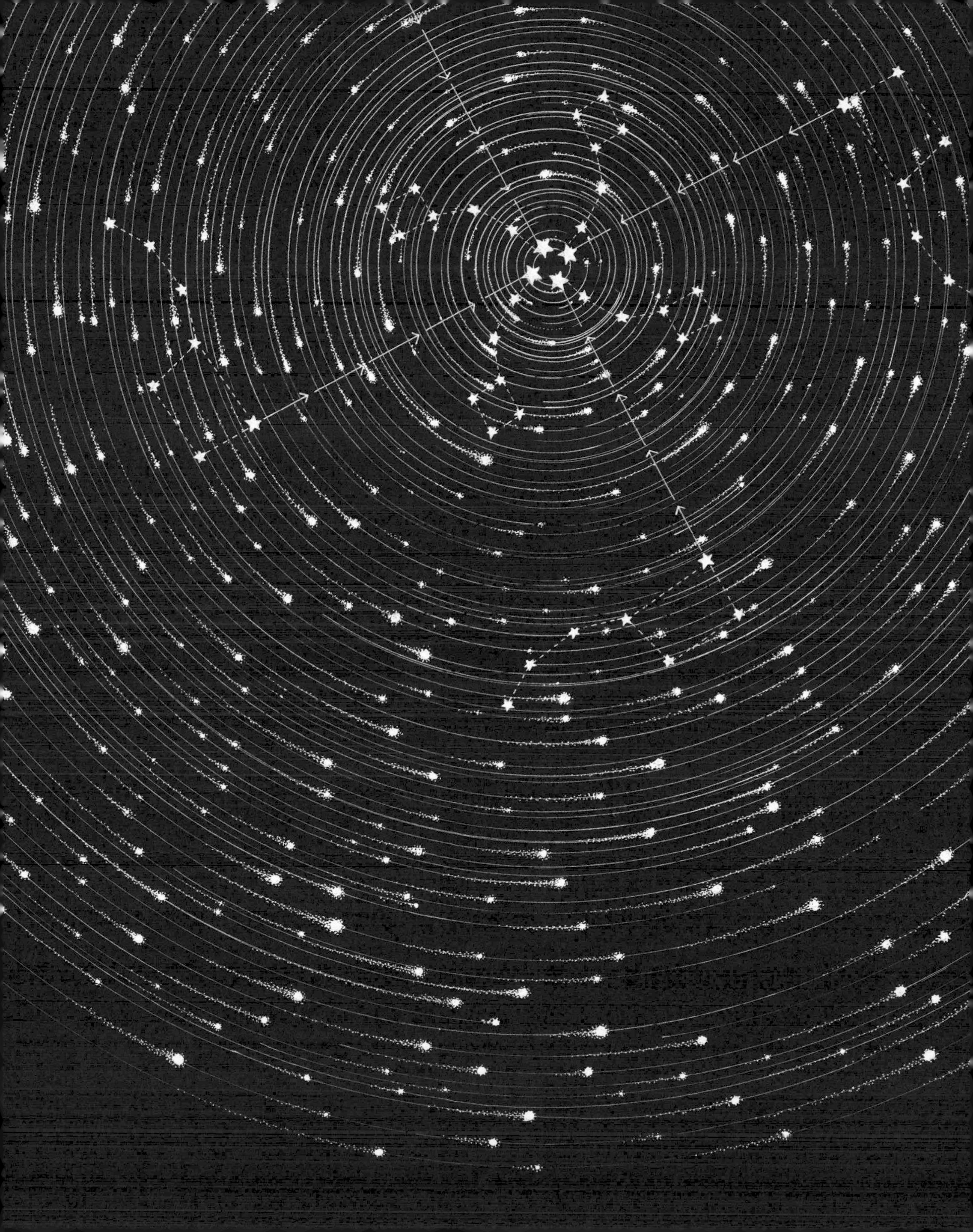

Chapter 9

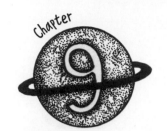

PIRATES OF THE ZODIAC

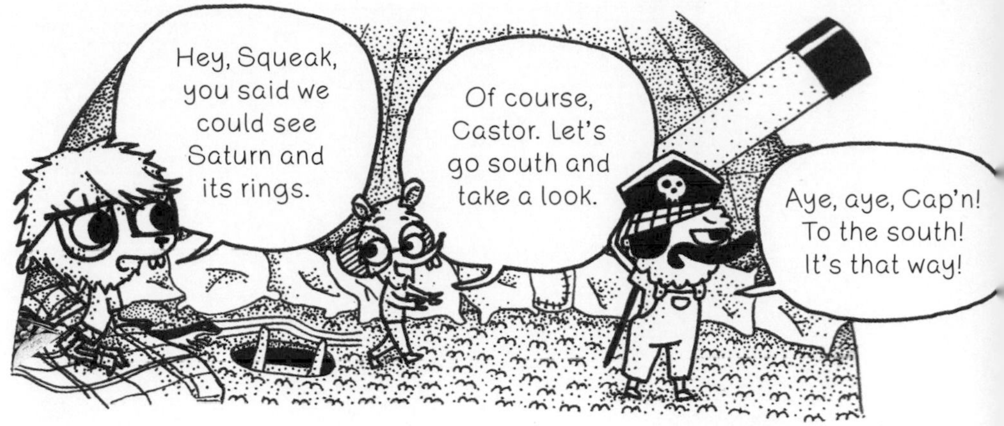

Hey, Squeak, you said we could see Saturn and its rings.
Of course, Castor. Let's go south and take a look.
Aye, aye, Cap'n! To the south! It's that way!

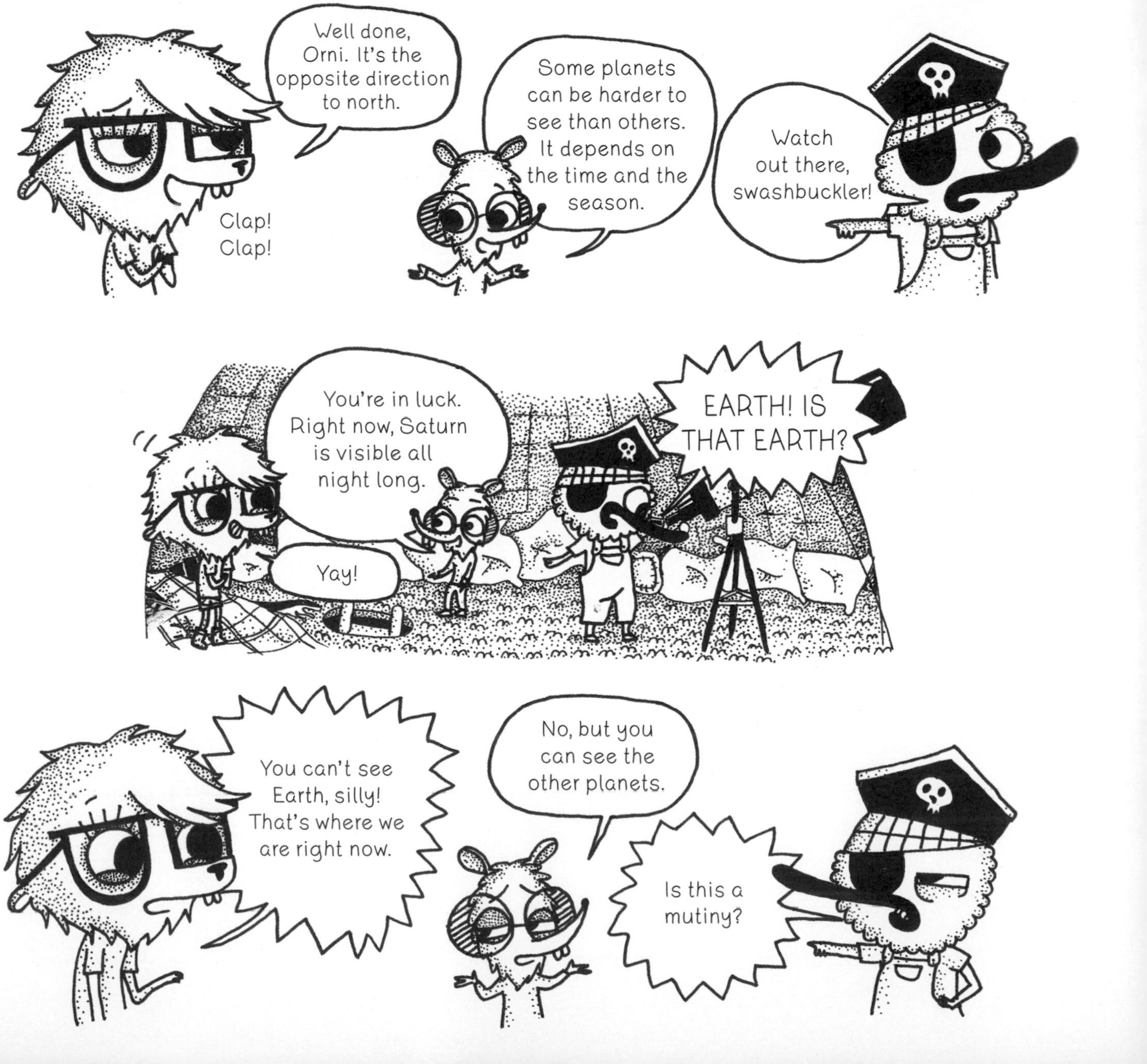

Well done, Orni. It's the opposite direction to north.
Clap! Clap!
Some planets can be harder to see than others. It depends on the time and the season.
Watch out there, swashbuckler!
You're in luck. Right now, Saturn is visible all night long.
Yay!
EARTH! IS THAT EARTH?
You can't see Earth, silly! That's where we are right now.
No, but you can see the other planets.
Is this a mutiny?

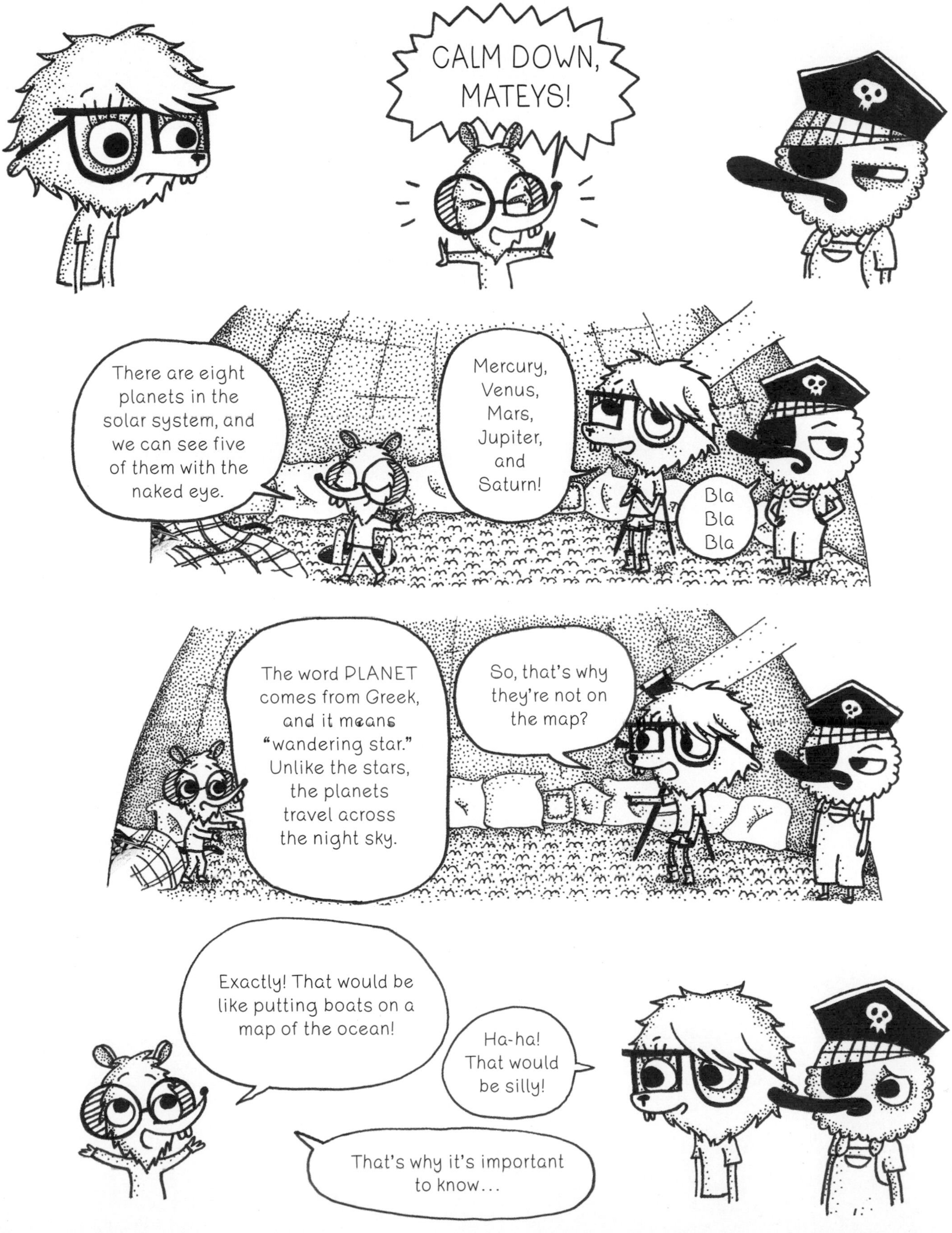
CALM DOWN, MATEYS!
There are eight planets in the solar system, and we can see five of them with the naked eye.
Mercury, Venus, Mars, Jupiter, and Saturn!
Bla Bla Bla
The word PLANET comes from Greek, and it means "wandering star." Unlike the stars, the planets travel across the night sky.
So, that's why they're not on the map?
Exactly! That would be like putting boats on a map of the ocean!
Ha-ha! That would be silly!
That's why it's important to know...

THE CONSTELLATIONS OF THE ZODIAC

There are 13 constellations of the zodiac, and they seem to move with the seasons across the night sky.

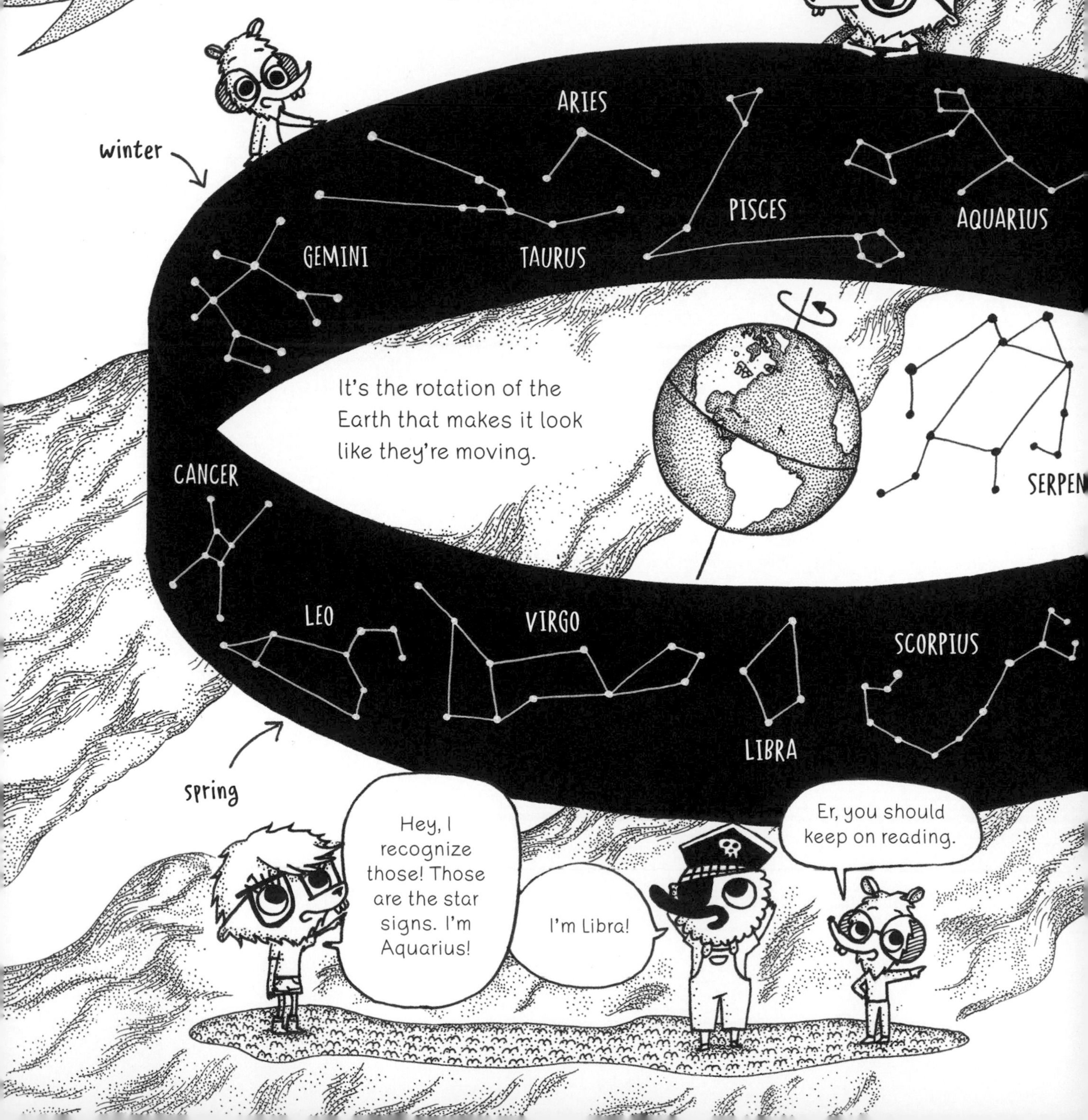

winter
ARIES
GEMINI
TAURUS
PISCES
AQUARIUS
It's the rotation of the Earth that makes it look like they're moving.
CANCER
SERPEN
LEO
VIRGO
SCORPIUS
LIBRA
spring
Hey, I recognize those! Those are the star signs. I'm Aquarius!
I'm Libra!
Er, you should keep on reading.

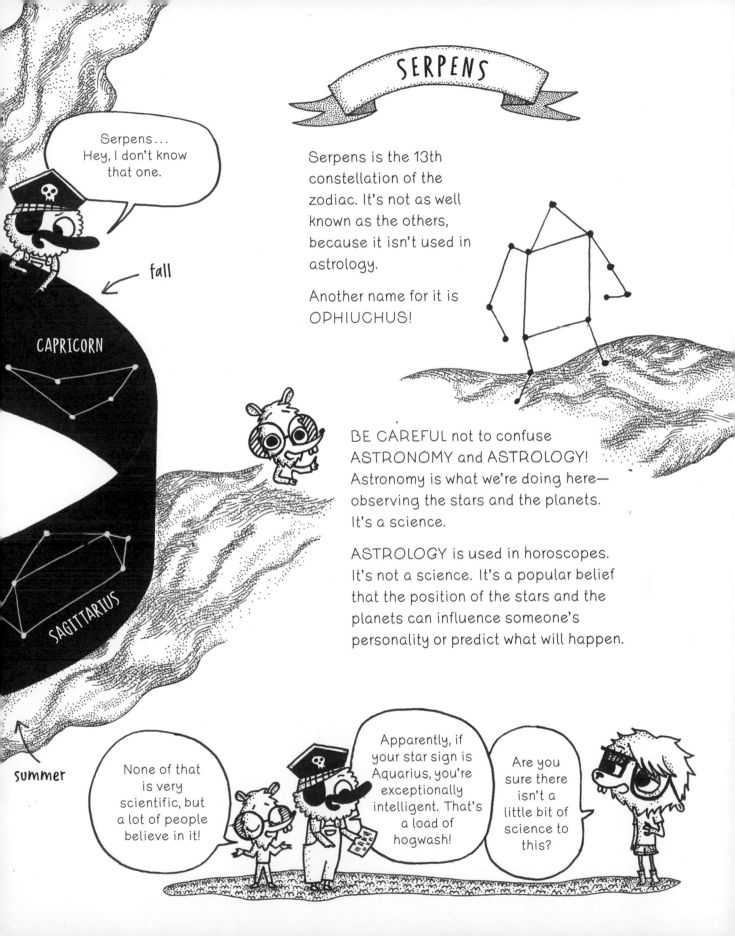

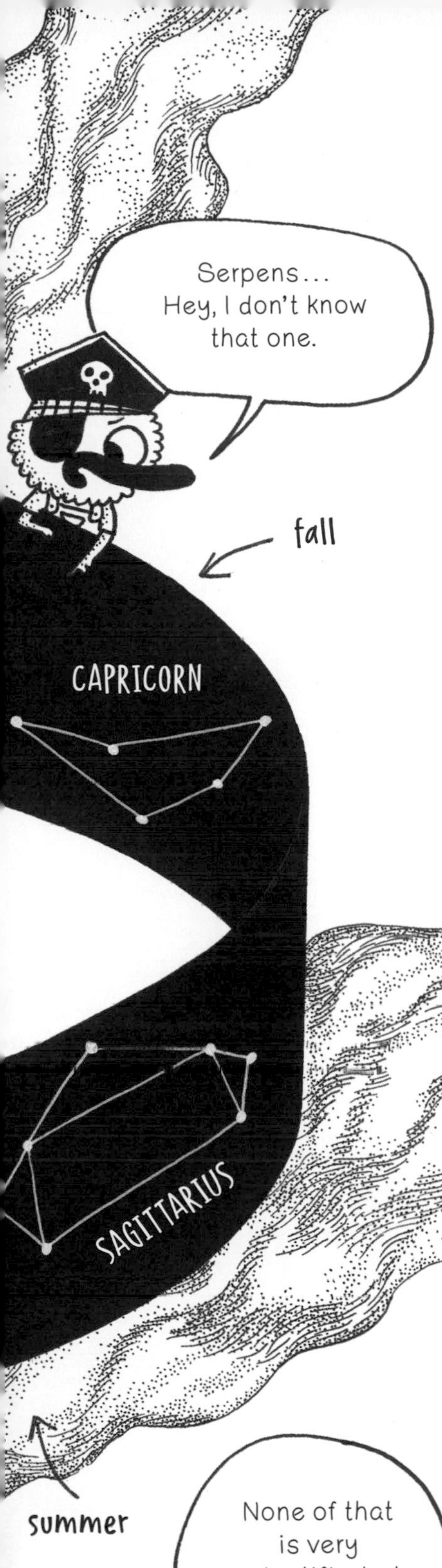
Serpens...
Hey, I don't know that one.
fall
CAPRICORN
SAGITTARIUS
summer

SERPENS

Serpens is the 13th constellation of the zodiac. It's not as well known as the others, because it isn't used in astrology.

Another name for it is OPHIUCHUS!

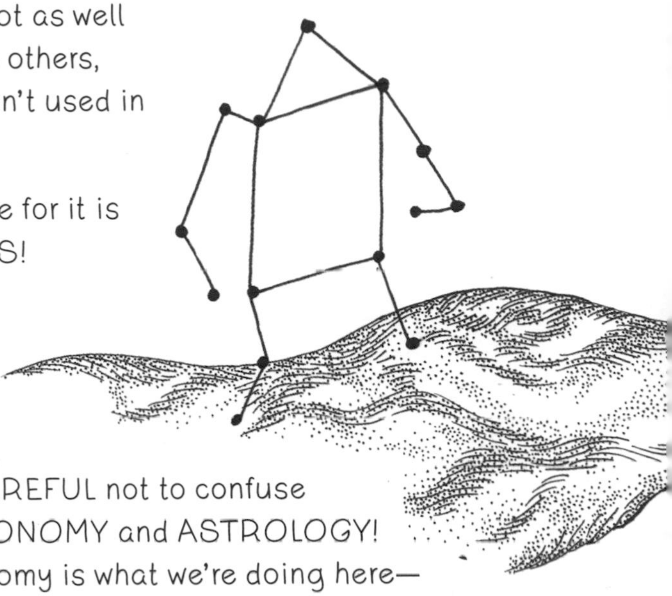

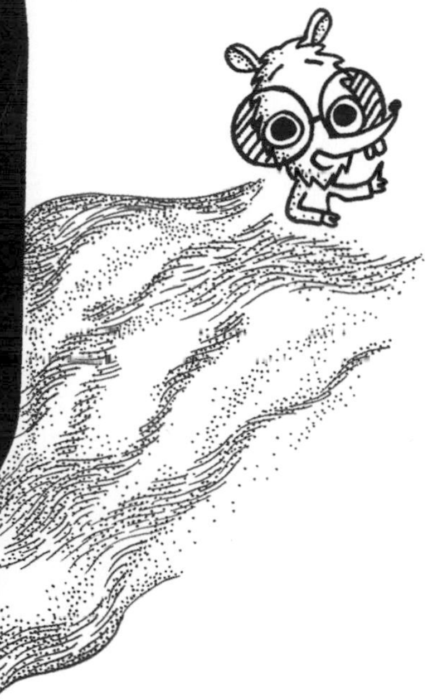

BE CAREFUL not to confuse ASTRONOMY and ASTROLOGY! Astronomy is what we're doing here—observing the stars and the planets. It's a science.

ASTROLOGY is used in horoscopes. It's not a science. It's a popular belief that the position of the stars and the planets can influence someone's personality or predict what will happen.

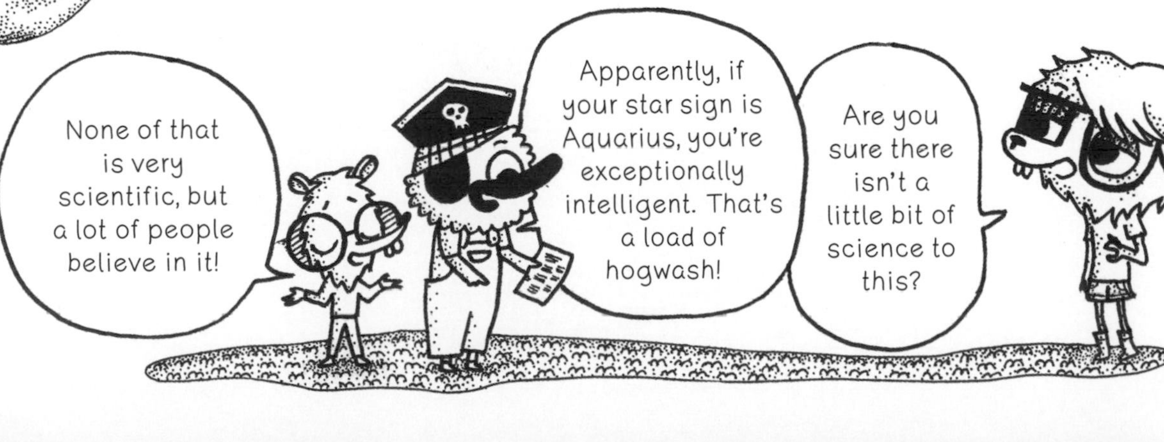
None of that is very scientific, but a lot of people believe in it!
Apparently, if your star sign is Aquarius, you're exceptionally intelligent. That's a load of hogwash!
Are you sure there isn't a little bit of science to this?

Chapter 10

TO THE SOUTH

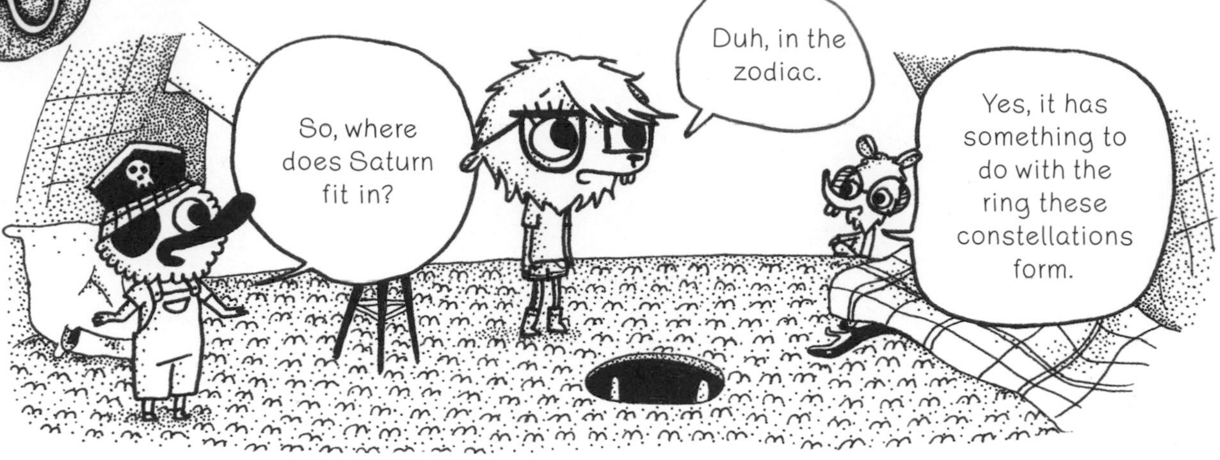
So, where does Saturn fit in?
Duh, in the zodiac.
Yes, it has something to do with the ring these constellations form.

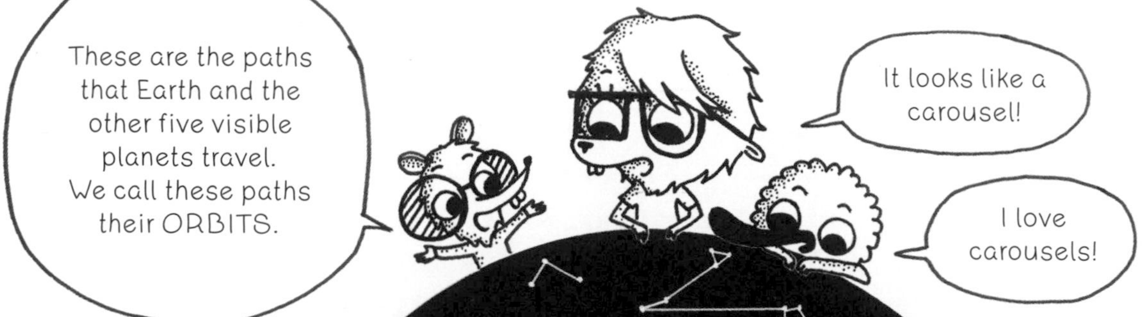
These are the paths that Earth and the other five visible planets travel. We call these paths their ORBITS.
It looks like a carousel!
I love carousels!

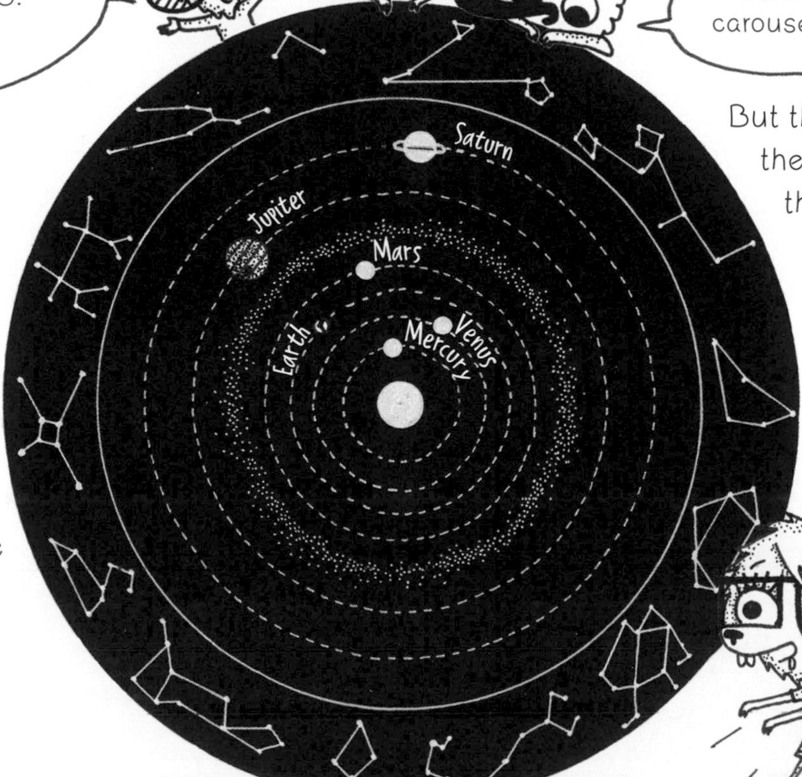
Saturn
Jupiter
Mars
Earth
Venus
Mercury

The constellations of the zodiac are like the things you see on the outside of the carousel. They don't move. The Sun in the middle doesn't move, either.

But the planets are like the things you ride on the carousel. They turn around the Sun on one plane. And that plane is as flat as a...

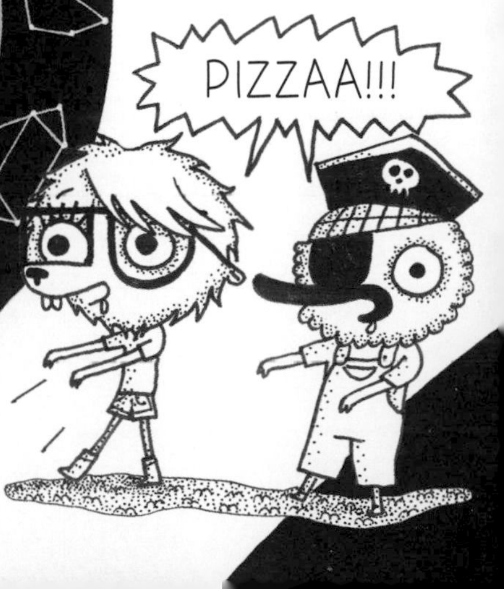
PIZZAA!!!

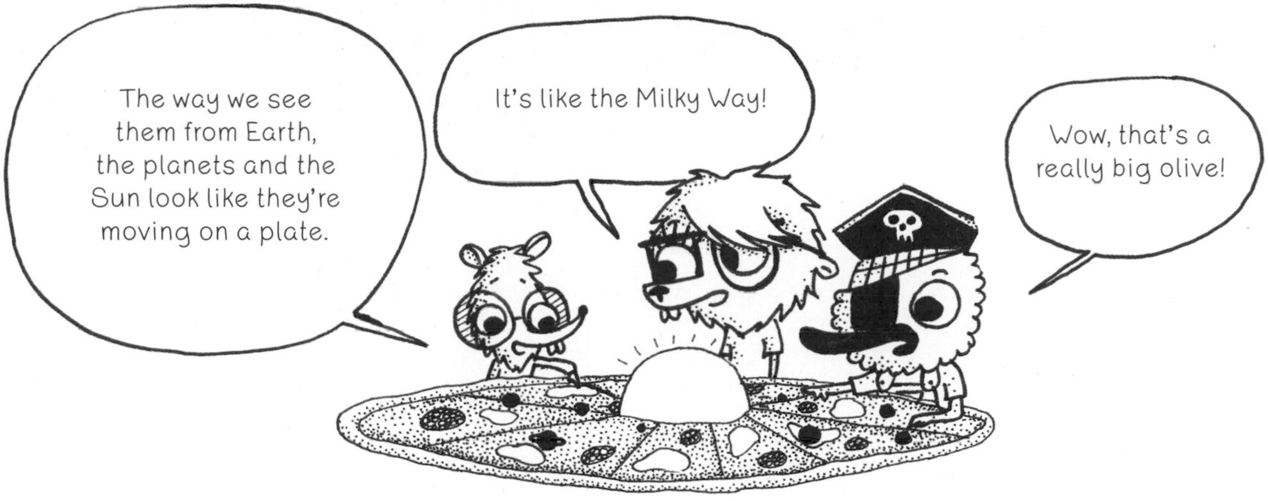
The way we see them from Earth, the planets and the Sun look like they're moving on a plate.
It's like the Milky Way!
Wow, that's a really big olive!

The Sun and the planets circle in the sky past the 13 constellations of the zodiac.

If we could see them all at once, it would look something like this.

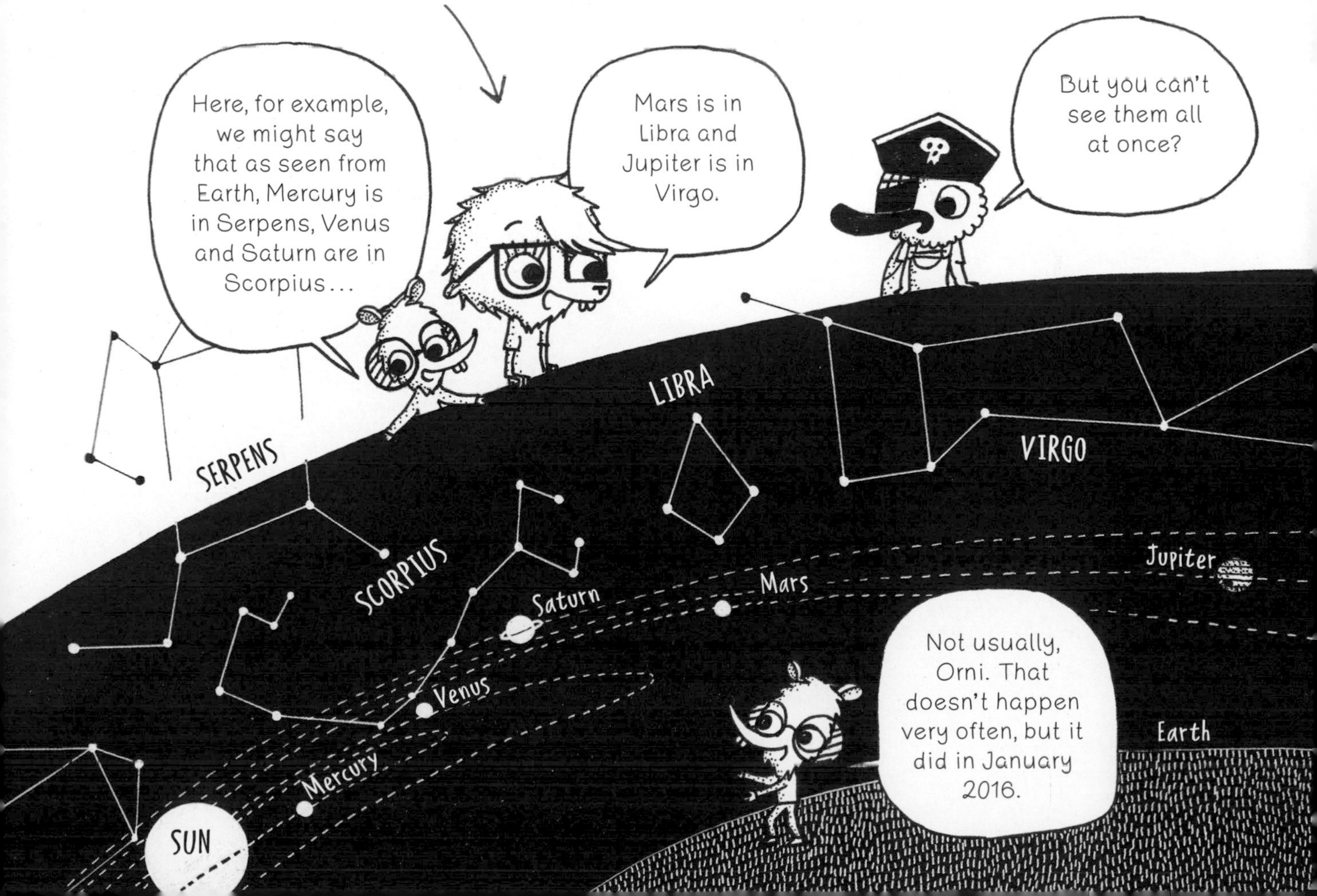
Here, for example, we might say that as seen from Earth, Mercury is in Serpens, Venus and Saturn are in Scorpius...
Mars is in Libra and Jupiter is in Virgo.
But you can't see them all at once?
Not usually, Orni. That doesn't happen very often, but it did in January 2016.
SERPENS
LIBRA
VIRGO
SCORPIUS
Jupiter
Mars
Saturn
Venus
Mercury
SUN
Earth

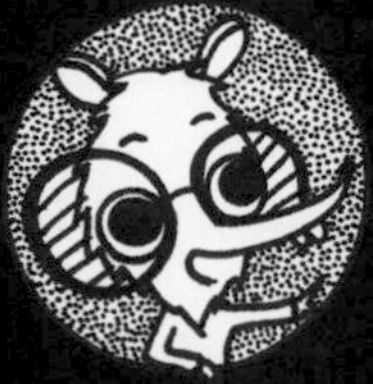

To the naked eye, the planets look a lot like stars. You need to know how to spot them!

HOW TO SPOT A PLANET

1. Look to the south (in the opposite direction of the pole star) and you'll find the zodiac.

2. Compare the constellations you see in the sky to the ones on the map, and look for the differences.

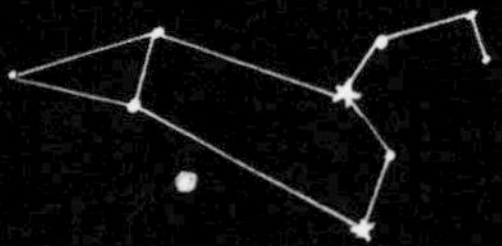

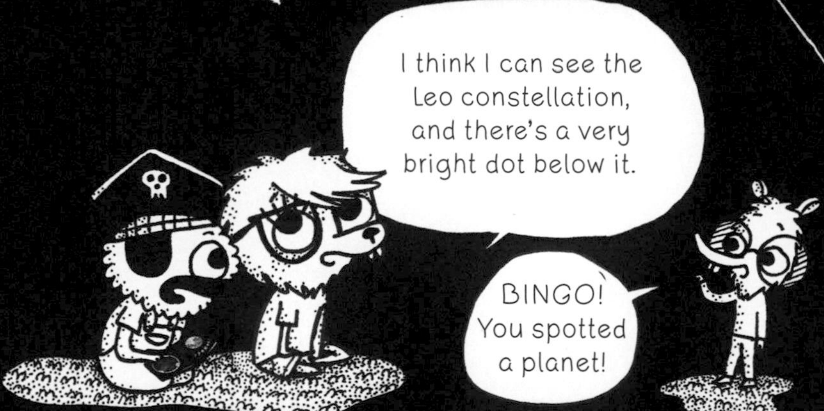
I think I can see the Leo constellation, and there's a very bright dot below it.
BINGO! You spotted a planet!

3. Use binoculars or a telescope to take a closer look at the planet.

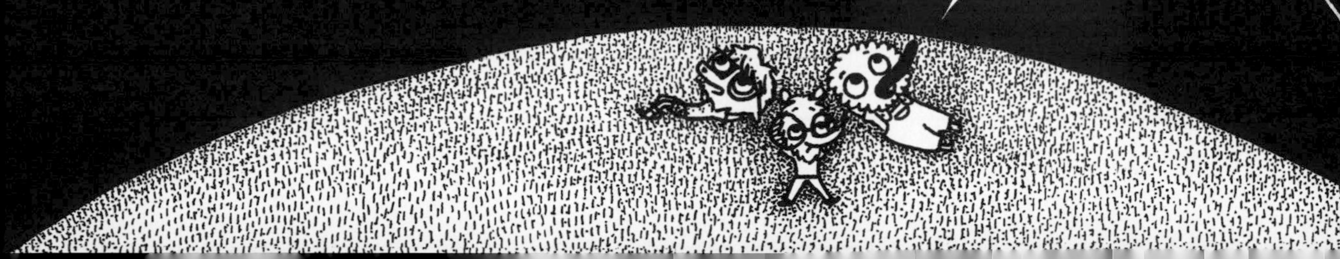
How do you know which planet you're looking at?

OBSERVING

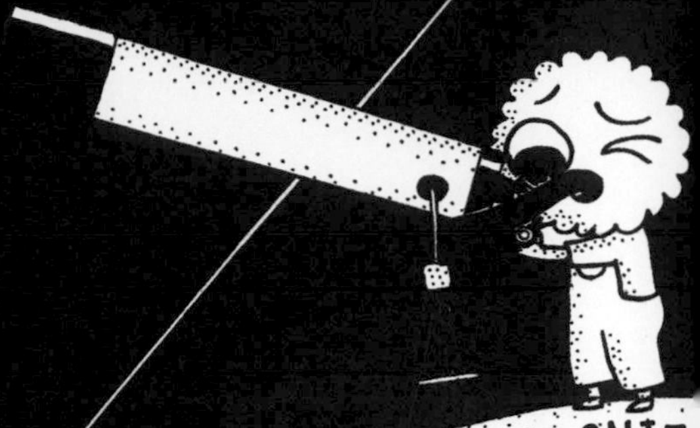

HOW TO RECOGNIZ

MERCURY is very close to the Sun.

⚠ Do not look at the Sun without a special filter!

VENUS is sometimes called the shepherd's star.

It's so bright, you can see it before the sky gets dark, or in the morning!

MARS is red because its surface is so rich in IRON.

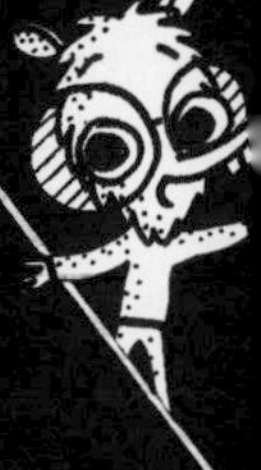

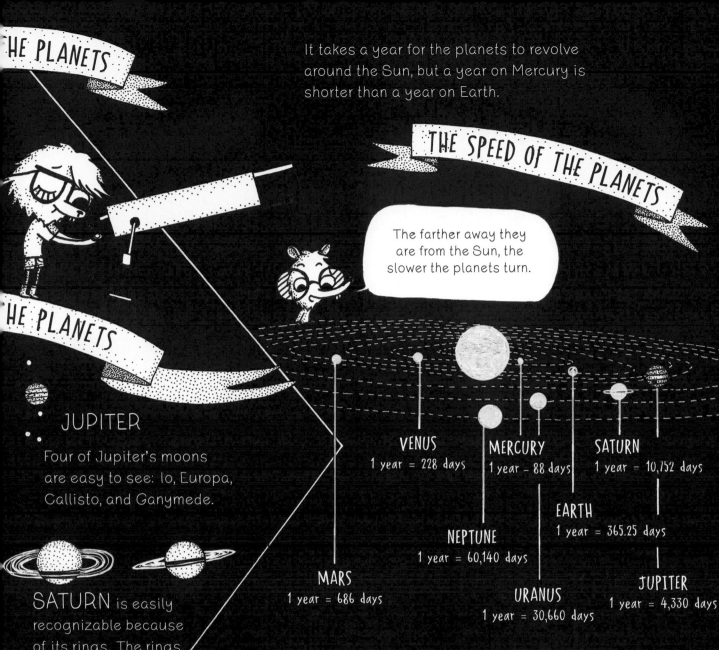

HE PLANETS

It takes a year for the planets to revolve around the Sun, but a year on Mercury is shorter than a year on Earth.

THE SPEED OF THE PLANETS

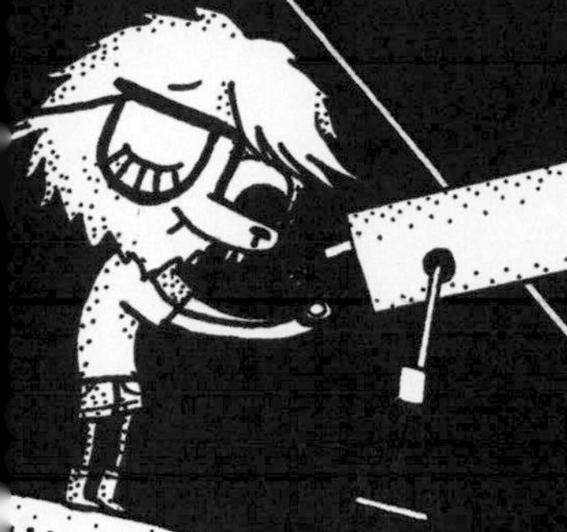

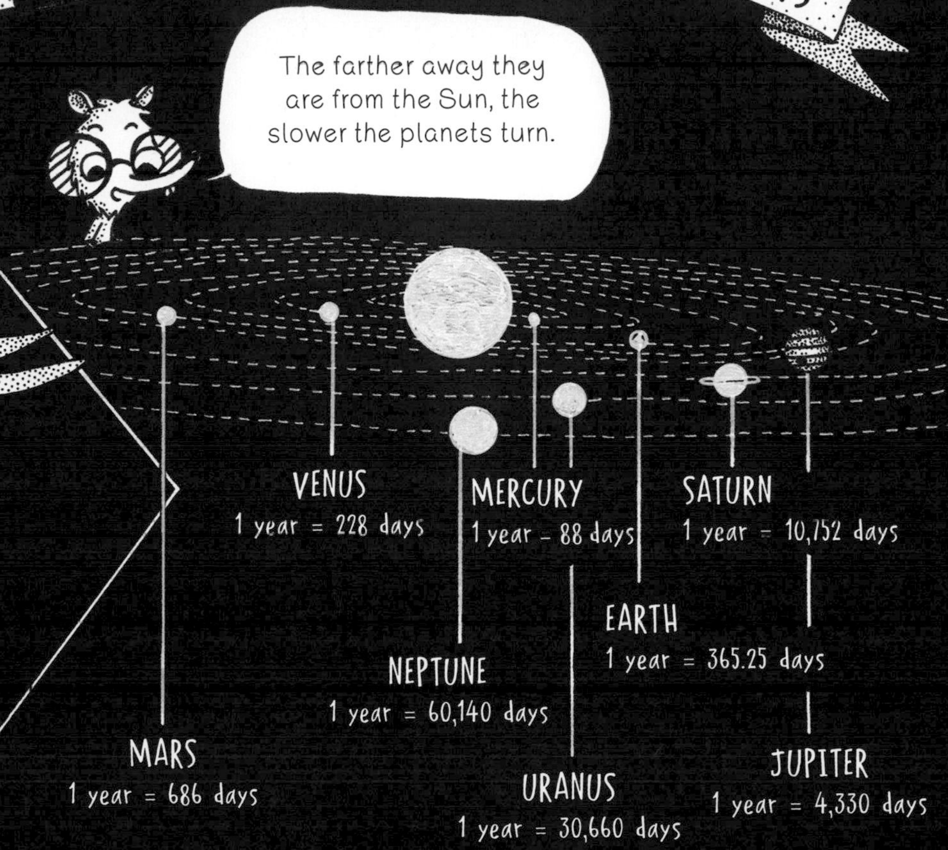

The farther away they are from the Sun, the slower the planets turn.
VENUS
1 year = 228 days
MERCURY
1 year = 88 days
SATURN
1 year = 10,752 days
EARTH
1 year = 365.25 days
NEPTUNE
1 year = 60,140 days
MARS
1 year = 686 days
URANUS
1 year = 30,660 days
JUPITER
1 year = 4,330 days

HE PLANETS

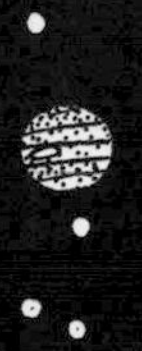

JUPITER

Four of Jupiter's moons are easy to see: Io, Europa, Callisto, and Ganymede.

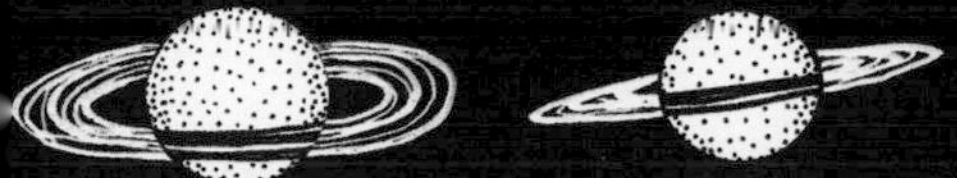

SATURN is easily recognizable because of its rings. The rings can be easier to spot depending on the angle you see them from.

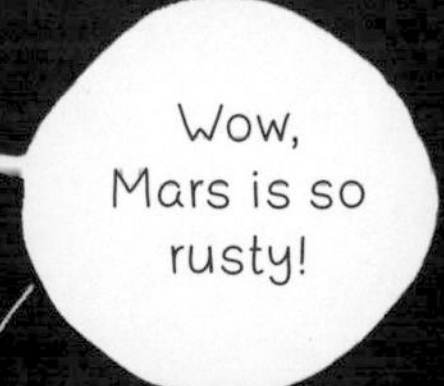

Wow, Mars is so rusty!

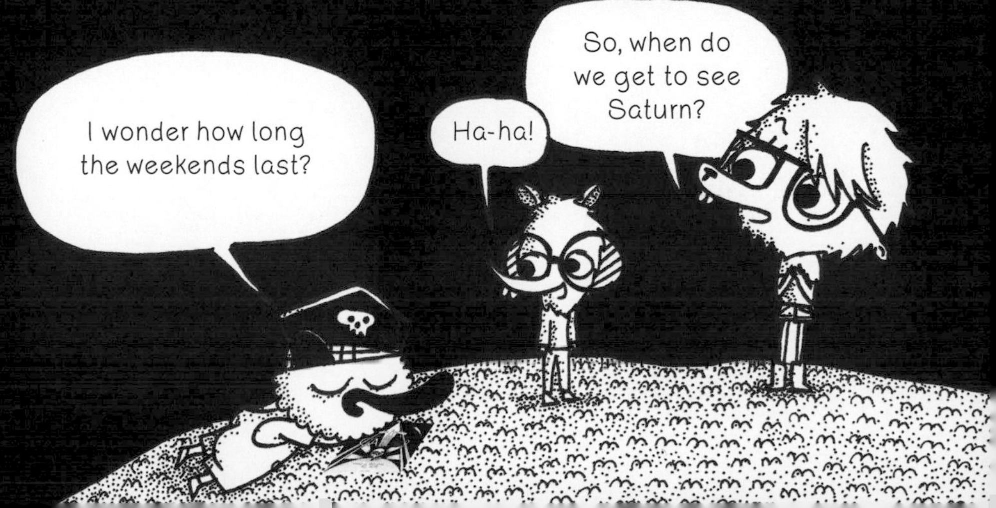

I wonder how long the weekends last?
Ha-ha!
So, when do we get to see Saturn?

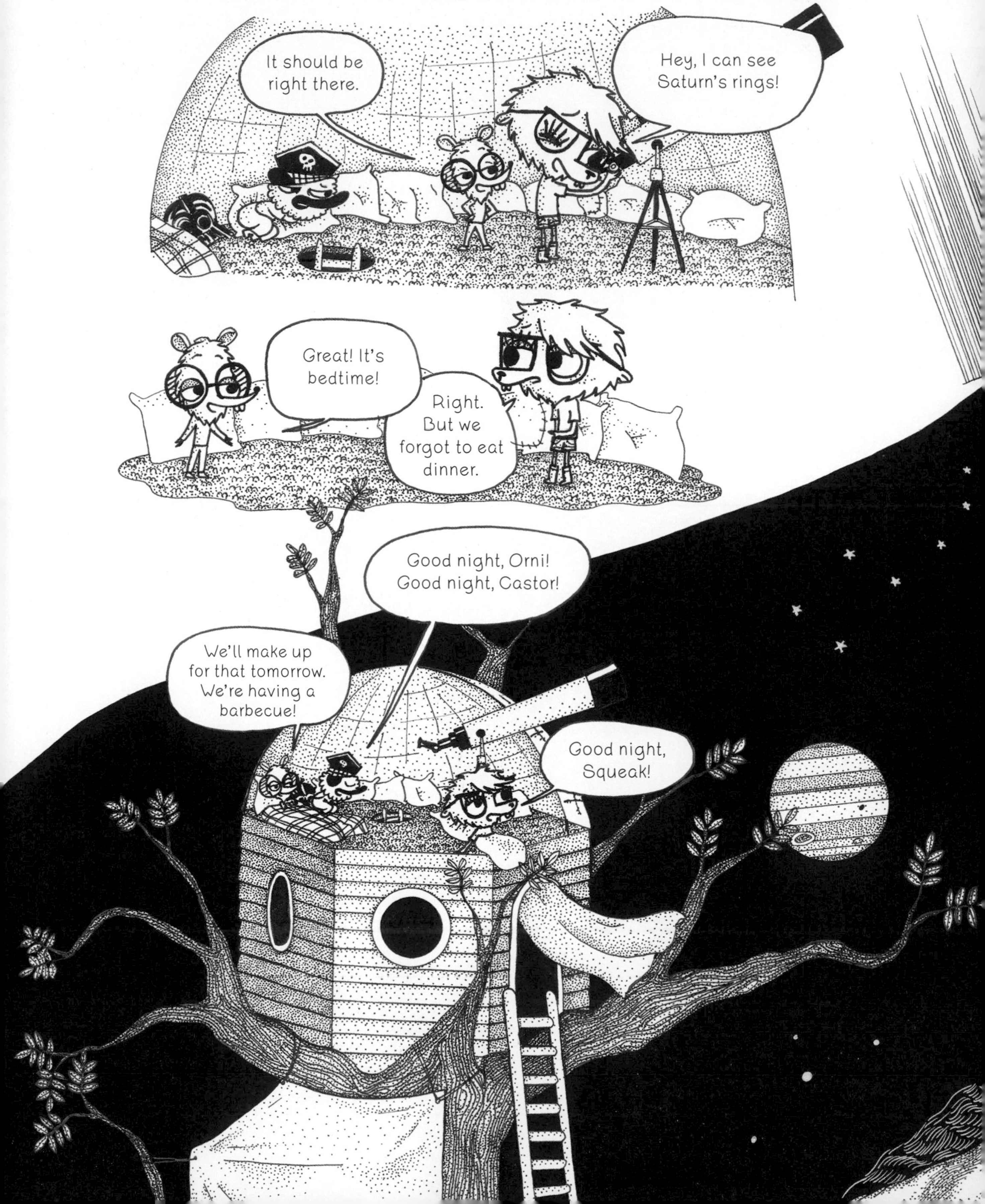
It should be right there.
Hey, I can see Saturn's rings!
Great! It's bedtime!
Right. But we forgot to eat dinner.
Good night, Orni! Good night, Castor!
We'll make up for that tomorrow. We're having a barbecue!
Good night, Squeak!

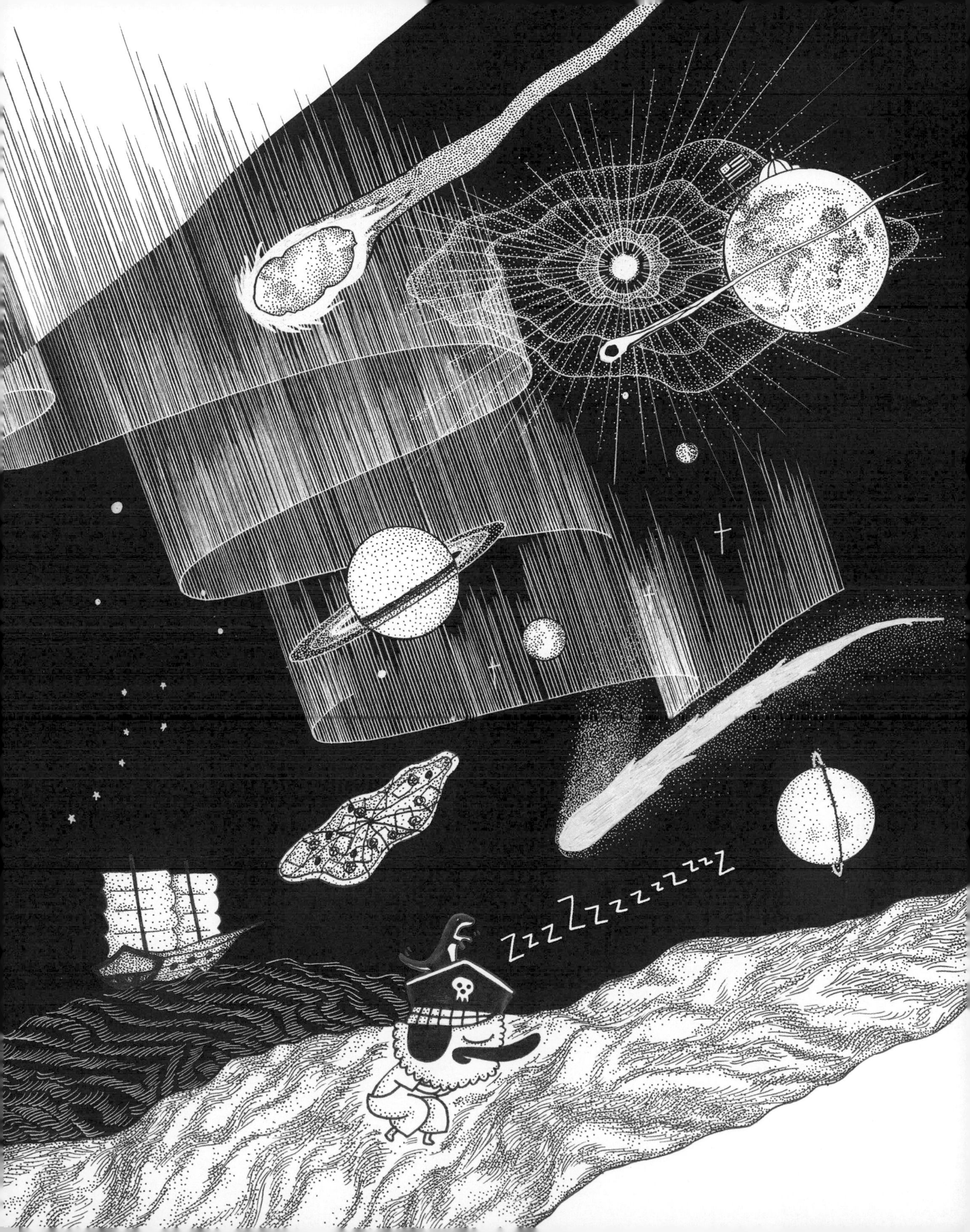
ZzzZzzzzZzzZ

Chapter 11

BARBECUE SPECTROMETRY

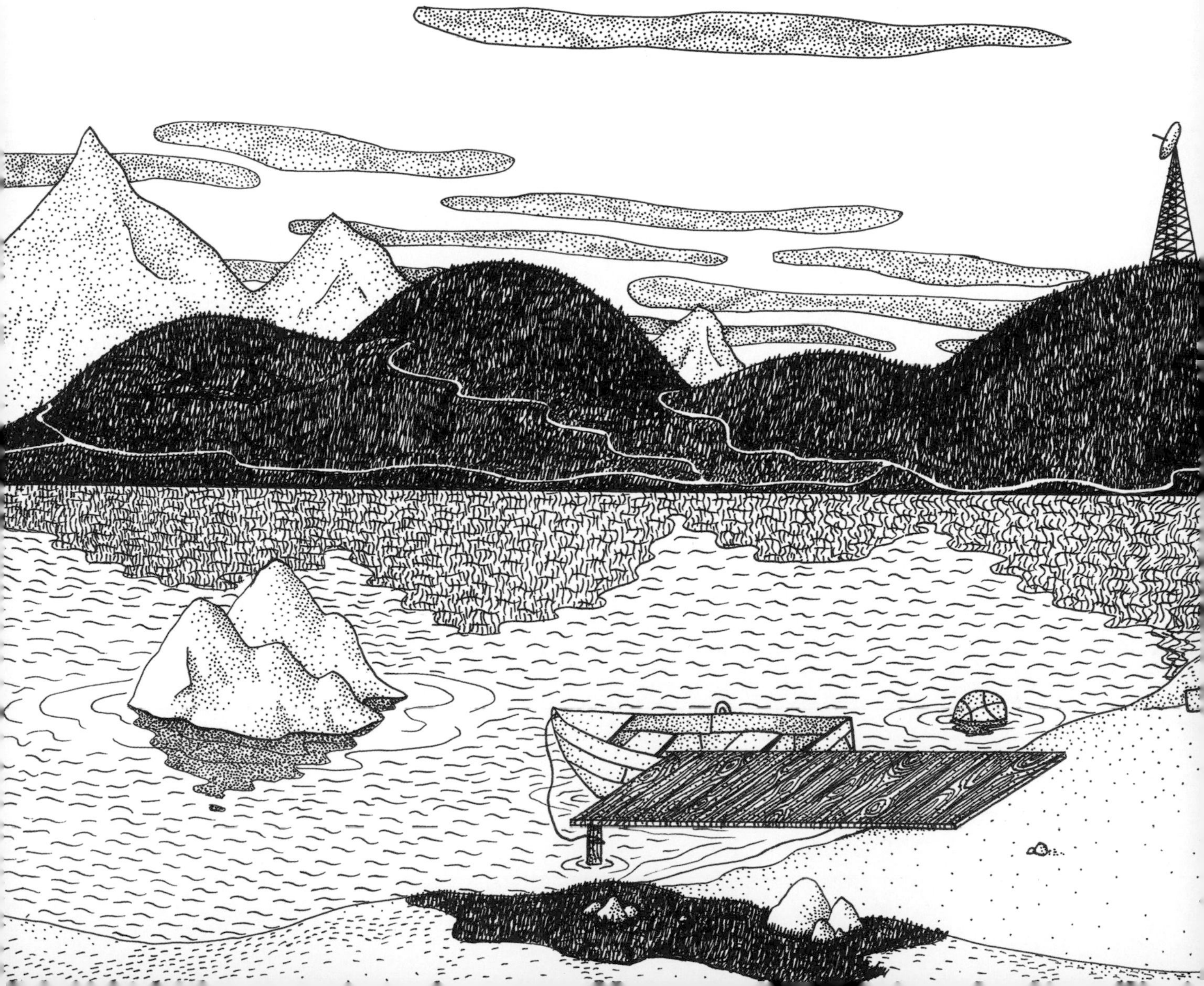

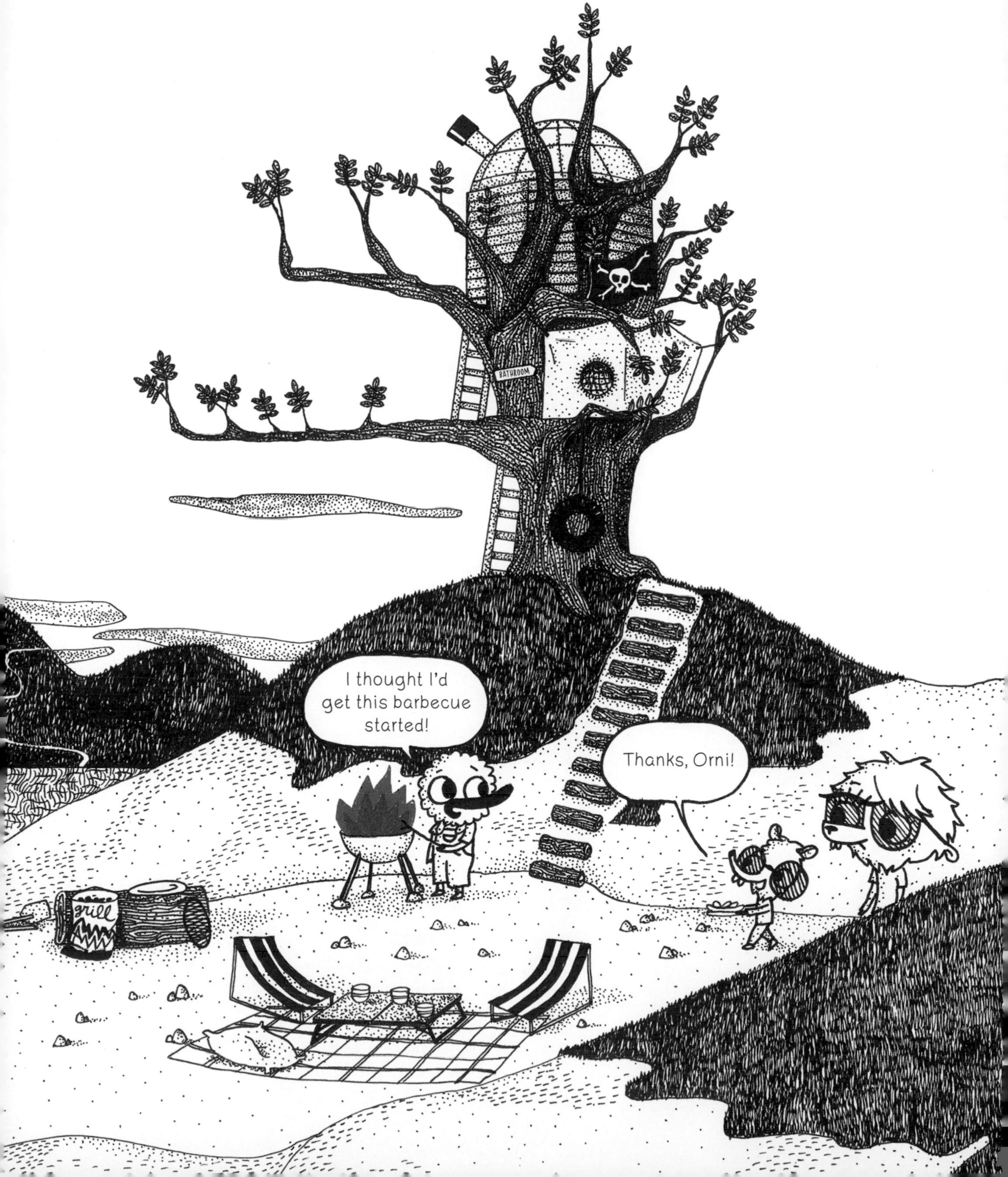
BATHROOM
I thought I'd get this barbecue started!
Thanks, Orni!
grill

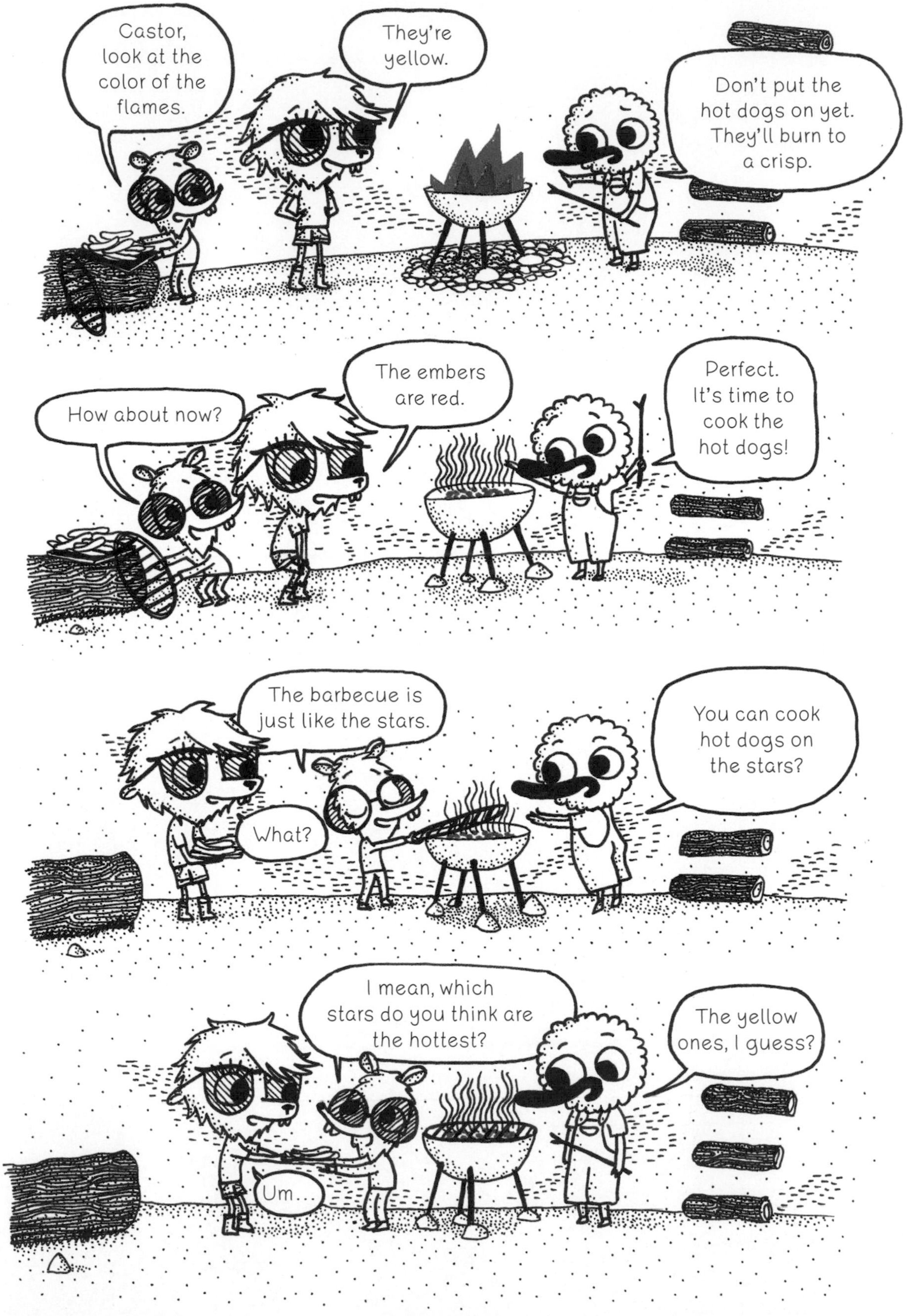
Castor, look at the color of the flames.
They're yellow.
Don't put the hot dogs on yet. They'll burn to a crisp.
How about now?
The embers are red.
Perfect. It's time to cook the hot dogs!
The barbecue is just like the stars.
What?
You can cook hot dogs on the stars?
I mean, which stars do you think are the hottest?
Um...
The yellow ones, I guess?

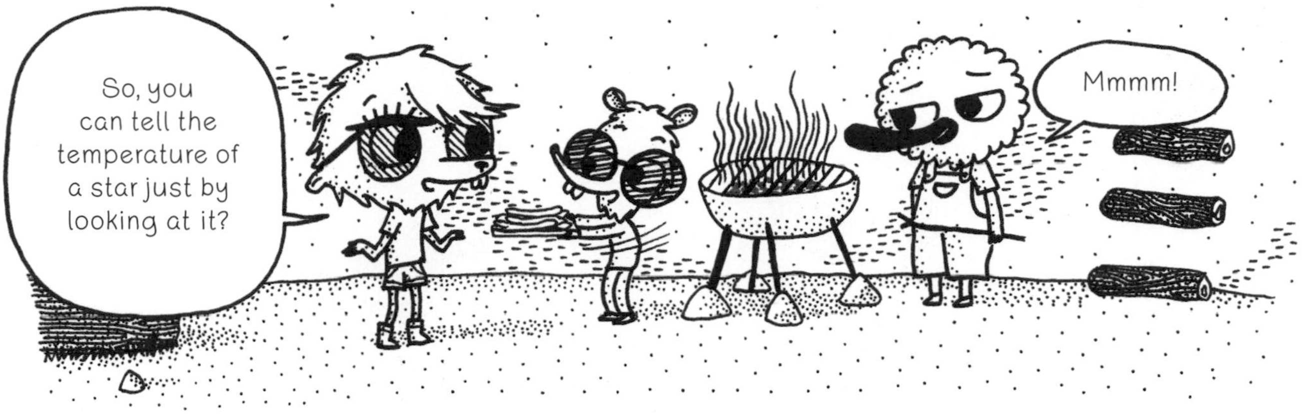
So, you can tell the temperature of a star just by looking at it?
Mmmm!

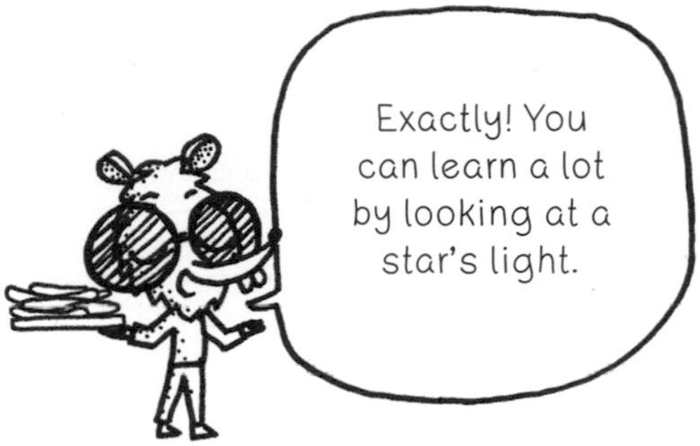
Exactly! You can learn a lot by looking at a star's light.

ITS TEMPERATURE, of course.
But also ITS MASS.
This is called SPECTROMETRY.

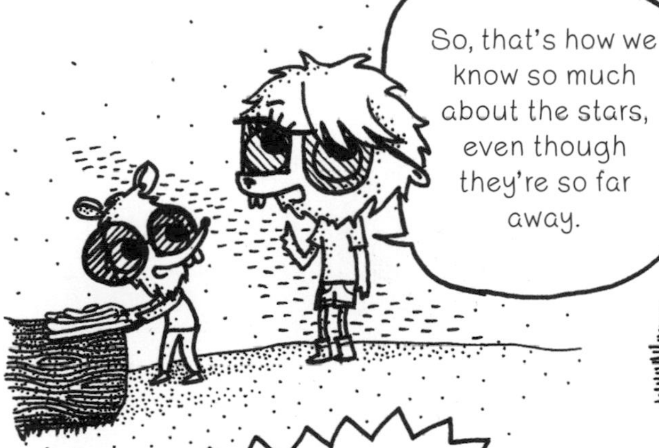
So, that's how we know so much about the stars, even though they're so far away.

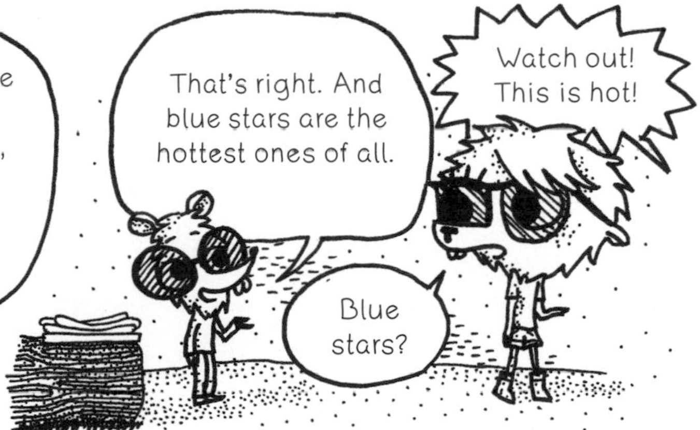
That's right. And blue stars are the hottest ones of all.
Watch out! This is hot!
Blue stars?

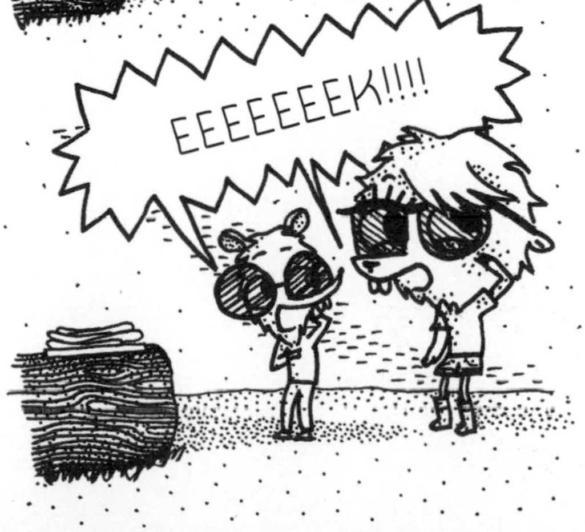
EEEEEEEK!!!!

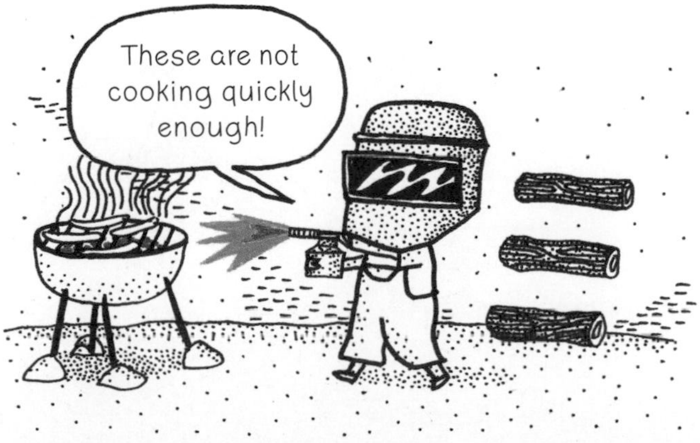
These are not cooking quickly enough!

Chapter 12

THE RAINBOW PRISM

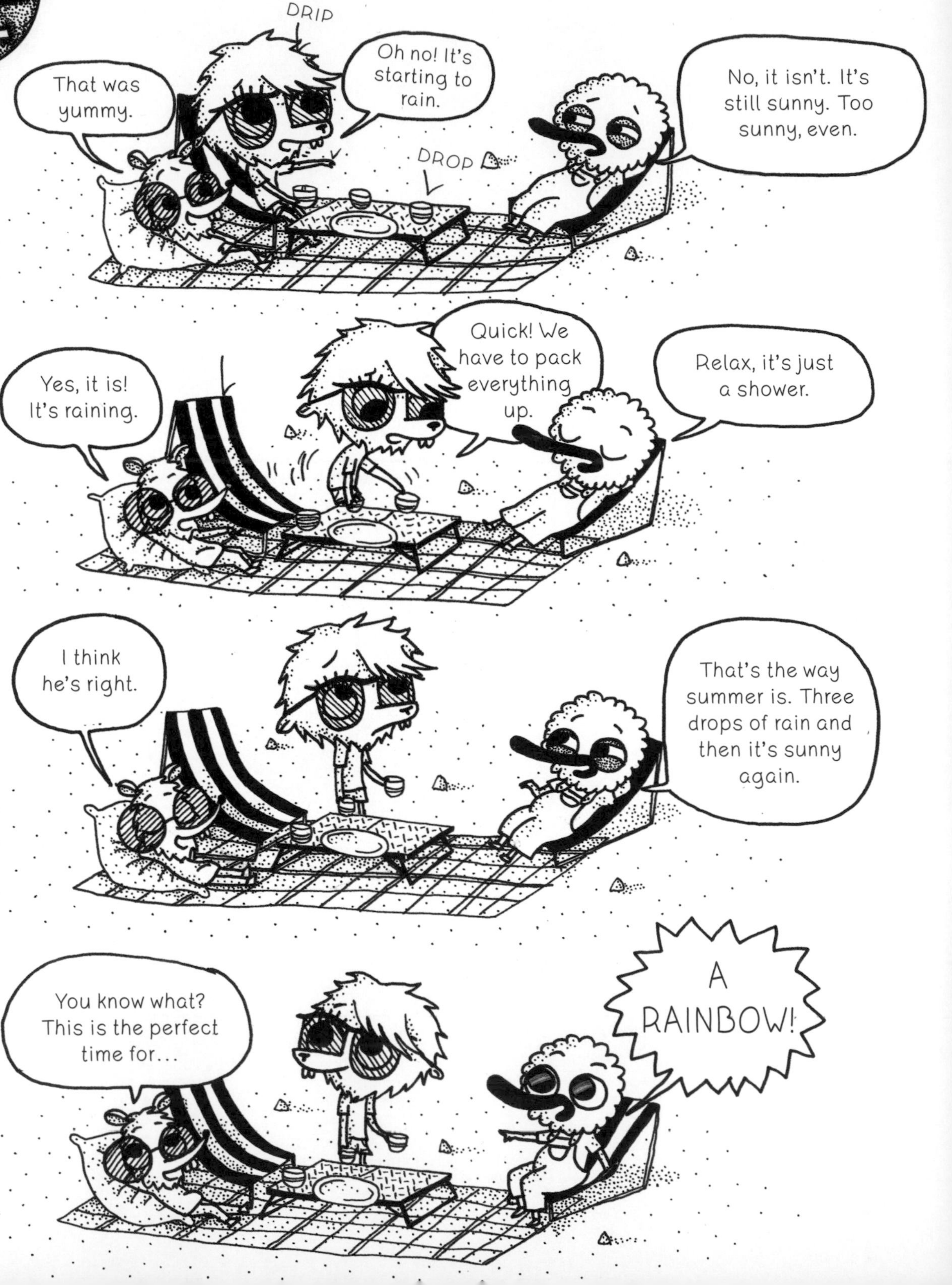
DRIP
That was yummy.
Oh no! It's starting to rain.
DROP
No, it isn't. It's still sunny. Too sunny, even.
Yes, it is! It's raining.
Quick! We have to pack everything up.
Relax, it's just a shower.
I think he's right.
That's the way summer is. Three drops of rain and then it's sunny again.
You know what? This is the perfect time for...
A RAINBOW!

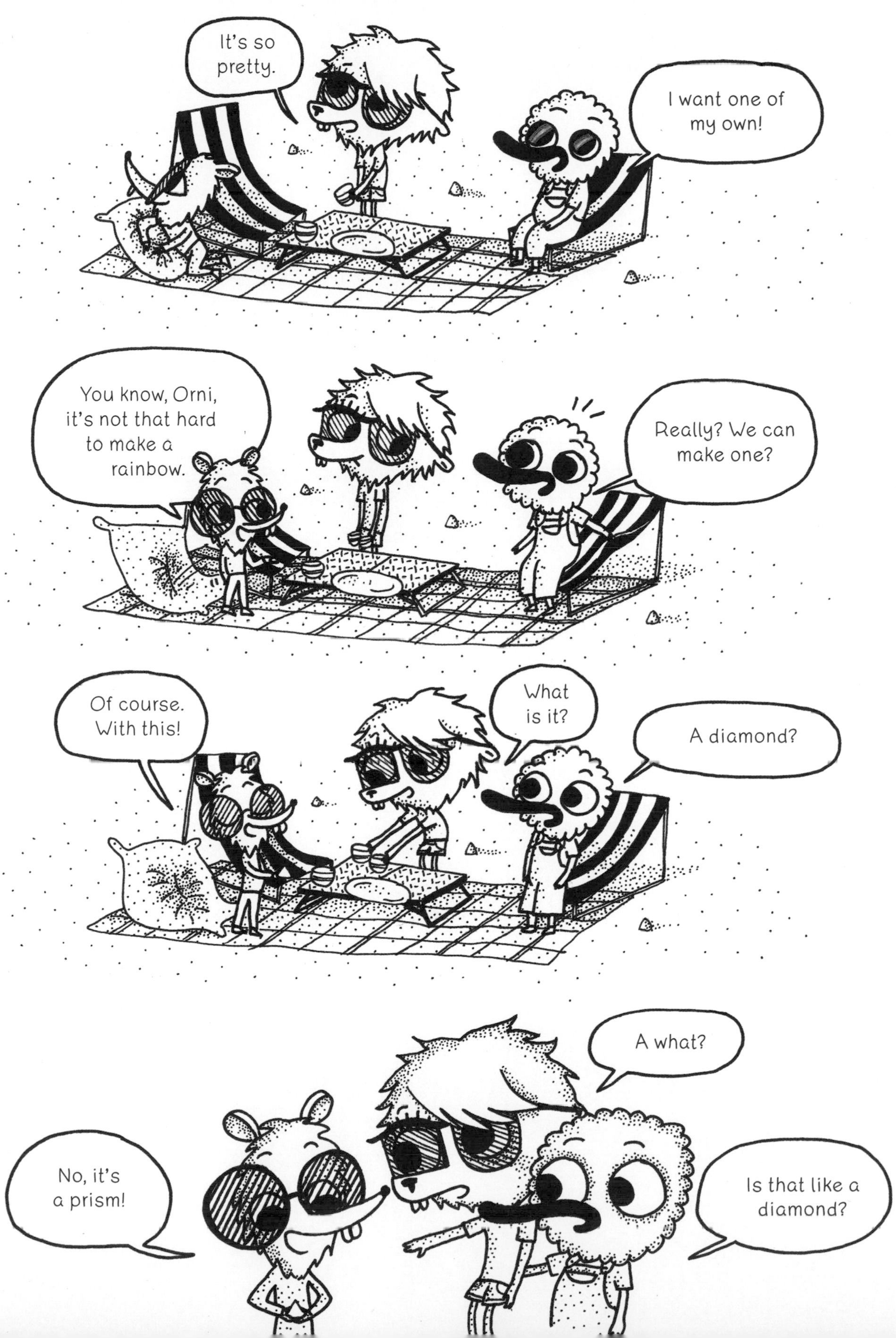
It's so pretty.
I want one of my own!
You know, Orni, it's not that hard to make a rainbow.
Really? We can make one?
Of course. With this!
What is it?
A diamond?
A what?
No, it's a prism!
Is that like a diamond?

VISIBLE LIGHT

A prism is an object made from cut glass that can split light.

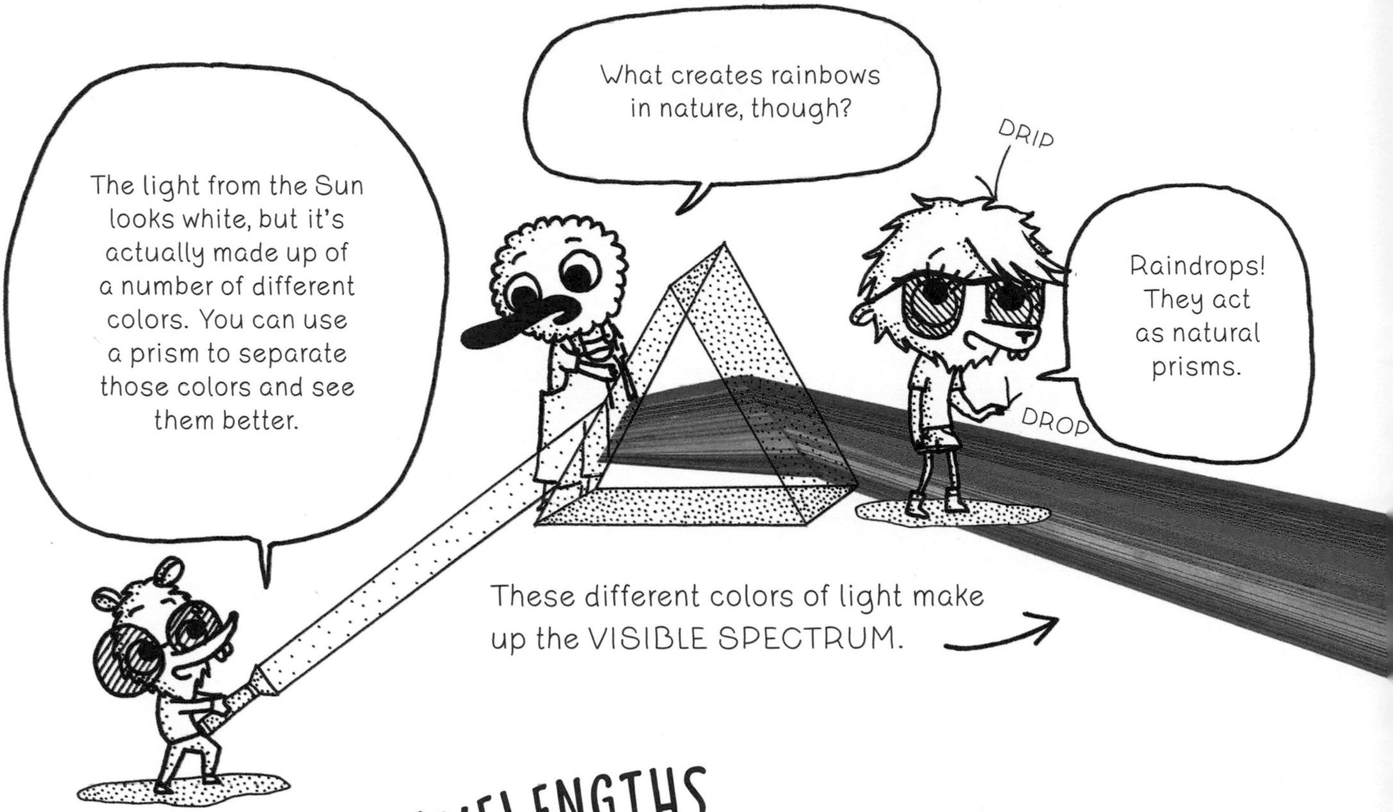

The light from the Sun looks white, but it's actually made up of a number of different colors. You can use a prism to separate those colors and see them better.
What creates rainbows in nature, though?
DRIP
Raindrops! They act as natural prisms.
DROP
These different colors of light make up the VISIBLE SPECTRUM.

WAVELENGTHS

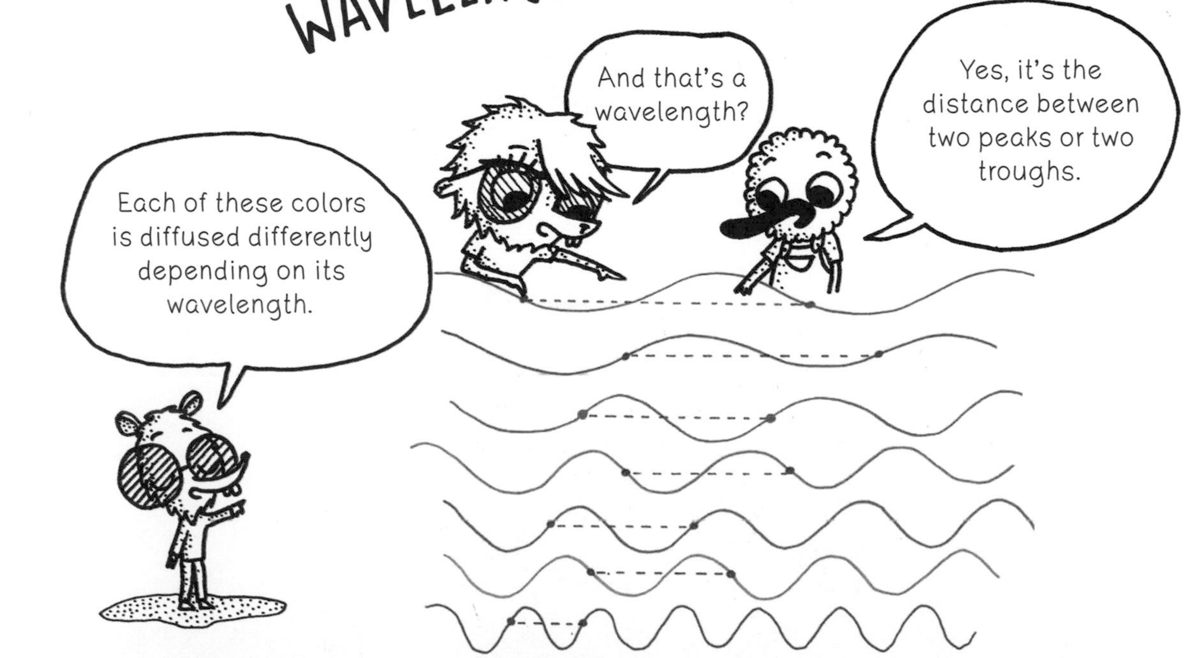

Each of these colors is diffused differently depending on its wavelength.
And that's a wavelength?
Yes, it's the distance between two peaks or two troughs.

The Earth is surrounded by a layer of gas called the ATMOSPHERE.

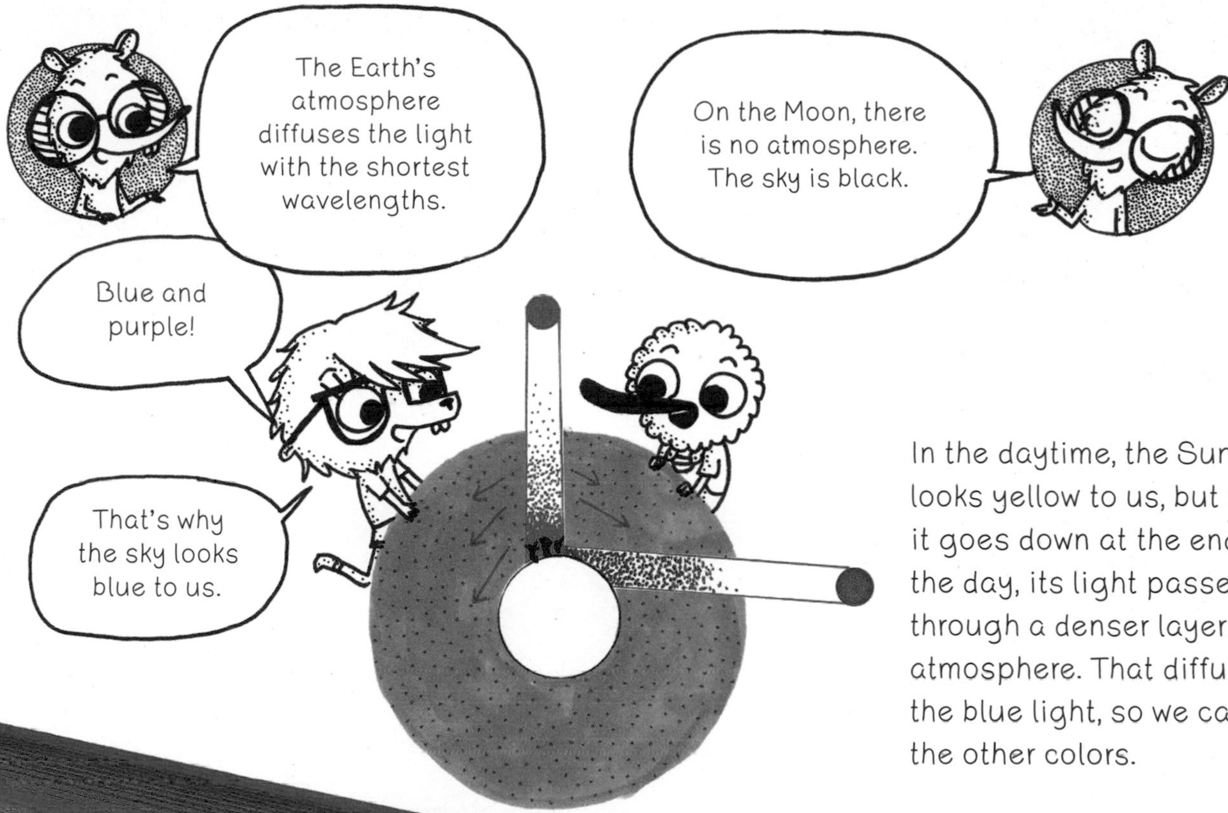
The Earth's atmosphere diffuses the light with the shortest wavelengths.
On the Moon, there is no atmosphere. The sky is black.
Blue and purple!
That's why the sky looks blue to us.

In the daytime, the Sun looks yellow to us, but when it goes down at the end of the day, its light passes through a denser layer of the atmosphere. That diffuses the blue light, so we can see the other colors.

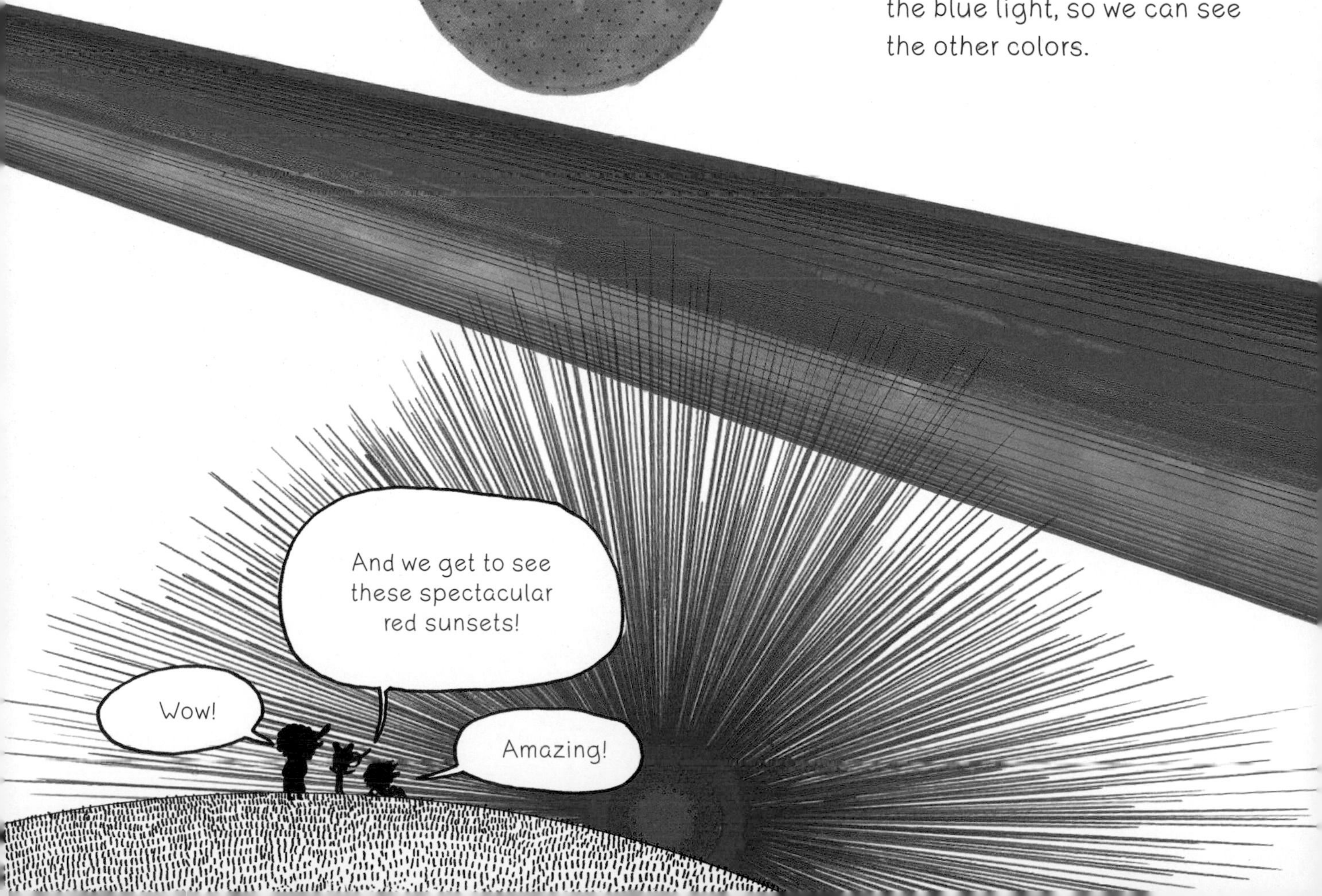
And we get to see these spectacular red sunsets!
Wow!
Amazing!

INVISIBLE LIGHT

The visible spectrum is the part of the light that we can see.

Right there.

GAMMA RAYS	X-RAYS	UV	INFRARED	MICRO-WAVES	RADIO WAVES

This is a very small part of the ELECTROMAGNETIC SPECTRUM, which is the whole range of waves.

Ha-ha! Like the microwaves that heat our food?

Yes, it's amazing! And radio waves, those are a kind of light as well.

X-RAYS

Eeeek!!!

Surprise!

X-rays are used in hospitals to take pictures of what's inside our bodies, and in airports to see what's in our baggage.

ULTRAVIOLET (UV) LIGHT

The wavelength of ultraviolet light is even shorter than purple's. This is what gives us a suntan in the summer.

Or a sunburn!

INFRARED LIGHT

Infrared has a wavelength even longer than red light.

The word INFRARED means "below red."

WILLIAM HERSCHEL
discovered it in
1900

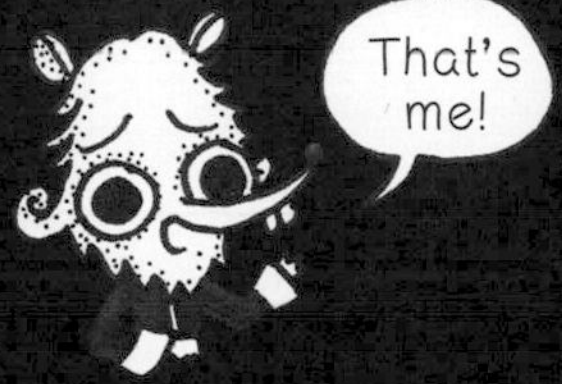
That's me!

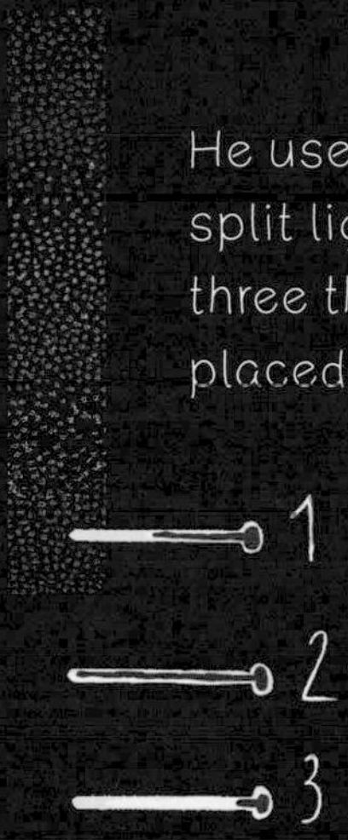
1
2
3

He used a prism to split light. Then he took three thermometers and placed:

1 one in the red light,

2 one right beside the red light, and

3 another one farther away.

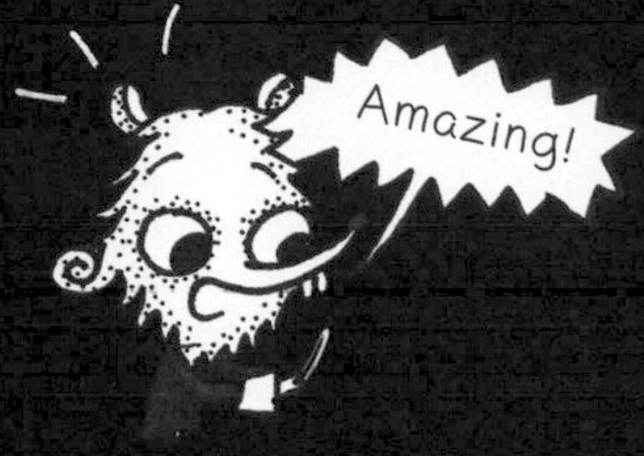
Amazing!

When he saw that the temperature on the second thermometer was the hottest, this proved that an INVISIBLE light existed!

THE CONSTELLATION OF ORION IN INFRARED

Infrared light is very useful in astronomy because it makes it possible to see heat. It reveals things that are invisible to the naked eye, including things that might be hidden behind dust clouds.

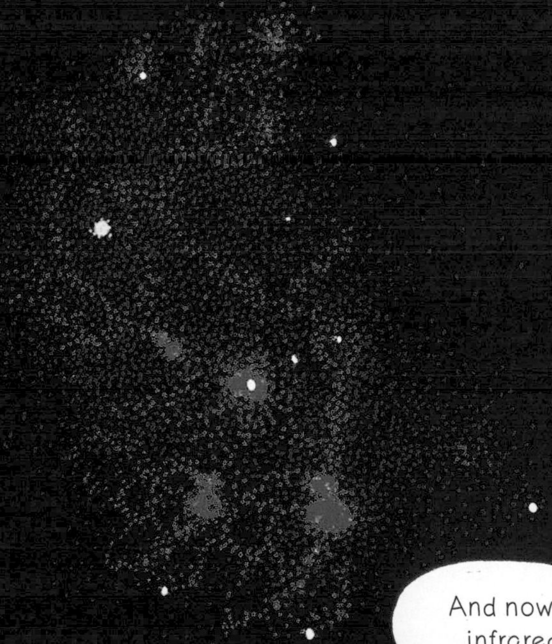

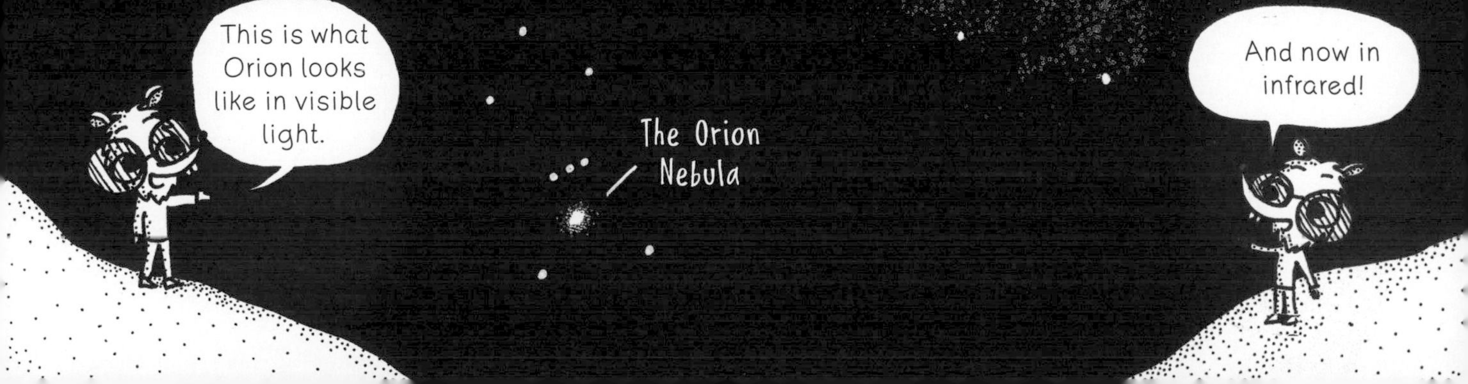
This is what Orion looks like in visible light.
The Orion Nebula
And now in infrared!

Chapter 13

SUPERLIGHT

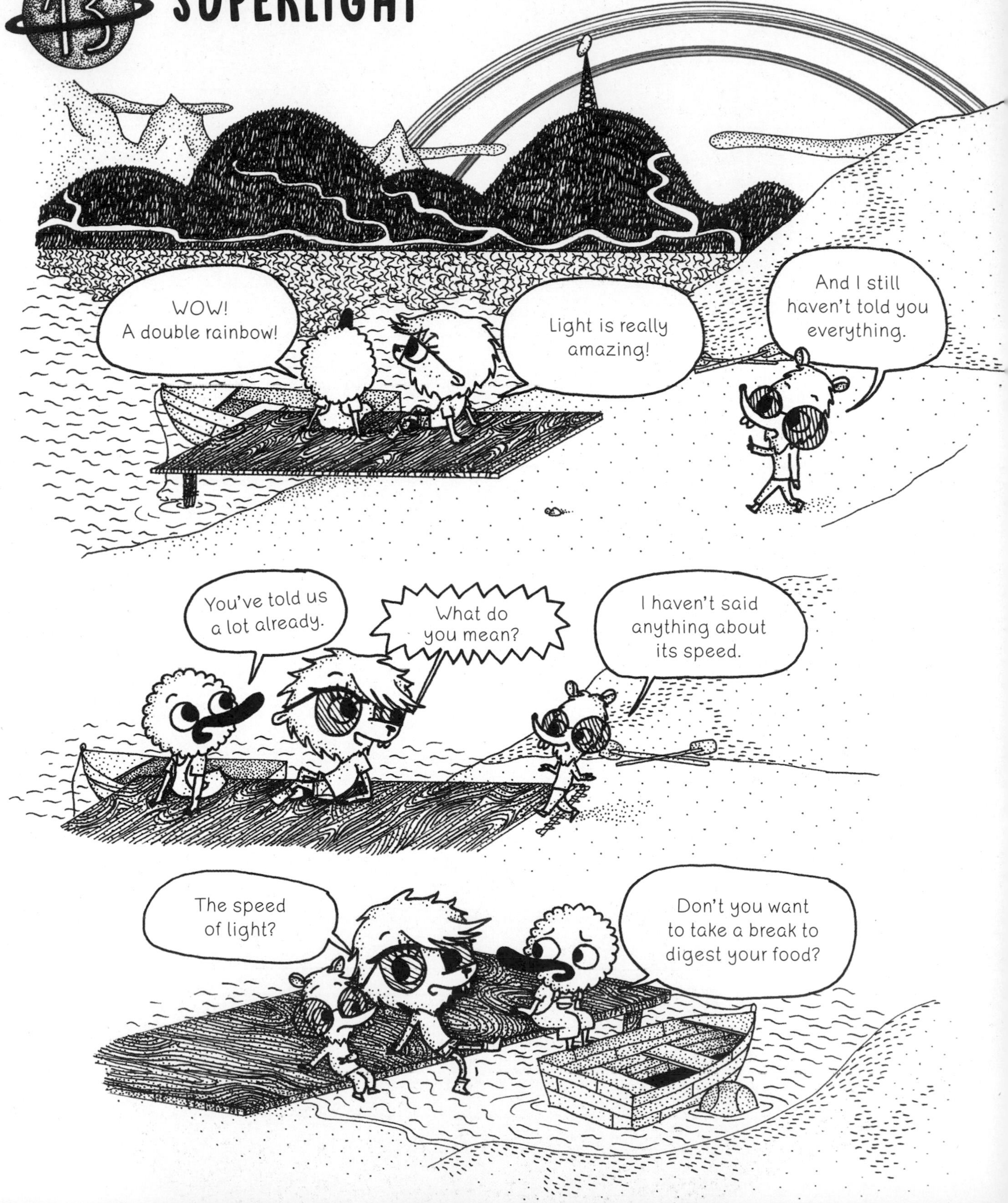
WOW!
A double rainbow!
Light is really amazing!
And I still haven't told you everything.
You've told us a lot already.
What do you mean?
I haven't said anything about its speed.
The speed of light?
Don't you want to take a break to digest your food?

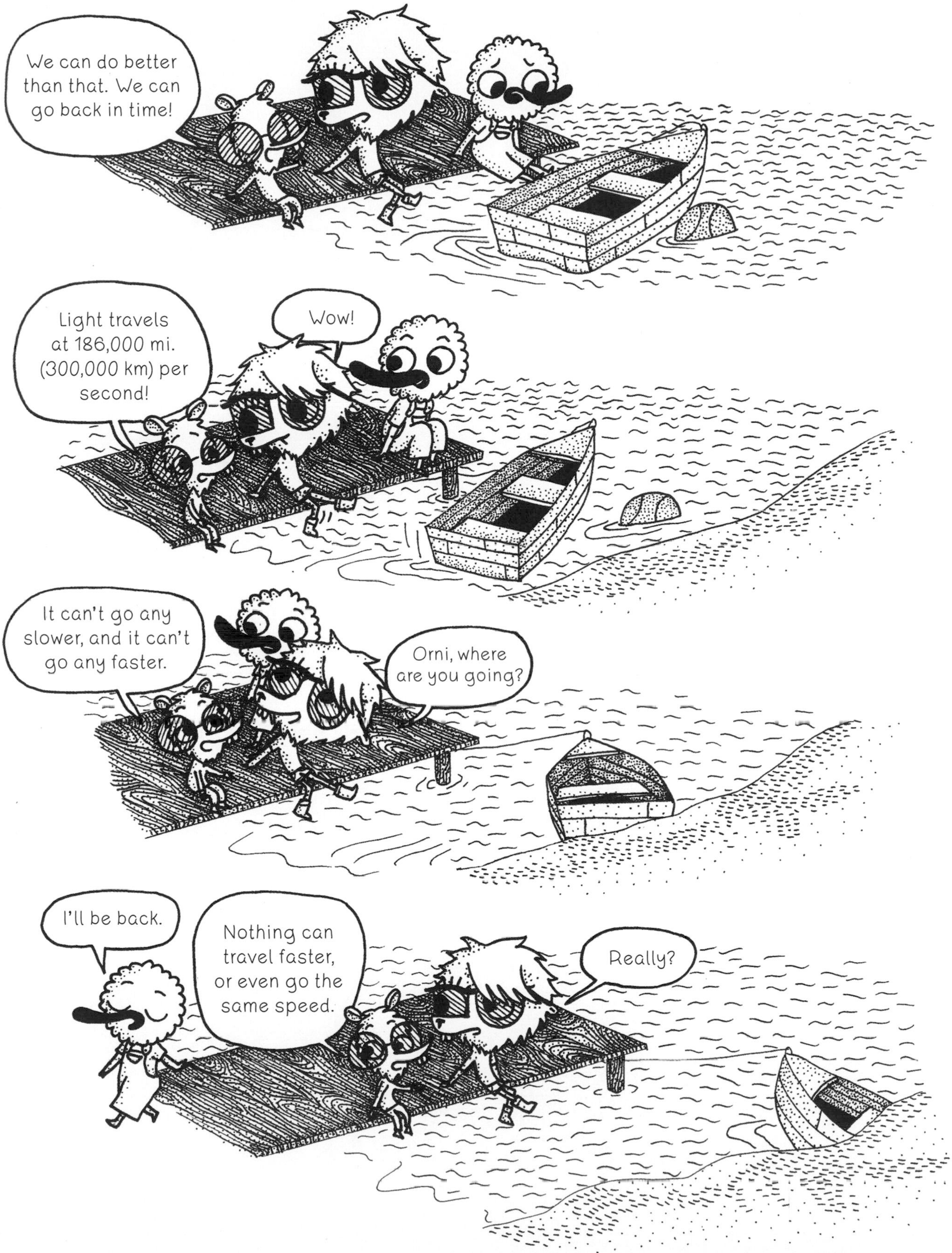
We can do better than that. We can go back in time!
Light travels at 186,000 mi. (300,000 km) per second!
Wow!
It can't go any slower, and it can't go any faster.
Orni, where are you going?
I'll be back.
Nothing can travel faster, or even go the same speed.
Really?

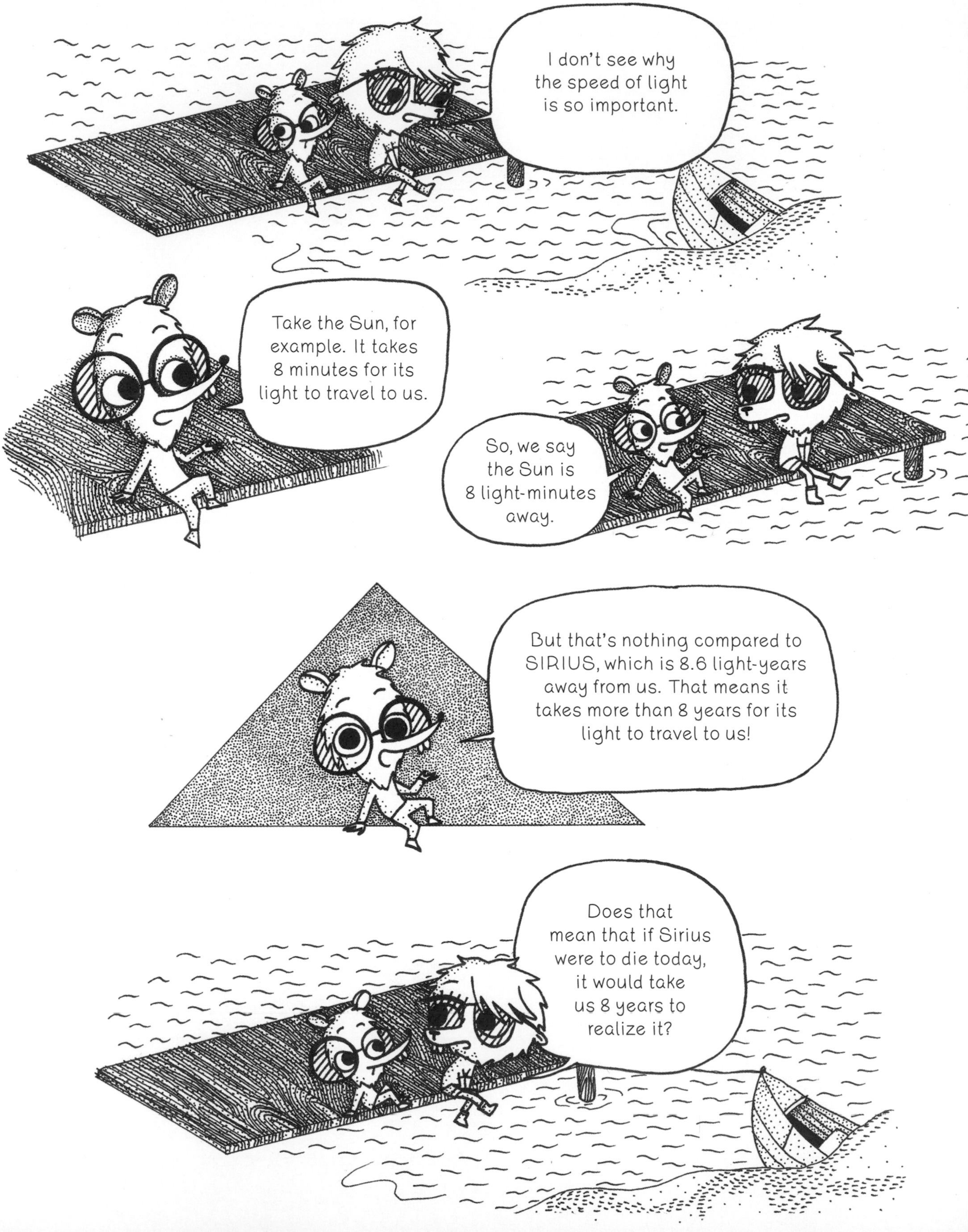
I don't see why the speed of light is so important.
Take the Sun, for example. It takes 8 minutes for its light to travel to us.
So, we say the Sun is 8 light-minutes away.
But that's nothing compared to SIRIUS, which is 8.6 light-years away from us. That means it takes more than 8 years for its light to travel to us!
Does that mean that if Sirius were to die today, it would take us 8 years to realize it?

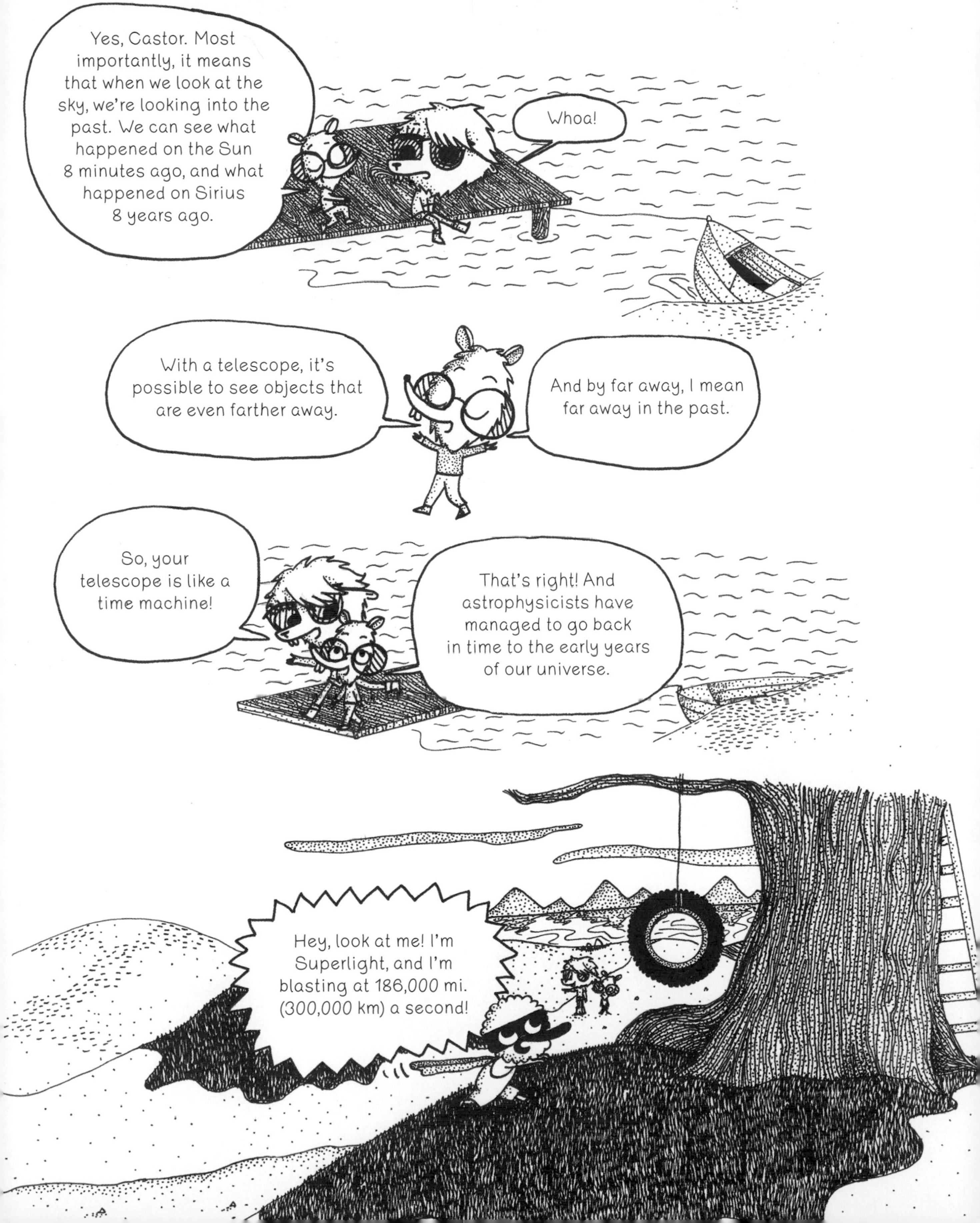
Yes, Castor. Most importantly, it means that when we look at the sky, we're looking into the past. We can see what happened on the Sun 8 minutes ago, and what happened on Sirius 8 years ago.
Whoa!
With a telescope, it's possible to see objects that are even farther away.
And by far away, I mean far away in the past.
So, your telescope is like a time machine!
That's right! And astrophysicists have managed to go back in time to the early years of our universe.
Hey, look at me! I'm Superlight, and I'm blasting at 186,000 mi. (300,000 km) a second!

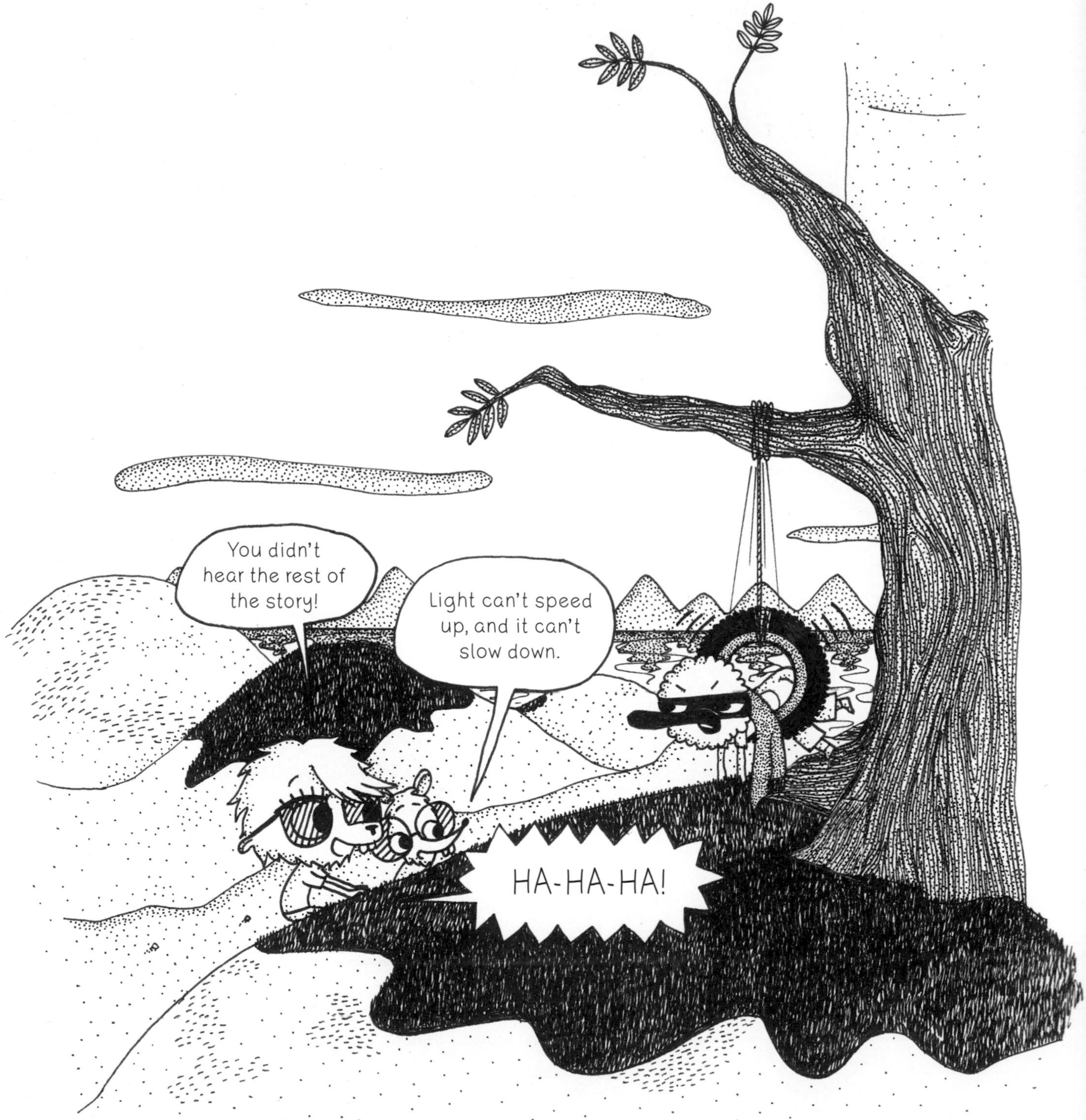
You didn't hear the rest of the story!
Light can't speed up, and it can't slow down.
HA-HA-HA!

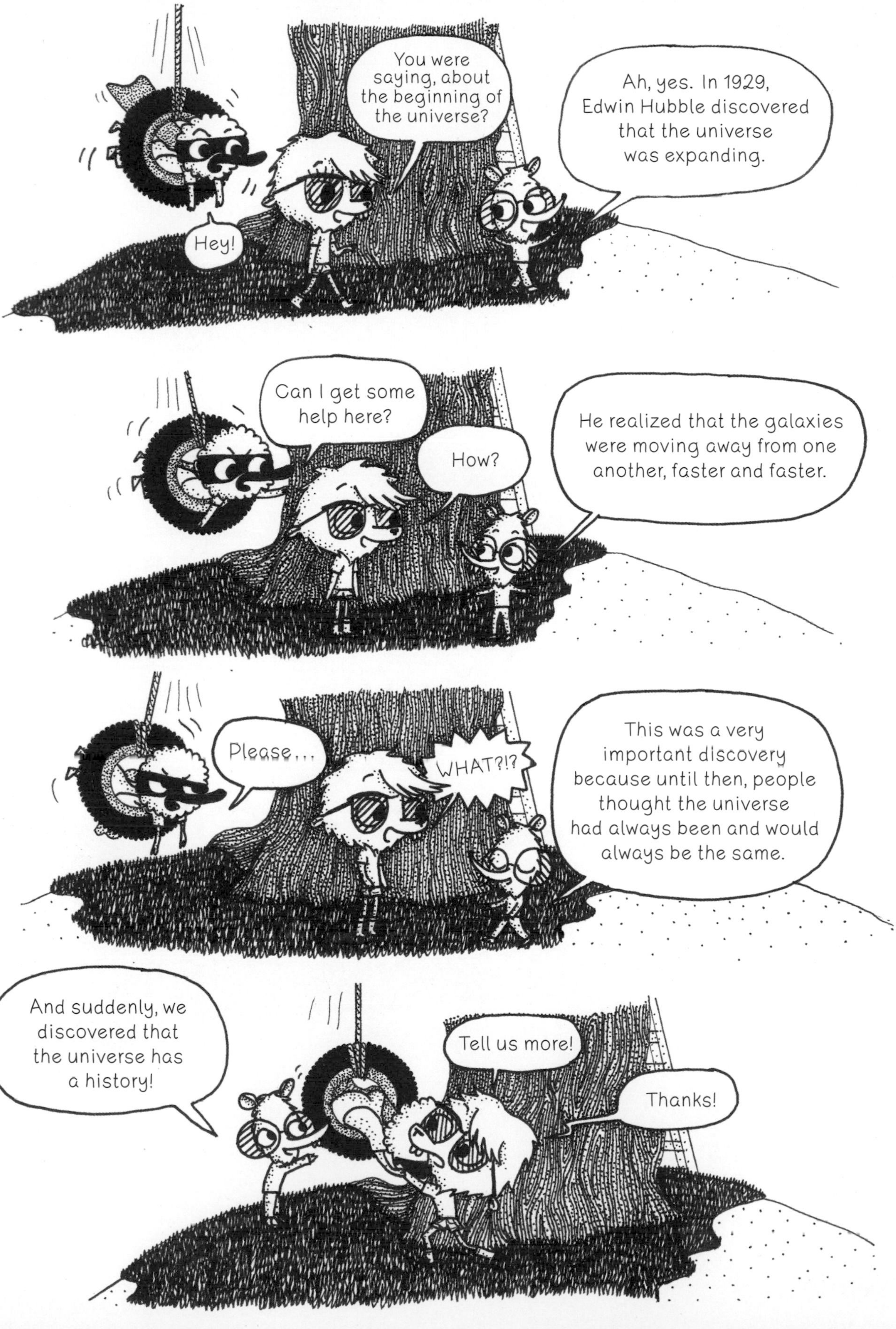
You were saying, about the beginning of the universe?
Ah, yes. In 1929, Edwin Hubble discovered that the universe was expanding.
Hey!
Can I get some help here?
How?
He realized that the galaxies were moving away from one another, faster and faster.
Please...
WHAT?!?
This was a very important discovery because until then, people thought the universe had always been and would always be the same.
And suddenly, we discovered that the universe has a history!
Tell us more!
Thanks!

Chapter 14

THE BIG BANG

The beginning of the universe is referred to as the big bang. Our universe is 13.6 billion years old, and we've managed to see a picture of it when it was 380,000 years old!

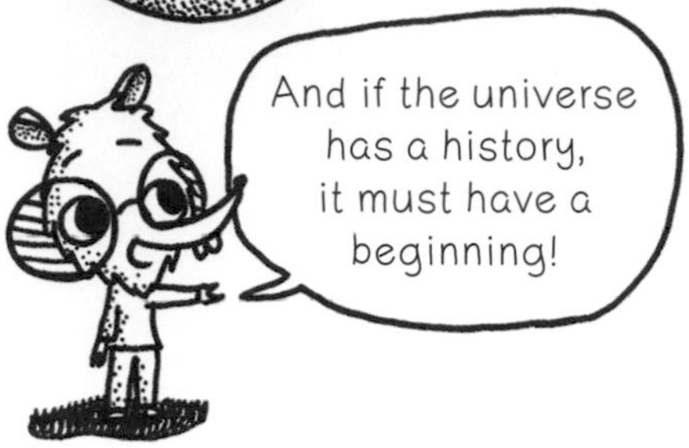
And if the universe has a history, it must have a beginning!

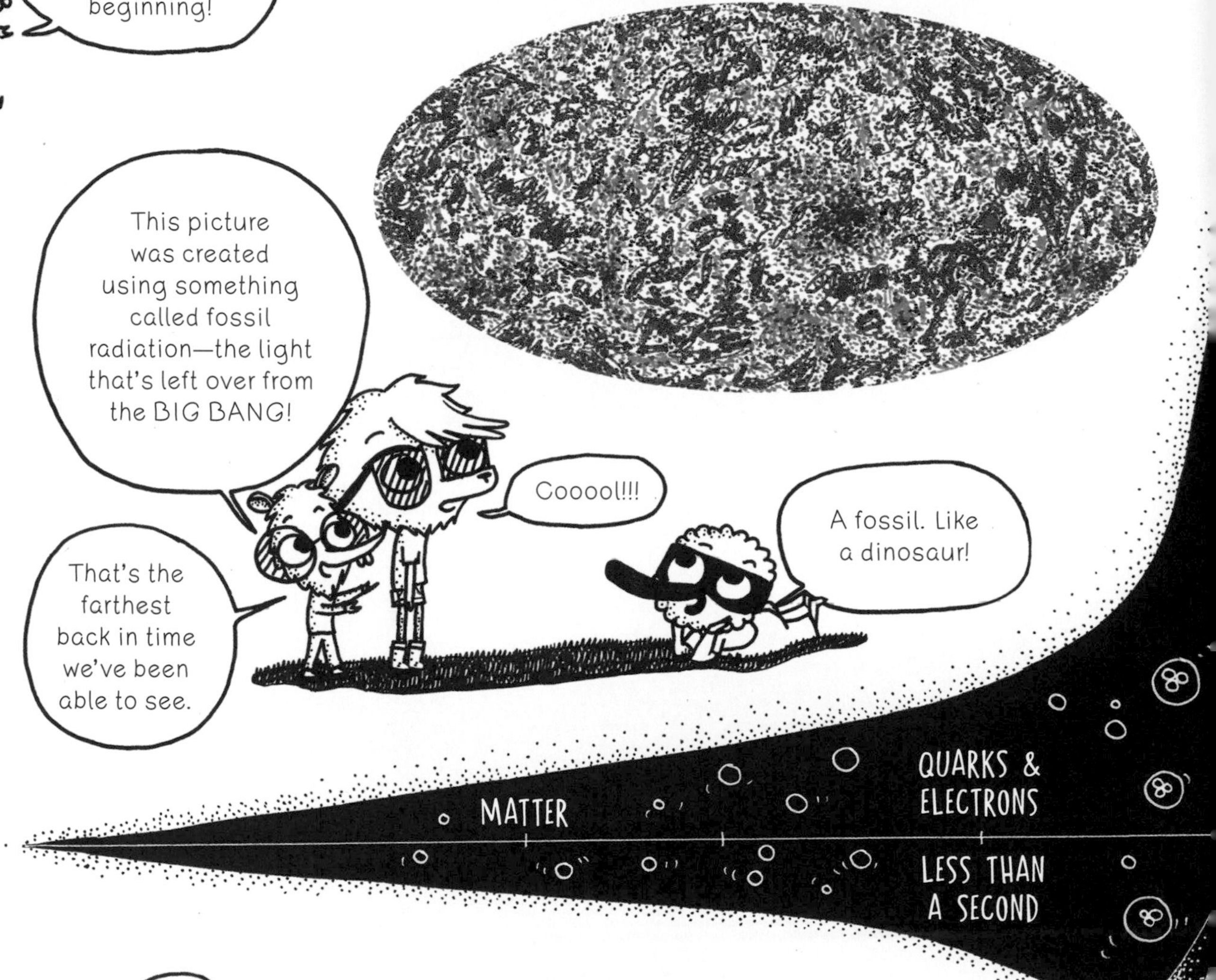
This picture was created using something called fossil radiation—the light that's left over from the BIG BANG!
Cooool!!!
A fossil. Like a dinosaur!
That's the farthest back in time we've been able to see.
MATTER
QUARKS & ELECTRONS
LESS THAN A SECOND

The term was first used by physicist FRED HOYLE, who was poking fun at this theory on the radio in England.

"I'll never believe the universe was created in a big bang!"

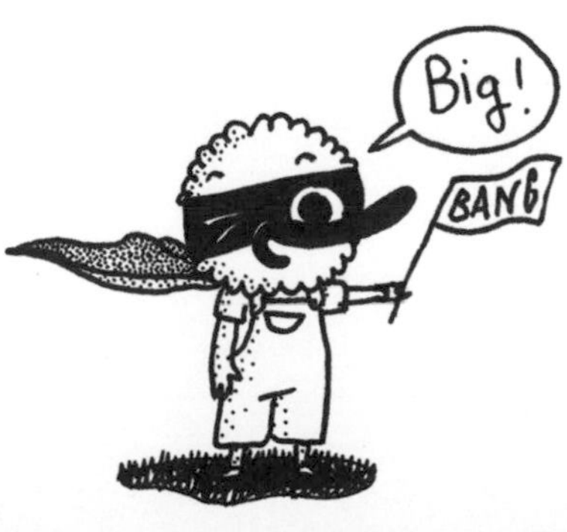
Big!
BANG

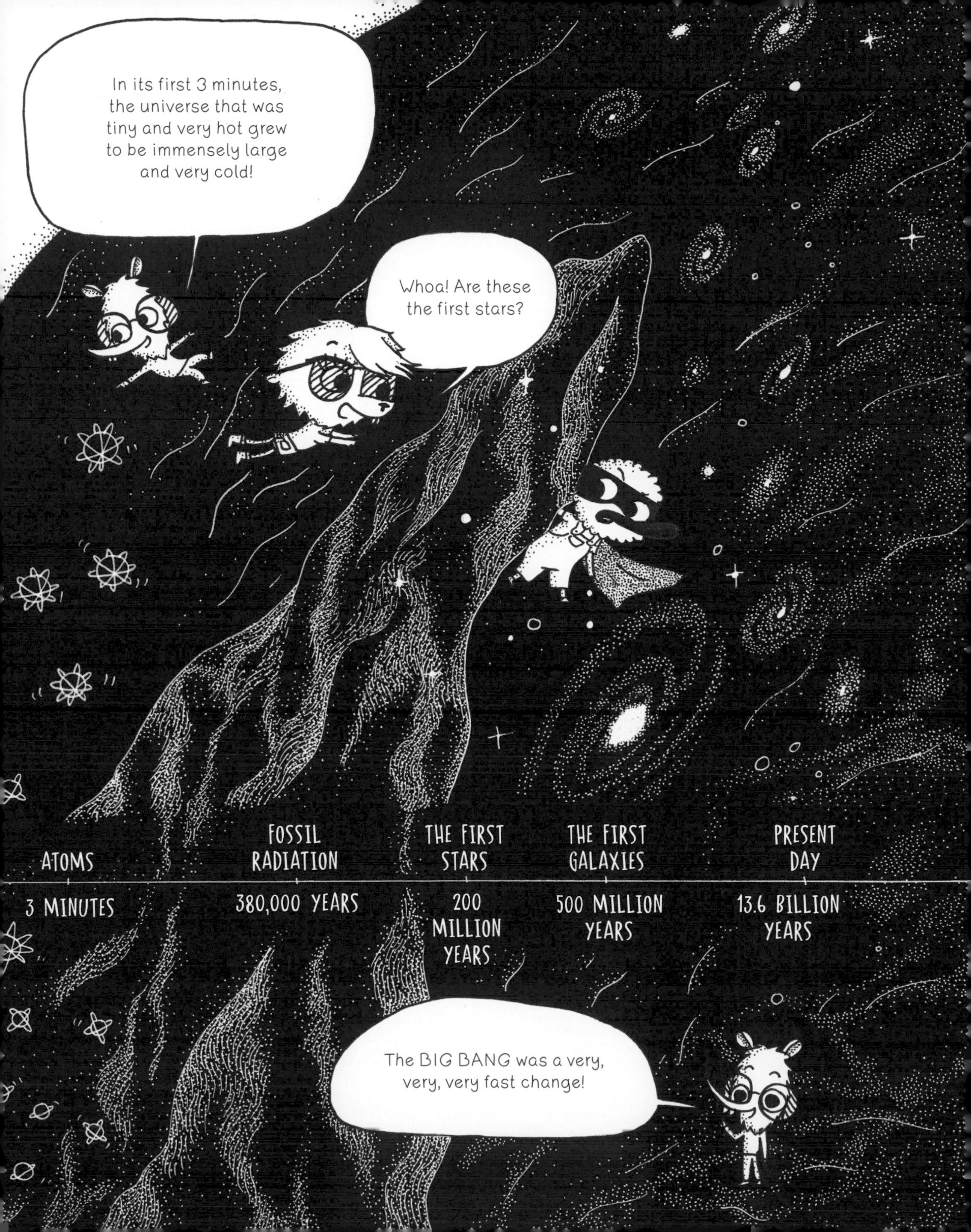
In its first 3 minutes, the universe that was tiny and very hot grew to be immensely large and very cold!
Whoa! Are these the first stars?
ATOMS
3 MINUTES
FOSSIL RADIATION
380,000 YEARS
THE FIRST STARS
200 MILLION YEARS
THE FIRST GALAXIES
500 MILLION YEARS
PRESENT DAY
13.6 BILLION YEARS
The BIG BANG was a very, very, very fast change!

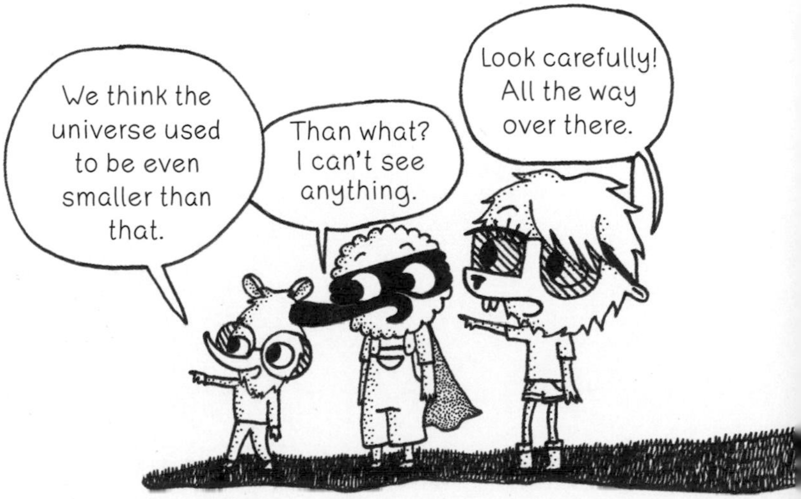
We think the universe used to be even smaller than that.
Than what? I can't see anything.
Look carefully! All the way over there.

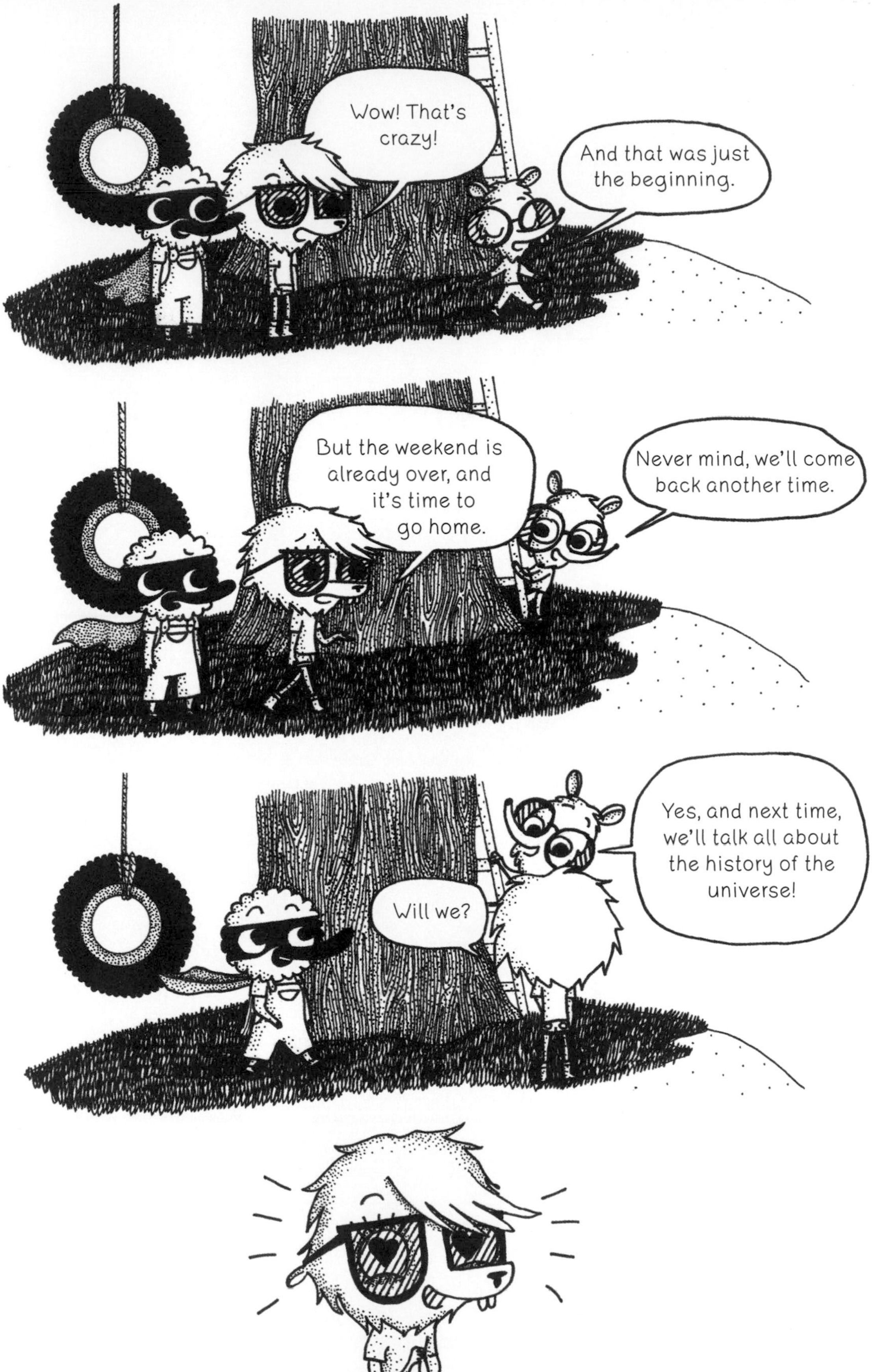
Wow! That's crazy!
And that was just the beginning.
But the weekend is already over, and it's time to go home.
Never mind, we'll come back another time.
Will we?
Yes, and next time, we'll talk all about the history of the universe!

CONCLUSION

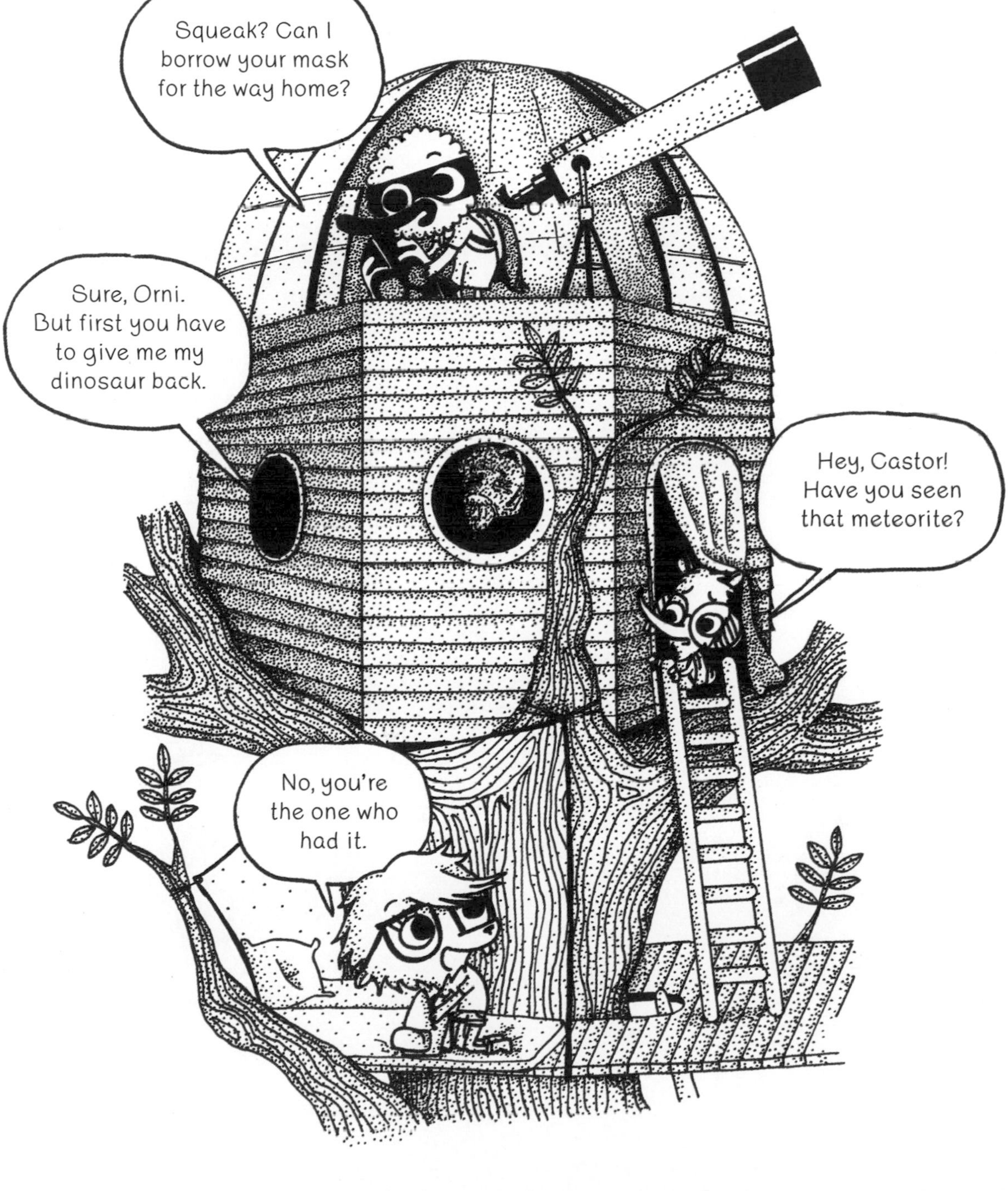

Squeak? Can I borrow your mask for the way home?
Sure, Orni. But first you have to give me my dinosaur back.
Hey, Castor! Have you seen that meteorite?
No, you're the one who had it.

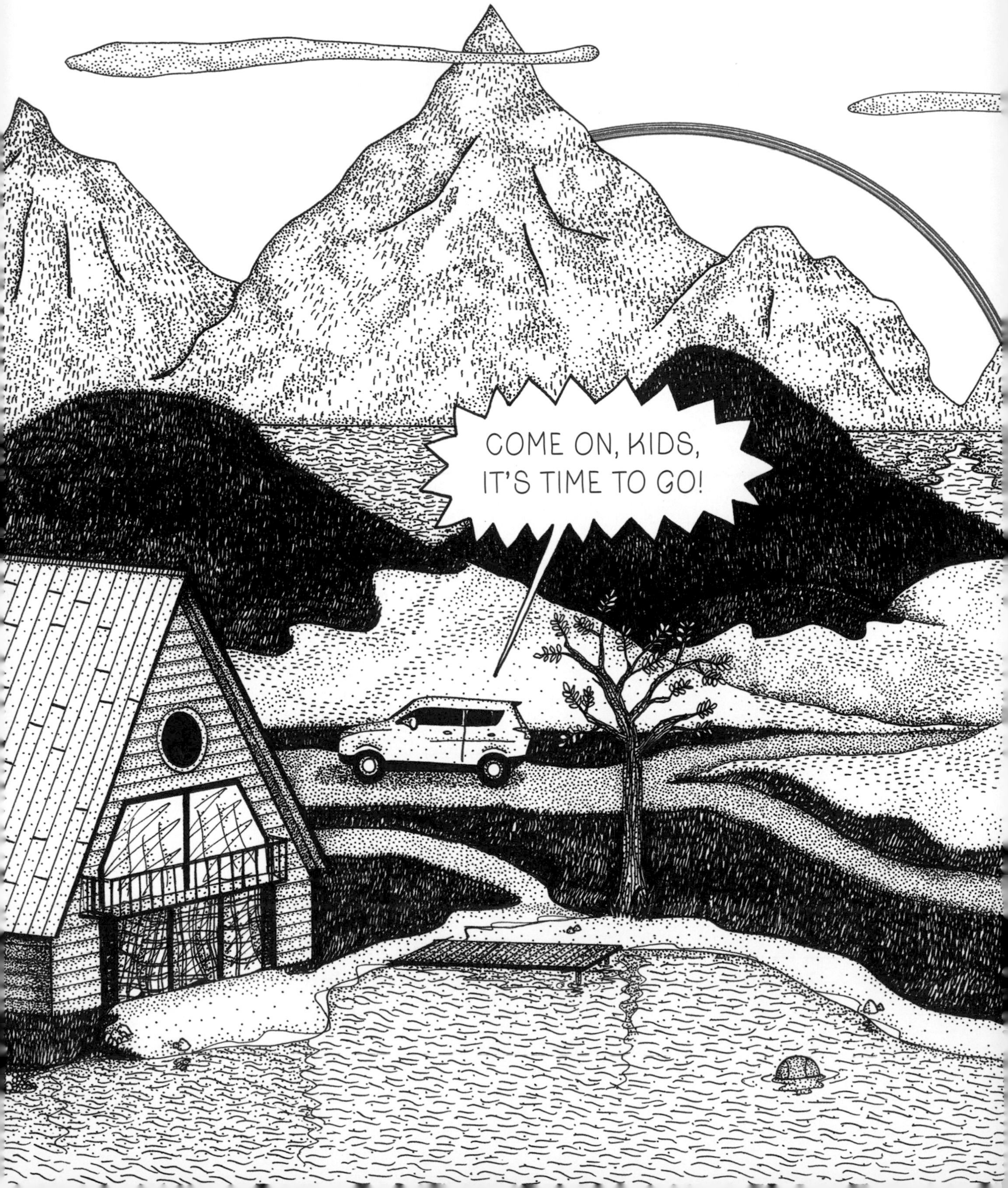
COME ON, KIDS, IT'S TIME TO GO!

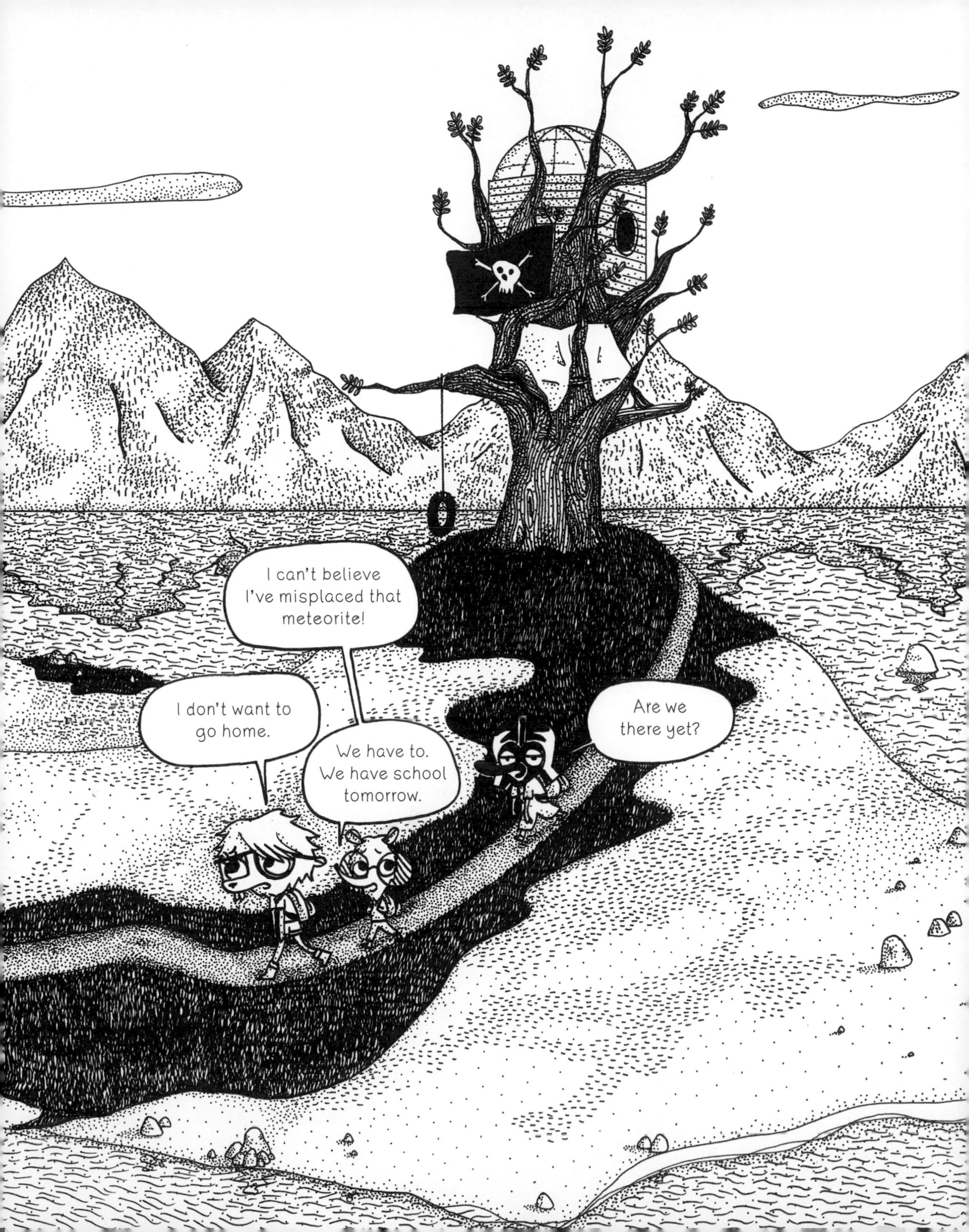
I can't believe I've misplaced that meteorite!
I don't want to go home.
We have to. We have school tomorrow.
Are we there yet?

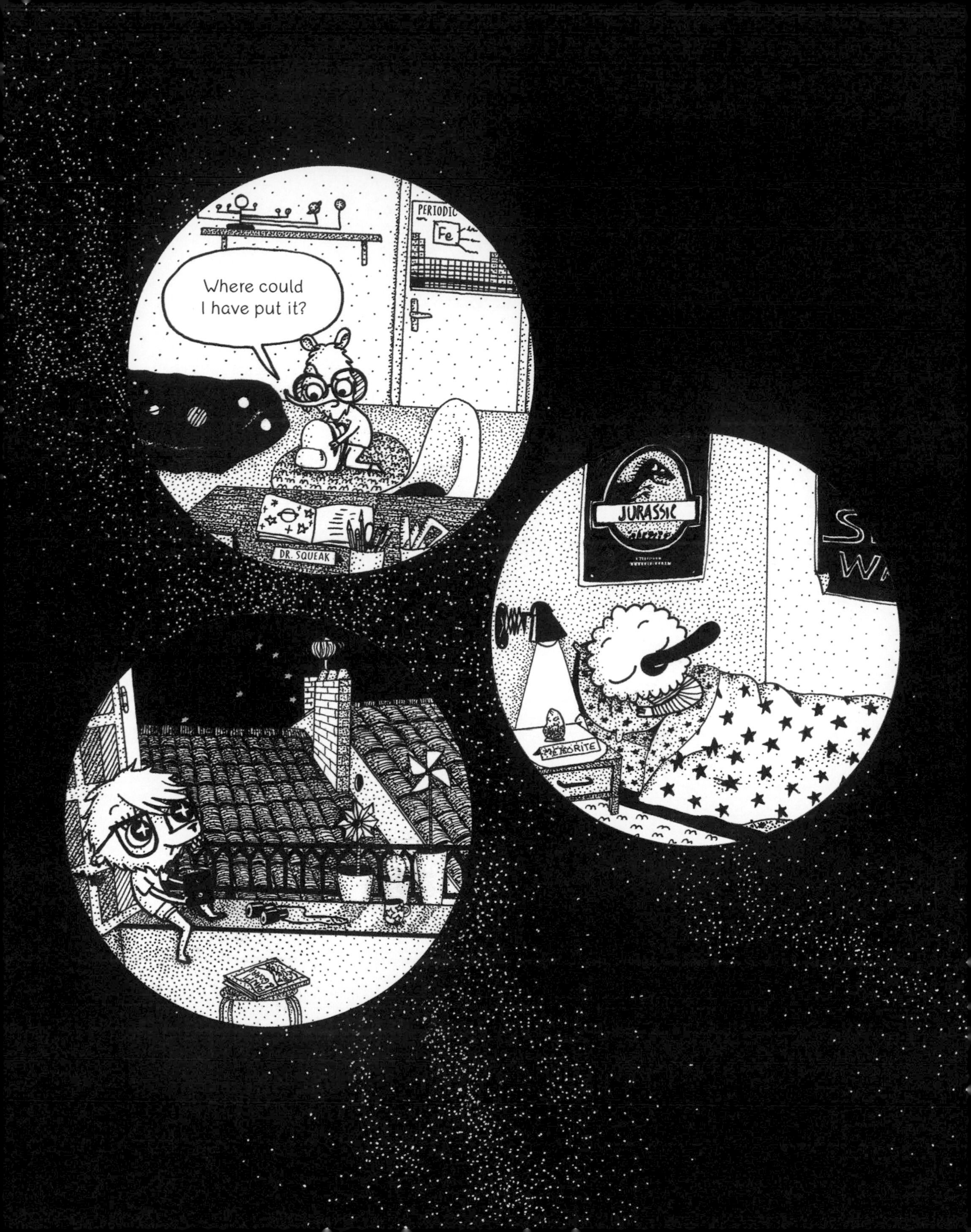
PERIODIC
Fe
Where could I have put it?
DR. SQUEAK
JURASSIC
METEORITE

Now it's your turn to be an ASTRONOMER!

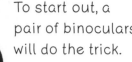

GET YOUR INSTRUMENTS

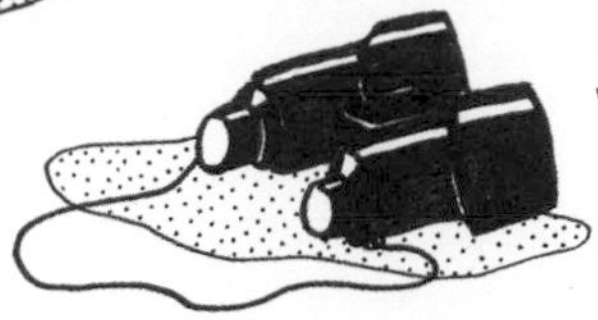

To start out, a pair of binoculars will do the trick.

Squeak has a
TELESCOPE
that uses a lens.

All these instruments are designed to capture light. The bigger the opening, the more stars you'll see in the sky. Remember: never look at the Sun without a special filter!

There are more powerful telescopes that use mirrors.

Align the axis of rotation with the pole star!

GET READY FOR OUR ADVENTURE IN ASTRONOMY

1. Make sure the sky is clear.

2. Before you go outside, check which constellations of the zodiac the planets are in.

3. Make sure there isn't a Full Moon because the light from it will hide most of the stars!

4. Move away from all light sources.

5. You'll need

- a map of the night sky

- binoculars

- a flashlight with a red bulb or something red to cover the lens (so it won't dazzle you, and you can still see your map!)

- a blanket

And this book!

And some cookies!

OBSERVE THE MOON

It's safe to look directly at the Moon with binoculars, because it doesn't produce its own light (unlike the Sun!).

You can see the craters more clearly in the First Quarter or Third Quarter than during a Full Moon.

First Quarter

Third Quarter

Full Moon

OBSERVE THE NIGHT SKY

Have fun finding...
- THE GREAT BEAR
- THE POLE STAR and
- THE LITTLE DIPPER

CASSIOPEIA

CEPHEUS

Isn't that a dinosaur?

Hey, Cepheus looks like a house!

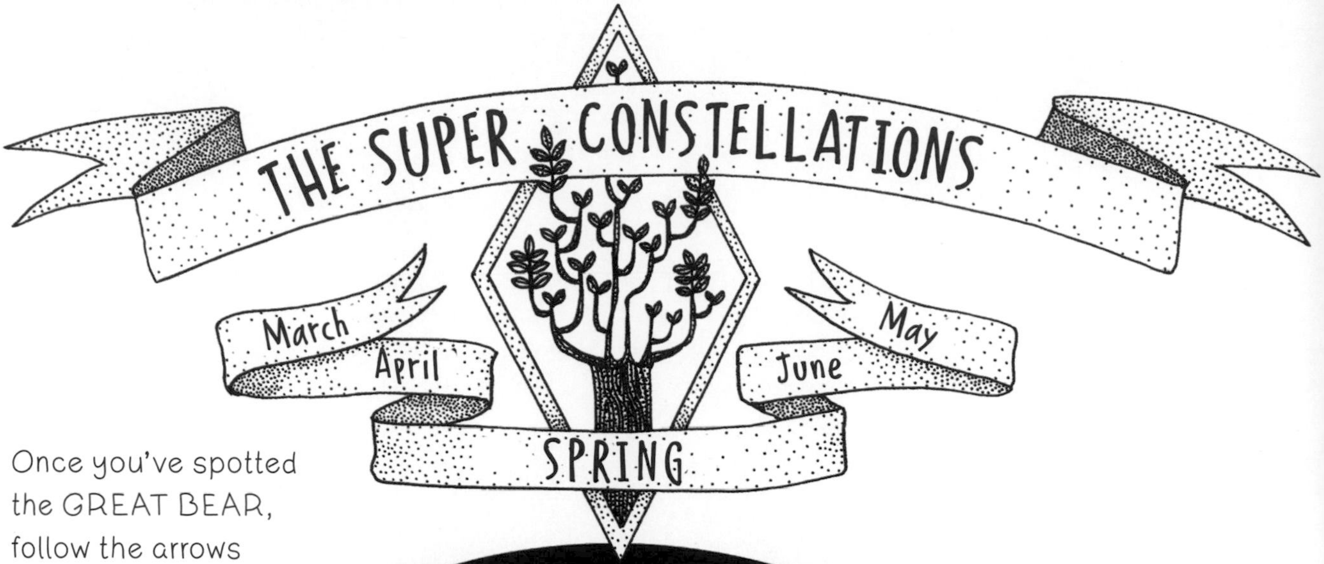
THE SUPER CONSTELLATIONS
March
April
May
June
SPRING

Once you've spotted the GREAT BEAR, follow the arrows to find the other constellations!

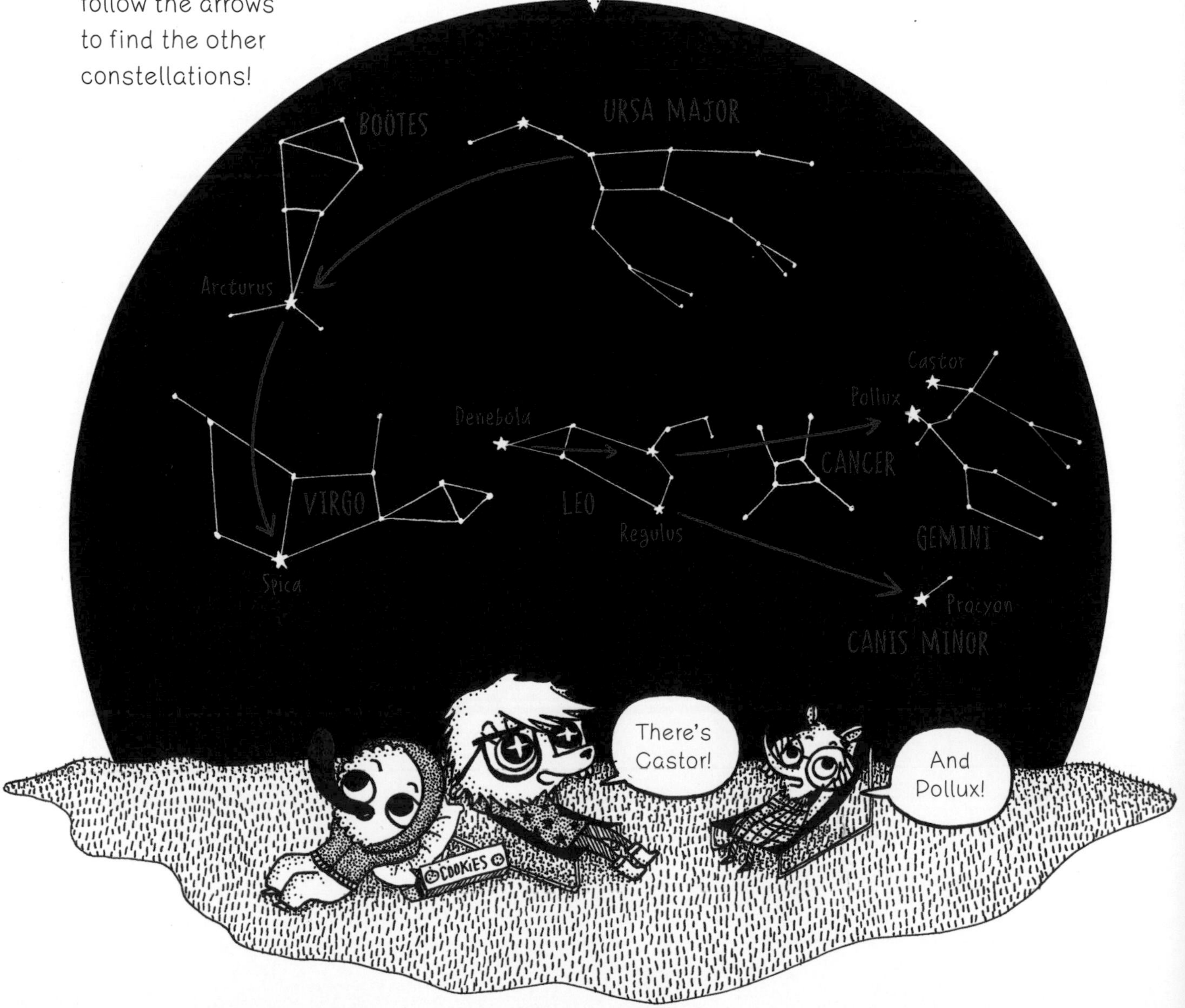
URSA MAJOR
BOÖTES
Arcturus
VIRGO
Spica
Denebola
LEO
Regulus
CANCER
Castor
Pollux
GEMINI
Procyon
CANIS MINOR
COOKIES
There's Castor!
And Pollux!

Summer is the sweetest season for stargazing!

And it's the best time to see shooting stars.

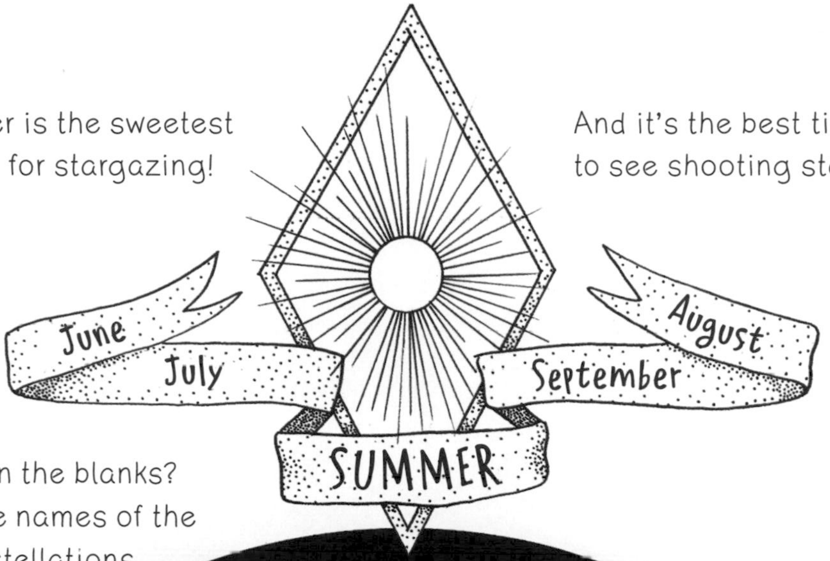
June
July
August
September
SUMMER

Can you fill in the blanks? You'll find the names of the missing constellations in this book.

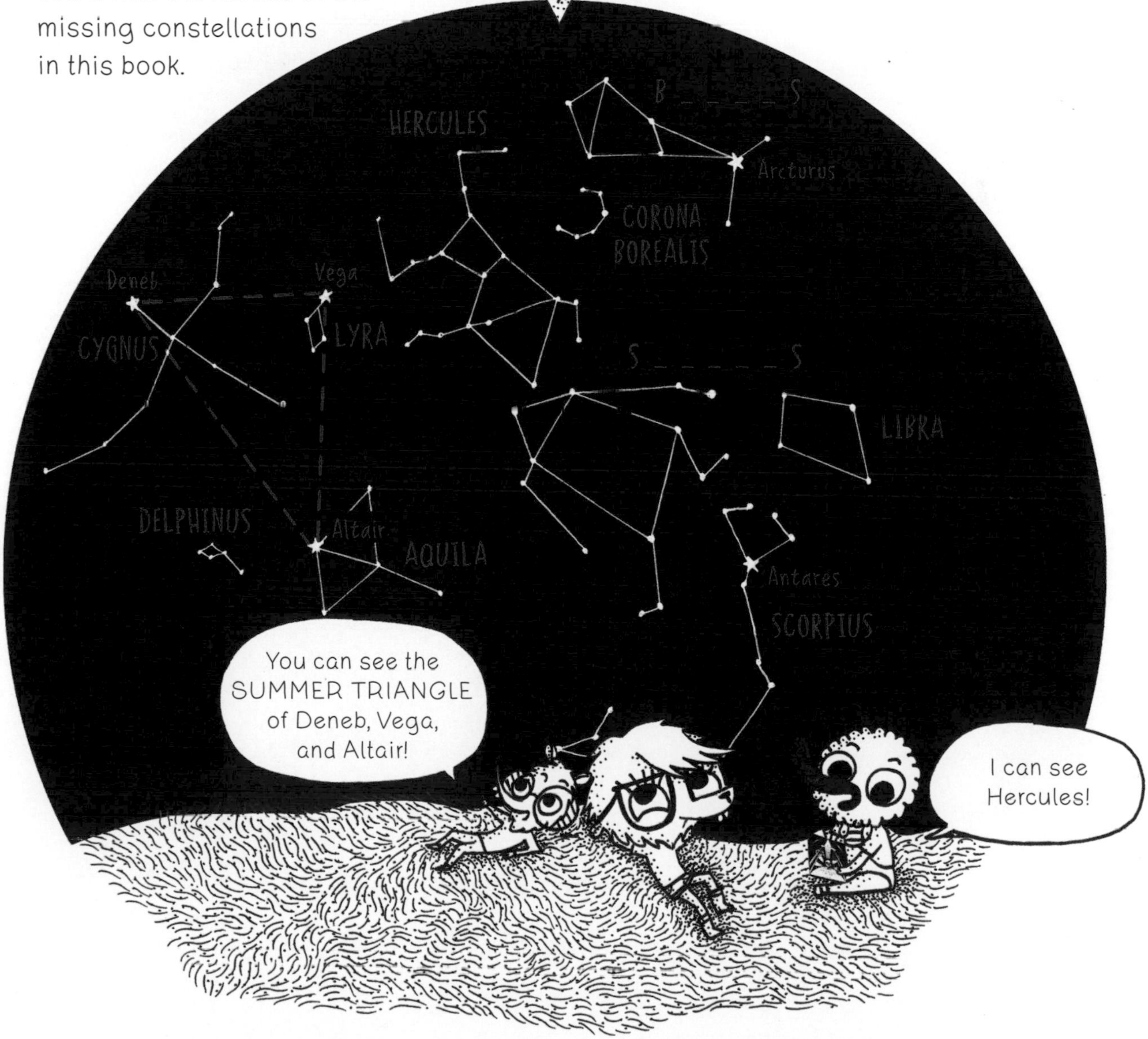
B _ _ _ _ S
HERCULES
Arcturus
CORONA BOREALIS
Deneb
Vega
LYRA
CYGNUS
S _ _ _ _ _ S
LIBRA
DELPHINUS
Altair
AQUILA
Antares
SCORPIUS
You can see the SUMMER TRIANGLE of Deneb, Vega, and Altair!
I can see Hercules!

In the fall, you can see ORION, TAURUS, and THE PLEIADES super clearly!

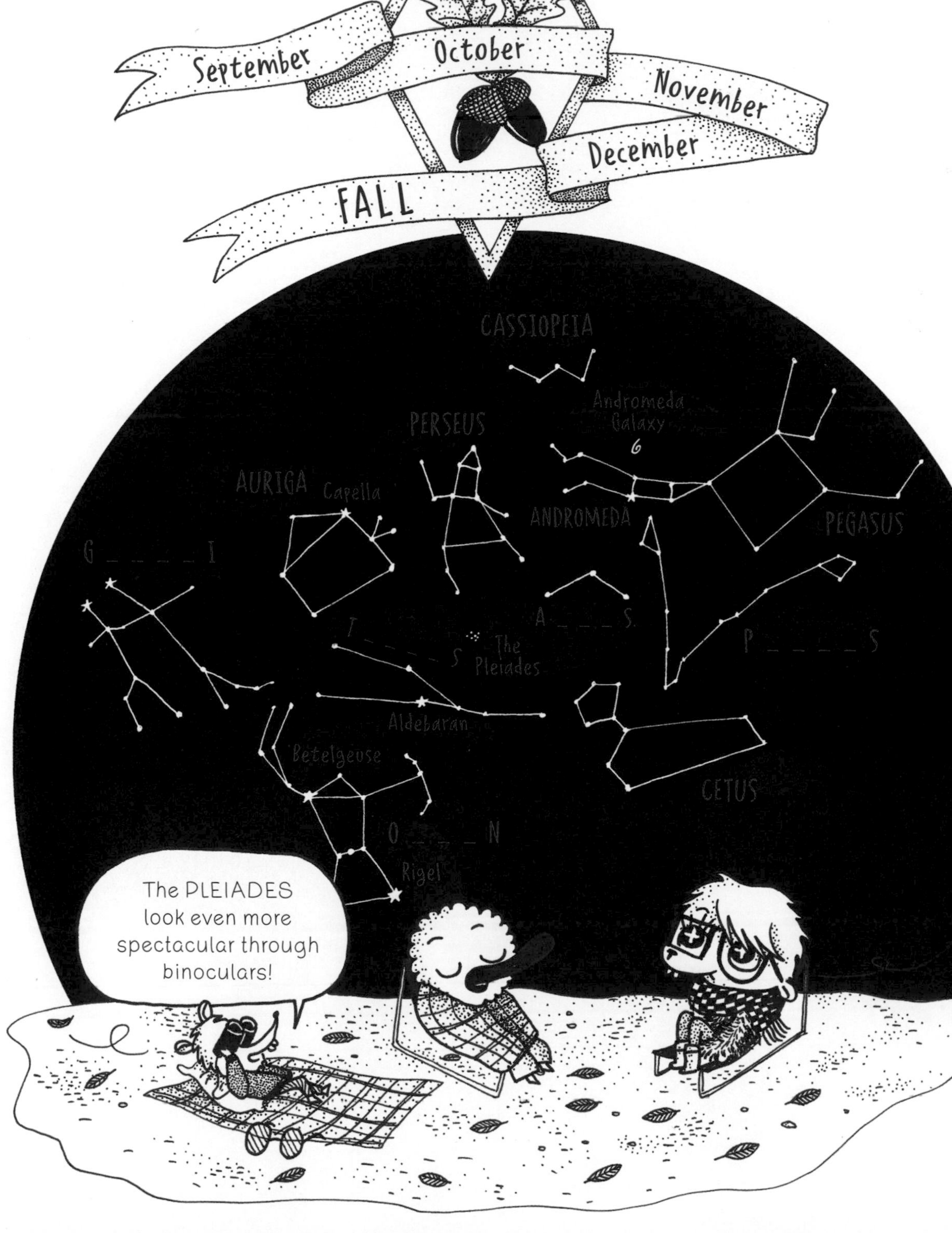
September
October
November
December
FALL
CASSIOPEIA
Andromeda Galaxy
PERSEUS
AURIGA
Capella
ANDROMEDA
PEGASUS
G _ _ _ _ I
A _ _ _ S
T _ _ _ _ S
The Pleiades
P _ _ _ _ S
Aldebaran
Betelgeuse
CETUS
O _ _ _ N
Rigel
The PLEIADES look even more spectacular through binoculars!

In winter, SIRIUS is very easy to spot. It's the second brightest star after the Sun!

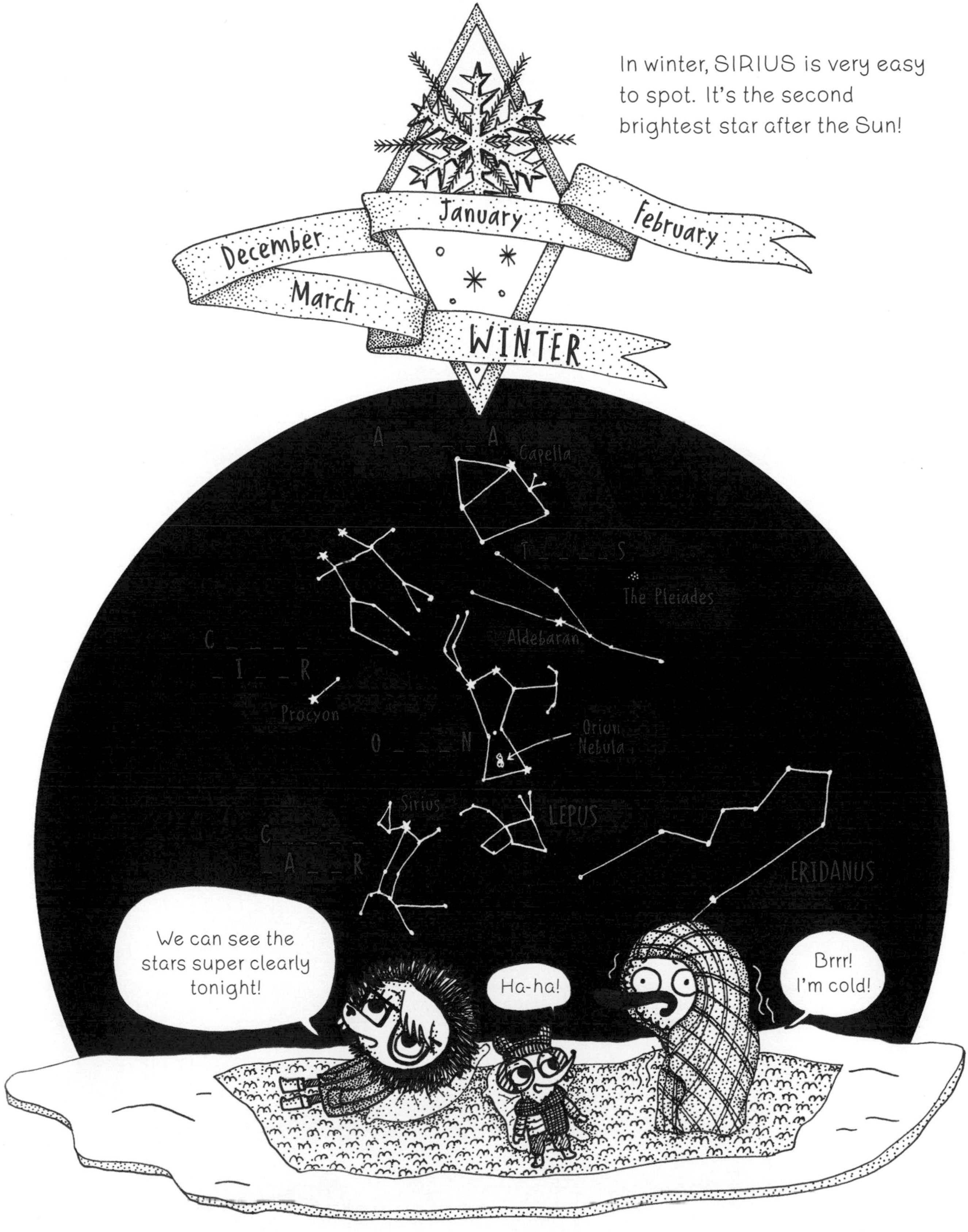
December
January
February
March
WINTER
Capella
The Pleiades
Aldebaran
Procyon
Orion Nebula
Sirius
LEPUS
ERIDANUS
We can see the stars super clearly tonight!
Ha-ha!
Brrr! I'm cold!

THANK YOU A THOUSAND TIMES!

THANK YOU to the Centre national du livre in France and to Auvergne-Rhône-Alpes Livre et Lecture for their support.

Thank you to Hélène Courtois for the proofreading and pointers, and for believing in this and being so helpful. Thank you to Jean-François Gonzalez, for the last-minute reread I found so reassuring.

Thank you to Simon Meyer for the follow-up, and to Walter Guyot and Anna Thibeau for spotting the scientific mediator in me. To Adrien Viciana for the advice, the insistence, and the 365.25. To Pania Rabipour for the light, to Julien Lambert for the ultimate proofread, and to all my mediation colleagues for their patience and explanations. To Assumpta Lopin for her support through thick and thin. And to everyone else for being so understanding and welcoming.

Thank you to Anne and Anne-Bénédicte for the listening ear, the respect for my project, the black and white, the splashes of color, the pages added, the words taken away, the surprises, the panicked emails, the last-minute possibilities, and the whims of a "star." Thank you to Frédéric Basset for his advice, his patience, the *black* black, and the *white* white. Thank you to Jo for believing in Castor right from the start and putting up with my spelling OCD.

Thank you to Pierrot for making me feel like writing this book and making it the best it can be. To Marie for the laughs and the vacation time. To my mom and my grandma—these planets of mine pull me away sometimes, but I love you so much. To Choulie for being my super platypus. To Elo, Chloé, Matthias, Aude, Dori, and Rob for the moral support. To Nico for the Carambar jokes. To Matï and Romain for the Photoshop. To Pierre for the spelling mistakes. Basically, to all my 101 friends for putting up with my little quirks, my excitement, my disappointment, and my songs. To Clairou and Jo for reading over my never-ending grant applications. To Panpi and Gorri for telling Maison Georges about their friend whose name was the inspiration for Castor. And thanks to the whole gang, Benjamin, Margaux, Nico, Estelle, Fraki, Denis, Grand Ju, Glob… I've filled your glasses with stars, and I'll keep on filling them.

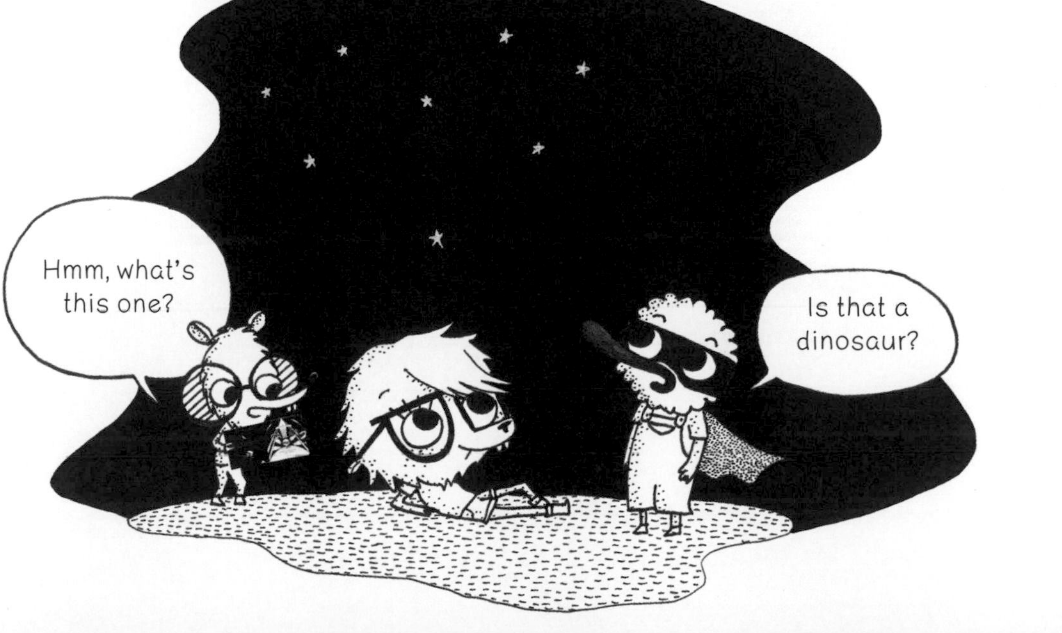
Hmm, what's this one?
Is that a dinosaur?

GAËLLE ALMÉRAS loves art and science, particularly astronomy and nature, and is a very active author and illustrator. In 2015, she started writing a series of popular science columns that then became *Super Space Weekend* (*Le Super week-end de l'espace*), which was awarded the Prix Brahic for best astronomy picture book for children in 2019 and was a finalist of the Montreuil Book Fair Pépites as well as France's Ministry of Higher Education's Prix le goût des sciences. She lives in Dompierre-les-Ormes, France.

DAVID WARRINER grew up in the United Kingdom with a passion for French language and culture, and lived in France and Quebec before deciding to call beautiful British Columbia home. He's been a professional translator for nearly half his life and has translated a range of fiction, nonfiction, and children's books for publishers on both sides of the Atlantic.

First published in English by Greystone Books in 2023
Originally published in French in 2018 as *Le Super week-end de l'espace* by Maison Georges.

23 24 25 26 27 5 4 3 2 1

Greystone Kids / Greystone Books Ltd.
greystonebooks.com

Cataloguing data available from Library and Archives Canada
ISBN 978-1-77840-066-7 (cloth)
ISBN 978-1-77840-109-1 (pbk.)
ISBN 978-1-77840-067-4 (epub)

Scientific proofreading: Hélène Courtois, astrophysicist and cosmographer;
Jean-François Gonzalez, planetologist
Photoengraver: Frédéric Basset

Editing by Linda Pruessen
Copy editing by Becky Noelle
Proofreading by Tracy Bordian
Cover design and interior typesetting by Jessica Sullivan

Printed and bound under a starry sky in China on FSC® certified paper at Shenzhen Reliance Printing. The FSC® label means that materials used for the product have been responsibly sourced.

Greystone Books thanks the Canada Council for the Arts, the British Columbia Arts Council, the Province of British Columbia through the Book Publishing Tax Credit, and the Government of Canada for supporting our publishing activities.

Canada

British Columbia | British Columbia Arts Council
An agency of the Province of British Columbia

Canada Council for the Arts Conseil des arts du Canada

MIX
Paper from responsible sources
FSC
www.fsc.org
FSC® C102842

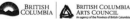

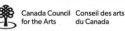

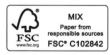

Greystone Books gratefully acknowledges the xʷməθkʷəy̓əm (Musqueam), Sḵwx̱wú7mesh (Squamish), and səlilwətaɬ (Tsleil-Waututh) peoples on whose land our Vancouver head office is located.

SCIENCE ADVENTURE CLUB

SUPER
OCEAN
WEEKEND
Adventures in Oceanography
Gaëlle Alméras
SCIENCE ADVENTURE CLUB

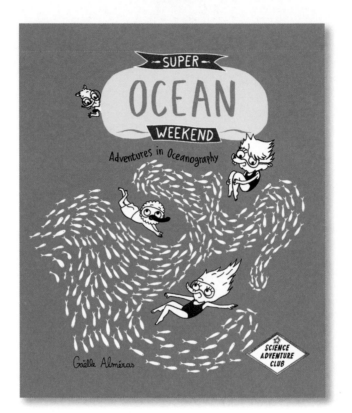

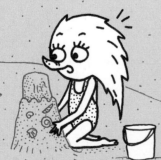

Don't miss
the next exciting adventure
with Squeak, Orni, and Castor!

SUPER OCEAN WEEKEND